CONTENTS

Cover Picture: The Salutation Inn, Herefordshire (page 163)

KEY TO SYMBOLS

14 rms Total number of rooms	**14 rms** Nombre de chambres	**14 rms** Anzahl der Zimmer
MasterCard accepted	MasterCard accepté	MasterCard akzeptiert
Visa accepted	Visa accepté	Visa akzeptiert
American Express accepted	American Express accepté	American Express akzeptiert
Diners Club accepted	Diners Club accepté	Diners Club akzeptiert
Quiet location	Un lieu tranquille	Ruhige Lage
Access for wheelchairs to at least one bedroom and public rooms	Accès handicapé	Zugang für Behinderte

(The 'Access for wheelchairs' symbol (&) does not necessarily indicate that the property fulfils National Accessible Scheme grading)

Chef-patron	Chef-patron	Chef-patron
M 20 Meeting/conference facilities with maximum number of delegates	**M** 20 Salle de conférences – capacité maximale	**M** 20 Konferenzraum-Höchstkapazität
Children welcome, with minimum age where applicable	Enfants bienvenus	Kinder willkommen
Dogs accommodated in rooms or kennels	Chiens autorisés	Hunde erlaubt
At least one room has a four-poster bed	Lit à baldaquin dans au moins une chambre	Himmelbett
Cable/satellite TV in all bedrooms	TV câblée/satellite dans les chambres	Satellit-und Kabelfernsehen in allen Zimmern
Fax available in rooms	Fax dans votre chambre	Fax in Schlafzimmern
No-smoking rooms (at least one no-smoking bedroom)	Chambres non-fumeur	Zimmer für Nichtraucher
Lift available for guests' use	Ascenseur	Fahrstuhl
Air Conditioning	Climatisation	Klimatisiert
Indoor swimming pool	Piscine couverte	Hallenbad
Outdoor swimming pool	Piscine de plein air	Freibad
Tennis court at hotel	Tennis à l'hôtel	Hoteleigener Tennisplatz
Croquet lawn at hotel	Croquet à l'hôtel	Krocketrasen
Fishing can be arranged	Pêche	Angeln
Golf course on site or nearby, which has an arrangement with the hotel allowing guests to play	Golf sur site ou à proximité	Golfplatz
Shooting can be arranged	Chasse / Tir	Jagd
Riding can be arranged	Équitation	Reitpferd
Hotel has a helicopter landing pad	Helipad	Hubschrauberlandplatz
Licensed for wedding ceremonies	Cérémonies de mariages	Konzession für Eheschliessungen

FOREWORD

In this guide you will find traditional inns, excellent restaurants and smaller hotels. Most are privately owned or in the hands of reputable brewers or small groups.

Our inspectors annually visit every recommended establishment in addition to the many hotels, inns, country houses and business meeting venues which regularly apply for inclusion. Only those that match our standards of diversity and excellence can be recommended.

The new millennium editions of our guides include the launch of 'Recommended Hotels & Game Lodges Southern Africa Mauritius The Seychelles'. You will find these exciting new recommendations together with those for North America and Europe in the index at the back of this guide.

A complete reference to our year 2000 recommendations representing 40 countries may be found together with a direct on line availability service (DOLAS) on our Internet site www.johansens.com The guides are also available on CD-ROM. We hope that you enjoy these recommendations and our thanks go to the many thousands of you who have sent us 'Guest Survey Reports' that are invaluable to maintaining our standards and are also available at the back of this guide.

Your experience has proved that to mention that you use Johansens when making a booking is a positive benefit to the enjoyment of your stay.

We wish you many more of them.

Andrew Warren
Managing Director

JOHANSENS AWARDS FOR EXCELLENCE
RECOMMENDED TRADITIONAL INNS, HOTELS & RESTAURANTS

The 1999 Awards for Excellence winners at the Dorchester

The Johansens Awards for Excellence were presented at the Johansens Annual Dinner held at The Dorchester on November 2nd 1998. The Most Excellent Traditional Inn Award was presented to **The New Inn at Coln** in Gloucestershire whose exceptional qualities were identified by scores of guests who sent in Johansens report forms after an enjoyable stay at the inn.Congratulations to The New Inn at Coln and thank you to everyone who sent in Guest Survey Report forms.

Each year we rely on the appraisals of Johansens guests, alongside the nominations of our team of inspectors, as a basis for making all our awards, not only to our Recommended Traditional Inns and Restaurants but also to our Country Houses and Hotels in Great Britain & Ireland, Recommended Hotels – Europe and the Mediterranean and Recommended Hotels & Inns – North America, Bermuda & The Caribbean. In these categories the award winners for 1999 were:

Johansens Most Excellent City Hotel Award:
Channings, Edinburgh, Scotland

Johansens Most Excellent Service Award:
Burpham Country Hotel, West Sussex

Johansens Most Excellent Country House Award:
Caragh Lodge, Co. Kerry, Ireland

Johansens Most Excellent Country Hotel Award:
Summer Lodge, Dorset

Johansens Most Excellent London Hotel Award:
The London Outpost of the Carnegie Club

Johansens Most Excellent Value for Money Award:
Beechwood Hotel, North Walsham, Norfolk

Johansens Most Excellent Restaurant Award:
Ynyshir Hall, Machynlleth, Wales

Johansens Special Award for Outstanding Excellence and Innovation:
Hotel du Vin Group of Hotels

Johansens – Europe: The Most Excellent Waterside Resort Hotel:
The Marbella Club, Marbella, Spain

Johansens – Europe: The Most Excellent Country Hotel:
Schlosshotel Igls, Igls, Austria

Johansens – Europe: The Most Excellent City Hotel:
La Tour Rose, Lyon, France

Johansens – North America: Special Award for Excellence:
The Lodge at Moosehead Lake, Greenville, Maine

Johansens – North America: Most Excellent Inn:
Carter House, Eureka, California

Johansens – North America: Most Excellent Hotel:
Monmouth Plantation, Natchez, Mississippi

Bottled at source, Broughton, Hampshire
„FOR BEST BEFORE DATE SEE CAP"
750mle
WELL... DE GUSTIBUS
NON EST DISPUTANDUM
HILDON
Hildon Ltd., Broughton, Hampshire SO20 8DG, 01794 - 301 747
STUDIO BRUSIUS

Published by

Johansens Limited, Therese House, Glasshouse Yard, London EC1A 4JN

Tel: 020 7566 9700 Fax: 020 7490 2538

Find Johansens on the Internet at: **http://www.johansens.com**

E-Mail: admin@johansen.u–net.com

Publishing Director:	Peter Hancock
P.A. to Publishing Director:	Carol Sweeney
Editorial Manager:	Yasmin Razak
Regional Inspectors:	Christopher Bond
	Geraldine Bromley
	Robert Bromley
	Julie Dunkley
	Martin Greaves
	Joan Henderson
	Marie Iversen
	Pauline Mason
	John O'Neill
	Mary O'Neill
	Fiona Patrick
	Brian Sandell
Production Manager:	Daniel Barnett
Production Controller:	Kevin Bradbrook
Senior Designer:	Michael Tompsett
Designer:	Sue Dixon
Copywriters:	Claire-Louise Baxter
	Simon Duke
	Norman Flack
Sales and Marketing Manager:	Laurent Martinez
Marketing Executive:	Stephen Hoskin
Sales Administrator:	Susan Butterworth
Webmaster:	John Lea
P.A. to Managing Director :	Glenda Walshaw
Managing Director:	Andrew Warren

Whilst every care has been taken in the compilation of this guide, the publishers cannot accept responsibility for any inaccuracies or for changes since going to press, or for consequential loss arising from such changes or other inaccuracies, or for any other loss direct or consequential arising in connection with information describing establishments in this publication.

Recommended establishments, if accepted for inclusion by our inspectors, pay an annual subscription to cover the costs of inspection, the distribution and production of copies placed in hotel bedrooms and other services.

Copyright © 1999 Johansens Limited

Johansens is a subsidiary of the Daily Mail & General Trust plc

ISBN 1 861017 7107

Printed in England by St Ives plc
Colour origination by East Anglian Engraving

Distributed in the UK and Europe by Johnsons International Media Services Ltd, London (direct sales) & Biblios PDS Ltd, West Sussex (bookstores). In North America by Hunter Publishing, New Jersey. In Australia and New Zealand by Bookwise International, Findon, South Australia

HOW TO USE THIS GUIDE

If you want to find a Traditional Inns, Hotel or Restaurant in a particular area you can

• Turn to the Maps on pages 196–202

• Search the Indexes on pages 207–210

• Look for the Town or Village where you wish to stay in the main body of the Guide. This is divided into Countries. Place names in each Country appear at the head of the pages in alphabetical order.

The Indexes list the Traditional Inns, Hotels and Restaurants by Countries and by Counties, they also show those with amenities such as fishing, conference facilities, swimming, golf, etc.

The Maps cover all regions. Each Traditional Inns, Hotel and Restaurant symbol (a red triangle) relates to a property in this guide situated in or near the location shown.

Green Squares show the location of Johansens Recommended Country Houses & Small Hotels. If you cannot find a suitable Traditional Inn, Hotel or Restaurant near where you wish to stay, you may decide to choose one of these establishments as an alternative. They are all listed by place names on pages 204–205.

Blue dots show the location of Johansens Recommended Hotels which can be found in our other publication Johansens Recommended Hotels, Great Britain & Ireland.

Properties which did not feature in our last (1999) edition are identified with a "NEW" symbol at the top of the page.

The prices, in most cases, refer to the cost of one night's accommodation, with breakfast, for two people. Prices are also shown for single occupancy. These rates are correct at the time of going to press but always should be checked with the hotel before you make your reservation.

We occasionally receive letters from guests who have been charged for accommodation booked in advance but later cancelled. Readers should be aware that by making a reservation with a hotel, either by telephone, e-mail or in writing, they are entering into a legal contract. A hotelier under certain circumstances is entitled to make a charge for accommodation when guests fail to arrive, even if notice of the cancellation is given.

All guides are obtainable from bookshops or by Johansens Freephone 0800 269397 or by using the order coupons on pages 211–224.

INTRODUCTION

From The New Inn at Coln, Near Cirencester, Gloucestershire
Winner of the 1999 Johansens Most Excellent Inn Award

The New Inn at Coln has been a labour of love and to have been chosen as Johansens Most Excellent Inn 1999 is a great thrill.

My wife Sandra-Anne and I are particularly delighted for our wonderful staff, for it is they who made it possible. We feel enormous pride that this commitment has been further reflected by our current AA 'Courtesy and Care' Award.

Before we acquired The New Inn, Sandra-Anne had a wealth of conference organising experience, and subsequently worked with a top London interior designer. I had run a successful restaurant abroad, so it seemed a natural fusion of our experience when we discovered the Inn, were both mesmerised by its warmth and atmosphere, and bought it. Over the years we have gently enhanced these essential ingredients to complement the magic and tranquillity of the Cotswolds that surround us. I trust that Queen Elizabeth I, who decreed the building of the inn, would have approved.

We are most grateful to Johansens, whose inspectors we have always found professional and constructive, and also to our guests for nominating us for this award. We look forward to welcoming them back, as we do those who have yet to be our guests at The New Inn at Coln.

Brian Evans

MARSH
An **MMC** Company

Marsh, the world's leading insurance broker, is proud to be the appointed Preferred Insurance Provider to Johansens Members Worldwide

ARE YOU A HOTELIER?

There is never a spare moment when you're running a Hotel, Inn, Restaurant or Country House. If you're not with a customer, your mind is on stocktaking. Sound familiar?

At Marsh, we realise you have little time to worry about your insurance policy, instead, you require peace of mind that you are covered.

That is why for over 20 years Marsh have been providing better cover for businesses like yours.

Our unique services are developed specifically for establishments meeting the high standards required for entry in a Johansens guide.

CONTACT US NOW FOR DETAILS OF THE INSURANCE POLICY FOR JOHANSENS
01892 553160 (UK)

Insurance Policy for Johansens members arranged by:
Marsh UK Ltd.
Mount Pleasant House,
Lonsdale Gardens,
Tunbridge Wells, Kent TN1 1NY

ARE YOU AN INDEPENDENT TRAVELLER?

Insurance is probably the last thing on your mind. Especially when you are going on holiday or on a business trip. But are you protected when travelling? Is your home protected while you are away?

Marsh offer a wide range of insurances that gives you peace of mind when travelling.

FOR DETAILS ON THESE SERVICES RING (UK):

TRAVEL	**01462 428041**
PENSIONS & FINANCIAL SERVICES	**0171 357 3307**
HOUSEHOLD	**01462 428200**
MOTOR	**01462 428100**
HEALTHCARE	**01462 428000**

Johansens Recommended Traditional Inns, Hotels and Restaurants
England

England has so much to offer – castles, cathedrals, museums, magnificent country houses and the opportunity to stay in areas of great historical importance.

Castle Combe, Wiltshire

Regional Tourist Boards

Cumbria Tourist Board
Ashleigh, Holly Road, Windermere
Cumbria LA23 2AQ
Tel: 015394 44444
England's most beautiful lakes and tallest mountains reach out from the Lake District National Park to a landscape of spectacular coasts, hills and dales.

East of England Tourist Board
Toppesfield Hall, Hadleigh
Suffolk IP7 5DN
Tel: 01473 822922
Cambridgeshire, Essex, Hertfordshire, Bedfordshire, Norfolk, Suffolk and Lincolnshire.

Heart of England Tourist Board
Woodside, Larkhill Road.
Worcester WR5 2EZ
Tel: 01905 763436
Gloucestershire, Hereford & Worcester, Shropshire, Staffordshire, Warwickshire, West Midlands, Derbyshire, Leicestershire, Northamptonshire, Nottinghamshire & Rutland. Represents the districts of Cherwell & West Oxfordshire in the county of Oxfordshire.

London Tourist Board
Glen House, Stag Place
London SW1E 5LT
Tel: 0171 932 2000
The Greater London area (see page 13)

Northumbria Tourist Board
Aykley Heads
Durham DH1 5UX
Tel: 0191 375 3000
The Tees Valley, Durham, Northumberland, Tyne & Wear.

North West Tourist Board
Swan House, Swan Meadow Road, Wigan Pier
Lancashire WN3 5BB
Tel: 01942 821222
Cheshire, Greater Manchester, Lancashire, Merseyside & the High Peak District of Derbyshire.

South East England Tourist Board
The Old Brew House, Warwick Park, Tunbridge Wells, Kent TN2 5TU
Tel: 01892 540766
East & West Sussex, Kent & Surrey

Southern Tourist Board
40 Chamberlayne Road, Eastleigh
Hampshire SO50 5JH
Tel: 01703 620006
East & North Dorset, Hampshire, Isle of Wight, Berkshire, Buckinghamshire & Oxfordshire.

West Country Tourist Board
60 St David's Hill, Exeter
Devon EX4 4SY
Tel: 01392 425426
Bath & NE Somerset, Bristol, Cornwall and the Isles of Scilly, Devon, Dorset (Western), North Somerset & Wiltshire.

Yorkshire Tourist Board
312 Tadcaster Road
York YO2 2HF
Tel: 01904 707961
Yorkshire and North & North East Lincolnshire.

Further Information

English Heritage
23rd Floor, Portland HouseStag Place
London SW1E 5EE
Tel: 0171-973 3000
Offers an unrivalled choice of properties to visit.

Historic Houses Association
2 Chester Street
London SW1X 7BB
Tel: 0171-259 5688
Ensures the survival of historic houses and gardens in private ownership in Great Britain

The National Trust
36 Queen Anne's Gate
London SW1H 9AS
Tel: 0171-222 9251
Cares for more than 590,000 acres of countryside and over 400 historic buildings.

THE GREYHOUND INN

STOCKS ROAD, ALDBURY, NR TRING, HERTFORDSHIRE HP23 5RT
TEL: 01442 851228 FAX: 01442 851495

Set in the glorious village of Aldbury, this former coaching inn overlooking a charming duck pond is now a popular location for film makers. The Greyhound Inn is surrounded by the beautiful Chiltern Hills with its wealth of footpaths and bridle paths, bird and nature attractions. The individually decorated bedrooms combine traditional décor such as antiques and pine furnishings with modern day comforts including television and en suite facilities. Breakfast, either continental or full English, is served in the oak-beamed restaurant. Guests may choose to dine here in the evening and savour the mouthwatering dishes but this inspired menu can also be enjoyed in any of the areas including the new light and airy garden room. The frequently changing menu is mainly based on fine English dishes with a strong emphasis on quality and the freshness of ingredients. During the summer months, the locally renowned bar snacks may be enjoyed in the courtyard garden. They are complemented by a local brew, Aldbury, made by the neighbouring Vale Brewery Company. Nearby attractions include the Rothschilds Museum, Whipsnade Zoo and Stocks, an excellent base for golf and horse riding. **Directions:** From M1, leave at junction 5 or 8. Exit M25 at junction 20 and take the new A41. Leave at the Tring exit and follow the signs for Aldbury. Price guide: Single £43–£55; double £49.50–£60; suites £60–£70. Weekend packages are also available.

THE DOLPHIN INN

THORPENESS, ALDEBURGH, SUFFOLK IP16 4NA
TEL: 01728 454994 FAX: 01728 454300

Recently refurbished, the Dolphin Inn is a traditional village hostelry at the heart of Thorpeness, a purposely designed holiday hamlet on Suffolk's heritage coast. Built in the 1920's and planned as a family holiday paradise, the village is hemmed in by a lake, the fragrant Suffolk wolds and the sea. Visitors marvel at the calmness, cleanliness and tranquillity that pervades Thorpeness and it does indeed feel as if time has stood still in this untainted corner of rural England. The Dolphin Inn is the quintessence of stylish and elegant simplicity. The rooms are bright, comfortable and superbly furnished, while the bar has timber floors and pine furniture. The food has an excellent reputation in the area and in the summer visitors can take advantage of the outdoor bar and barbecue facilities. Thorpeness seems to be tailor-made for the active holiday maker. The hamlet boasts a fine 18-hole golf course and seven tennis courts are available for hire at the local country club. From the sand and shingle beach, guests can take boat trips along Suffolk's breathtaking Heritage Coast. Oyster lovers will not miss the opportunity to visit nearby Orford, which is famed for the quality of its seafood. Ornithologists will also marvel at the many and varied species of bird to be seen in the vicinity. **Directions:** Travelling from the A12, take the turn for Aldeburgh and follow the signs for Thorpeness. Price guide: Single £45; double £60.

DEANS PLACE HOTEL

SEAFORD ROAD, ALFRISTON, EAST SUSSEX BN26 5TW
TEL: 01323 870248 FAX: 01323 870918

This breathtaking 14th century hotel is surrounded by beautiful acres of landscaped gardens. With the Sussex coast close by and towns such as Brighton, Eastbourne and Tunbridge Wells within easy driving distance, this hotel is the perfect setting for a weekend away! The hotel boasts Peter Dowding as their head chef, who was formerly a sous chef at The Dorchester, and after an excellent Sunday lunch, visitors are able to enjoy a relaxing walk in the extensive and exceptionally well looked after grounds. The hotel itself also has an outdoor heated swimming pool that is available to guests between May and September inclusive. However, for those who simply want to just relax, they will be spoilt for choice with various lounges to choose from! With its excellent public rooms and facilities, this hotel is a suitable venue for all occasions from wedding ceremonies and receptions to seminars and conferences. There is also a four poster bed available for that special celebration! Music lovers will be pleased to hear that the hotel is not far from the Glyndebourne festival and for those who prefer a quiet round of golf, there are plenty of local golf courses to choose from. **Directions:** The hotel can be found just off the A27 through the south side of the village of Alfriston, on the left. Price guide: Single from £59.50, double from £89.

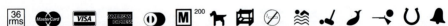

THE BOATHOUSE BRASSERIE

HOUGHTON BRIDGE, AMBERLEY, NR ARUNDEL, WEST SUSSEX BN18 9LR
TEL: 01798 831059 FAX: 01798 831063

This delightful informal restaurant is on the River Arun at the site of the ancient Houghton Wharf. It is under the same private ownership as the White Horse Inn at Sutton. The restaurant is Edwardian in style, full of character and strewn with charts and maritime bric-a-brac. Weather permitting, you may prefer to enjoy your meal out on the open wooden deck or under the verandah. The attractive staff are friendly and attentive. The Carvery, is without doubt, the speciality here – succulent roast meats are on display, carved for you by the chefs. There is a small but impressive à la carte menu and the fresh fish is a tempting alternative. Extra seasonal dishes are shown on the blackboard in the bar. There is a fine selection of sweets, a good cheeseboard and coffee of the highest class. The set price lunch (two-courses and coffee) is good value and very popular. On Sunday it is advisable to book well ahead. The wine list is well chosen and reasonably priced. Arundel Castle, Petworth House, Parham House, Chichester (Festival Theatre) and Goodwood Racecourse are all nearby. Being on the Southdowns Way there are some good walks to be had. The Amberley Chalkpits Industrial Museum is nearby. **Directions:** The Boathouse is on the B2139 (Arundel to Storrington Road) where it crosses the River Arun.

THE NEW DUNGEON GHYLL HOTEL

GREAT LANGDALE, AMBLESIDE, CUMBRIA LA22 9JY
TEL: 015394 37213 FAX: 015394 37666

The splendour of Lakeland's most majestic fells is the setting for The New Dungeon Ghyll Hotel. It is built on the site of an ancient Norse settlement, but was rebuilt as a Victorian Hotel in the 1830s. Bought by John Smith in 1991 and completely refurbished, the hotel stands in its own lawned gardens in a spectacular position beneath the Langdale Pikes and Pavey Ark. The comfortable bedrooms are all en suite and offer colour television, tea and coffee making facilities and direct dial telephones. There are two bars with open fires. The dining room enjoys panoramic views of the Valley and the Fells beyond. A table d'hôte menu is offered and includes a varied choice of both English and continental dishes. Generous portions are served to satisfy the hearty appetite of a keen walker. A good selection of wines is available to complement the cuisine. The Langdale Valley offers wonderful walking and climbing opportunities in England's most beautiful corner, with abundant wildlife and many places of historical and literary importance. From the hotel guests can walk up Stickle Ghyll to Stickle Tarn and onwards to Pavey Ark, Harrison Stickle and numerous other pikes. **Directions:** M6 junction 36 A591. Through Windermere to Ambleside. Follow A593 towards Coniston, turn right onto B5343 to Langdale. The hotel is two miles past Chapelstyle on the right. Price guide: Single £40–£45; double £59–£70.

THE ROYAL OAK INN

BONGATE, APPLEBY-IN-WESTMORLAND , CUMBRIA CA16 6UN
TEL: 017683 51463 FAX: 017683 52300 E-MAIL: ApplebyInn@aol.com

The Royal Oak has been a coaching inn since the 1600s and parts of the building are 750 years old. It is a well cared for, traditional hostelry, situated in the oldest part of the north Pennine town of Appleby-in-Westmorland. The oak panelling, beams, stone walls and open fires combine to give the inn its warm, inviting atmosphere. The bedrooms are all individually furnished and all have a private bathroom. Facilities for ironing and clothes-drying are available. Guests will find the owners hospitable and their staff attentive, providing an efficient service. An extensive selection of fresh fish, local meat and vegetarian dishes, together with some unusual specialities, are offered to suit all tastes. There are two dining rooms, one of which is non-smoking and an extensive wine list of over 70 bins. A full Westmorland breakfast is served to set visitors up for a day of sightseeing. The Royal Oak has held an AA rosette for its food since 1996. Hand-pumped ales plus malt whiskies are offered in the Snug and Taproom bars. The inn is well placed for visitors wishing to explore the celebrated scenery of the high moorlands, as well as the numerous castles and historic houses in the area. Running through Appleby is the Settle to Carlisle railway which traverses spectacular remote countryside. **Directions:** The inn can easily be located on the south-east approach to Appleby from the A66 Penrith-Scotch Corner road. Price Guide: Single £33–£53; double £72–£86.

RED LION INN

MAIN STREET, HOGNASTON, ASHBOURNE, DERBYSHIRE DE6 1PR
TEL: 01335 370396 FAX: 01335 370961 E-MAIL: lionrouge@msn.com

The Red Lion is a typical country inn which offers a traditional welcoming atmosphere of good hospitality and homely service. It is situated on the fringe of The Peak District in the main street of the tiny village of Hognaston, just a short drive from the attractive old market town of Ashbourne. With a log fire in the bar, cosy corners, good ales and rustic character, this is a welcome retreat for those wanting a relaxing break or for visitors seeking the opportunity to walk through beautiful countryside. Three individually styled and traditionally furnished bedrooms offer comfortable accommodation. Each bedroom has en suite facilities with a shower. Guests dine in a delightful, sunny conservatory or in the L-shaped bar where the menu is entirely "chalkboard". The choice is extensive and the food is good. Chef Hilary Heskin and her team show considerable expertise in the interesting and imaginative choice of ingredient combinations and sauces that they create and in the way they present them. This wonderful walking country is home to some of England's finest stately homes and National Trust properties such as Sudbury Hall and Kedleston Hall. Other attractions include boating and fishing at Carsington Water, Crich Tramway Museum and Alton Towers. **Directions:** From M1, exit at junction 25 and take A52 towards Derby and Ashbourne. Hognaston is situated on B5035 Ashbourne-Wirksworth road. Price guide: Single £45; double £75.

NEW

BEECHES COUNTRY RESTAURANT

WALDLEY, DOVERIDGE, NR ASHBOURNE, DERBYSHIRE DE6 5LR
TEL: 01889 590288 FAX: 01889 590559 E-MAIL: beechesfa@aol.com

Beeches Country Restaurant was opened in 1986 by Barbara and Paul Tunnicliffe in their home, then the centre of a thriving dairy farm. Much has changed since then. The farm has ceased activities – whilst the restaurant has proved so popular that it has been lovingly and carefully extended into an exceptional venue for both business and leisure visitors to the Derbyshire Dales. The bedrooms are spacious and have direct dial telephones, refreshment trays and televisions. The hotel offers business meeting facilities with access to its facsimile and photocopying machines. At the heart of The Beeches' popularity is Barbara's splendid cooking. Featuring bold flavours, some based on traditional recipes, some on new British ideas, she always uses the freshest ingredients. She regularly demonstrates at The Royal Argiculture and BBC Good Food Shows. Specialities include breasts of organically-fed duck glazed with honey and crushed peppercorns, served pink on spring onion mash on a rich rhubarb sauce or roast suckling pig on a hot Waldorf salad with a rich Calvados sauce – not for the faint hearted! Vegetarian, fresh fish and lighter dishes are also offered. Sudbury Hall, Calke Abbey, Tutbury Castle, the Potteries museums and Alton Towers are all nearby. **Directions:** The nearest motorways are M6, junction 15 or M1 junction 24. Once on A50, exit at Doveridge. Travel North to Waldley for 2 miles. Price guide: Single £48; double £62–£72.

TYTHERLEIGH COT HOTEL

CHARDSTOCK, AXMINSTER, DEVON EX13 7BN
TEL: 01460 221170 FAX: 01460 221291

Originally the village cider house, this 14th century Grade II listed building has been skilfully converted into a spacious modern hotel, idyllically situated in the secluded village of Chardstock on the Devon/Dorset/Somerset borders. The bedrooms, converted from former barns and outbuildings, are all individually designed, some with four-poster or half-tester beds and double Jacuzzis. The beautifully designed award winning restaurant is housed in a Victorian-style conservatory, overlooking an ornamental lily pond with cascading fountain and wrought-iron bridge. Special house parties are held at Christmas and New Year and bargain break weekends can be arranged. The hotel has an outdoor heated swimming pool, sauna, solarium and mini-gym. Riding, tennis, golf and clay pigeon shooting can be arranged locally. The hotel is ideally located for guests to explore the varied landscape of the South West with many historic houses and National Trust properties nearby, such as Forde Abbey, Shute Barton and Parnham House. **Directions:** From Chard take A358 Axminster road; Chardstock signposted on the right about 3 miles along. Price guide: Single £50; double/twin £65–£85.

THE WINDMILL AT BADBY

MAIN STREET, BADBY, NR DAVENTRY, NORTHAMPTONSHIRE NN11 6AN
TEL: 01327 702363 FAX: 01327 311521

The Windmill Inn Hotel was first established as an inn in the 17th century and is situated in the heart of the pretty village of Badby. A traditional thatched country pub, complete with log fires, The Windmill offers good food and a range of cask-conditioned ales. The owners, with their extensive experience of hotel and pub management, have plenty of ideas for regular activities. Winter Sportsmen's Dinners and theme nights with entertainment are popular events. The en suite bedrooms provide comfortable accommodation and the whole hotel is ideally suitable for house party weekends from 12–14 guests. Under the skilled eye of Gavin Baxter the award-winning kitchen prepares a varied range of freshly cooked dishes. The sumptuous menu includes a delicious traditional Sunday Luncheon at £7.50 which offers excellent value for money. Stilton mushrooms, chargrilled Cajun chicken, steak and kidney pie and poached salmon with new potatoes are amongst the many highly recommended specialities. Weddings, functions and business meetings and conferences are catered for with ease. Places to visit include Althorp, Sulgrave Manor (home of the Washingtons), Bleinheim Palace, Silverstone Circuit, Warwick and Stratford-upon-Avon. **Directions:** Situated in the centre of Badby, a village located off the A361, three miles south of Daventry on the Banbury road. Price guide: Single £52.50–£55; double £69–£79.

THE VICTORIA HOTEL

FRONT STREET, BAMBURGH, NORTHUMBERLAND NE69 7BP
TEL: 01668 214431 FAX: 01668 214404

Overlooked by the impressive castle, this excellent hotel provides a welcome of the highest standard. Tucked away in the Northumberland village of Bamburgh, the surrounding area is steeped in history and offers much recreation for golfers, bird watchers, horse-riders, water sport fanatics and those who simply enjoy walking and admiring the local scenery. Families with children of all ages will be spoilt for choice; from exploring the beach and frolicking in the rock pools to visiting the Bird Sanctuary on the Farne Islands, there is something for everyone.

Inside the hotel, parents will welcome the sight of a soft play den for the under 10's. The bedrooms are individually named and tastefully decorated, each with its own character. The hotel has a Brasserie restaurant offering a refreshingly different environment with superb food, using the best regional produce. **Directions:** Turn off the A1 north of Alnwick onto the B1342 near Belford and follow the signs to Bamburgh. The hotel can be found at the top of the village opposite the green. Price guide: Single £40–£55; double/twin £60–£80.

THE PHEASANT

BASSENTHWAITE LAKE, NR COCKERMOUTH, CUMBRIA CA13 9YE
TEL: 017687 76234 FAX: 017687 76002

This famous 17th century coaching inn is set in lovely gardens and woodlands just 100 yards from the shores of Bassenthwaite Lake. Renowned for its friendly hospitality, The Pheasant has 20 light and airy bedrooms, each comfortably furnished and with private facilities. Three are located in the bungalow next to the hotel. Guests have three sitting rooms to choose from when they want to enjoy a quiet morning coffee or a real Cumbrian afternoon tea with home-made specialities including scones with brandy butter. The bar, with its polished walls and oak settles, is said to be one of the best known in the Lake District. With its traditional setting and convivial atmosphere, this is the perfect place to enjoy a drink before moving on to dinner. The food served in the lovely beamed dining room comprises many local Cumbrian specialities, in addition to traditional English food and a wide selection of fine wines. A daily changing menu includes culinary delights to cater for all. The Pheasant is within easy reach of the whole Lake District. Usually chosen for its idyllic and peaceful location, the hotel makes a convenient base for guests on fishing, bird-watching or sporting expeditions. **Directions:** Just off the A66, The Pheasant is 6 miles east of Cockermouth and 8 miles north-west of Keswick. Price guide: Single £59–£79; double £90–£120.

THE WOOLPACK INN

BECKINGTON, NR BATH, SOMERSET BA3 6SP
TEL: 01373 831244 FAX: 01373 831223

Situated in the centre of the village of Beckington, on the borders of Somerset, Avon and Wiltshire, The Woolpack is a small coaching inn dating from the 16th century. Legend has it that condemned criminals were allowed a final drink here before being led away to the local gallows. The inn has been thoughtfully decorated and furnished to recapture the original character of the building. On the ground floor is the bar area, with its stone floor and open log fire, where fine traditional ale is served. There is also a small lounge. Awarded two AA Rosettes, the attractive restaurant serves an interesting menu prepared with fresh, local produce. Guests may start with a warm bruschetta of mozzarella, tomato, scallions and pesto before indulging in a veal escalope with wild mushrooms, roasted shallots and a white wine butter sauce. Desserts include iced tiramisu with a coffee and nut sauce and traditional sticky toffee pudding with a rum butter sauce. Each of the 12 bedrooms has been individually renovated, each having an en suite bathroom and all modern comforts. There are places to visit nearby in abundance: the Georgian city of Bath, the cathedral cities of Salisbury and Wells, Longleat House and Safari Park, the stone circles at Stonehenge and Avebury and the tropical bird gardens at Rode. **Directions:** Beckington, recently bypassed, is on A36 Bath–Southampton road on the borders of Somerset and Wiltshire. Price guide: Single £55; double £65–£85.

THE BLUE BELL HOTEL

MARKET PLACE, BELFORD, NORTHUMBERLAND NE70 7NE
TEL: 01668 213543 FAX: 01668 213787 E-MAIL: bluebel@globalnet.co.uk

This beautifully restored old coaching inn stands in the centre of Belford, near the old Market Cross. The sophisticated Georgian-style interiors are decorated to complement the original features. Luxurious bedrooms provide every modern comfort and are all unique. There is an elegant residents' lounge and two bars, well stocked with fine malts, rare brandies and vintage ports. The hotel also has three acres of walled terraced grounds, with a putting lawn and an organic vegetable and herb garden. The emphasis is on freshness with fruit and vegetables from the hotel gardens, combined with an excellent supply of fresh local produce such as Cheviot lamb, Tweed salmon and Craster kippers, creating a range of delicious seasonal dishes.

Frequently changing à la carte and table d'hôte menus are served in the garden restaurant, which is furnished with locally crafted tables. For a more simple but substantial menu, try the Buttery. There is much to discover along Northumberland's scenic coastline – the Farne Islands, Lindisfarne and Berwick-upon-Tweed are among the many interesting attractions. Sporting activities which can be enjoyed locally include shooting, fishing, riding and golf. **Directions:** Midway between Berwick and Alnwick, about 14 miles south of Berwick and two minutes from the A1. From A1 turn off at Belford/Wooler junction to join the B6349. The hotel is situated in the centre of the village. Price guide: Single £38–£60; double £76–£98.

CATHERINE WHEEL

BIBURY, NR CIRENCESTER, GLOUCESTERSHIRE GL7 5ND
TEL: 01285 740250 FAX: 01285 740779

The 15th century Catherine Wheel is located centrally in Bibury, the Cotswold village described by William Morris as "the most beautiful in England". Straddling the River Coln, this pre-Roman settlement was listed in the Domesday Book: amongst today's attractions are the trout farm and Arlington Mill Museum, just a stroll down the hill from the inn. In the main bar area there is clear evidence of former 15th century dwellings and recent refurbishment has retained many original features entirely in keeping with its history, including the many exposed ships' timber beams. The Arlington Bar commemorates Old Bibury in fine prints and old photographs and its warm hospitality is reflected in the large open fires that blaze in wintertime.

Equally popular in summer is the ancient apple and pear orchard which provides plenty of shaded seating for a refreshing drink. The two double and two family bedrooms have thoroughly modern en suite bathrooms, colour televisions and complimentary hot drink trays. The extensive dining areas are run on informal lines, offering a wide choice of traditional British Pub fare. The fresh Bibury trout are perennially popular: fine roast beef for Sunday lunch and daily chef's special dishes provide an array of alternatives. Nearby are the ancient cottages of Arlington Row and the wonderful gardens of Barnsley House. **Directions:** Bibury stands on B4425 between Cirencester and Burford. Price guide: from £40 per room plus £5 per head for breakfast.

THE FISHERMAN'S COT

BICKLEIGH, NR TIVERTON, DEVON EX16 8RW
TEL: 01884 855237/855289 FAX: 01884 855241

This picturesque, rambling, thatched inn, surrounded by thickly wooded hillsides, stands on the west bank of the River Exe. Bickleigh Bridge nearby dates from the middle ages. The charming traditional bars and comfortable, rooms combined with tasteful furnishings create a relaxing atmosphere which tempts guests to return again and again. The Fisherman's Cot is excellent value for money with the 21 en suite bedrooms having every home-from-home facility. They vary in size, but all enjoy the character of old world charm. Superbly prepared cuisine can be enjoyed in the warmly panelled restaurant which in the summer months opens onto a terrace overlooking the river. The inn is an ideal base for guests who enjoy walking, riding and fishing. For those who like history, Bickleigh Castle is nearby along with Tiverton Castle and Tiverton Canal with its horse-drawn barges. **Directions:** From the M5 exit at junction 27. At Tiverton take the A396 to Bickleigh. Alternatively, follow the A396 from Exeter city centre. Price guide: Single from £49; double/twin from £69.

STAG & HOUNDS

FOREST ROAD, BINFIELD, NR BRACKNELL, BERKSHIRE RG12 9HA
TEL: 01344 483553 FAX: 01344 423620

The Stag & Hounds is a charming 14th century inn with a fascinating history. It has strong hunting connections and was a favourite with Henry VIII on his regular hunting trips to Great Windsor Park and the surrounding areas. It is also believed that Elizabeth I enjoyed watching the locals dancing round the maypole from the windows of the inn. A tree stump in front of the inn marks the original centre of the Great Park and it is now a protected monument. Visitors to the Stag & Hounds can expect a very warm welcome and excellent hospitality. It is full of character, tastefully decorated, comfortably furnished and has retained many original features - all that is best in a British pub, complemented by delicious dishes from a comprehensive menu and a superb selection of beers and wines. Binfield village, with its 14th century church, is ideally situated for exploring the many delights of Berkshire. Nearby is Ascot and its popular racecourse, Eton with its famous college and historic Windsor. **Directions:** From the M4, exit at junction 10. Take the A329 towards Bracknell and at the first exit turn left onto the B3408. Continue through Binfield village and turn left at the mini roundabout, signed Bracknell and Warfield. The Stag & Hounds is approximately half a mile further on.

WHITE HORSE HOTEL

4 HIGH STREET, BLAKENEY, HOLT, NORFOLK NR25 7AL
TEL: 01263 740574 FAX: 01263 741303

The White Horse was formerly an 18th century coaching inn and in the early 1900s became the first hotel in Blakeney, a popular boating centre with a main street of brick and flint buildings and a waterfront crowded with sailing craft and cruisers. Set around a shady courtyard, the hotel has ten simple and uncluttered en suite bedrooms, some with good views across the harbour, the National Trust reserve and marshes. All have colour television, telephone and tea and coffee making facilities. A comfortable residents sitting room is available. The area is much favoured by artists and the hotel has its own gallery with regularly changing exhibitions. No dogs. Situated in the former stables which overlook the walled garden, the restaurant is light and airy and has an attractive relaxed style. Chef Christopher Hyde offers a seasonal à la carte menu using local fare. Lobsters, sea bass, pheasant and pigeons are favourites with special dishes introduced daily on the restaurant blackboard. Bar food includes whitebait, herring roes, crab salads and mussels. The meals are complemented by a good choice of wines and ales. The sandy resorts of Sheringham and Cromer, boat trips to Blakeney Point Nature Reserve, the Norfolk Coast Path, Blickling Hall and Holkham Hall are all nearby. There is sailing, fishing, riding and golf at Cromer and Sheringham. **Directions:** From Norwich, take A140 to Cromer and then A149 coastal road west for approx. 12m. Price guide: Single £35; double £70; suite £80.

DIAL HOUSE

**THE CHESTNUTS, HIGH STREET, BOURTON-ON-THE-WATER , GLOUCESTERSHIRE GL54 2AN
TEL: 01451 822244 FAX: 01451 810126 E-MAIL: info@dialhousehotel.co.uk**

In the heart of the Cotswolds lies Dial House Hotel, a small 17th century country house which combines the charm and elegance of a bygone era with all the facilities of a modern hotel. Proprietors Lynn and Peter Boxall have many years experience in the hotel industry and extend a warm welcome to their guests. The hotel is open throughout the year and roaring log fires burn throughout the winter months. In the summer, lunches are served in the delightful and secluded walled garden. Chef Callam Williamson creates delicious, freshly-cooked food for the à la carte restaurant, which creates an aura of old England with its inglenook fireplace and oak beams. Dial House has received 2 AA Rosettes for its cuisine and every care is taken by friendly staff to provide guests with an interesting choice of dishes and good quality wines. An open fire in the comfortable lounge creates an ideal setting to finish off an evening with coffee and liqueurs. The décor of the bedrooms is light and cheery. Some have antique four-poster beds and overlook the garden. All are en suite, centrally-heated and equipped with tea and coffee making facilities. Bargain breaks available. Stratford-Upon-Avon, Bath and Cirencester, Warwick Castle, Blenheim Palace, Cheltenham, Slimbridge Wildfowl Trust and Oxford are all nearby. **Directions**: Bourton-on-the-Water is 4 miles south west of Stow-on-the-Wold off A429. Price Guide: Single from £49.50; double from £99.

THE MANOR HOTEL

WEST BEXINGTON, DORCHESTER, DORSET DT2 9DF
TEL: 01308 897616 FAX: 01308 897035 E-MAIL: themanorhouse@bt.connect.com

The Manor Hotel, winner of the 1997 Johansens Most Excellent Inn Award and also mentioned in the Domesday Book, is in a wonderful setting, overlooking the beautiful Dorset countryside and spectacular Lyme Bay. The friendly atmosphere is apparent immediately on entering the inn, while the oak-panelling, stone walls and original fireplaces remind guests they are in the midst of history. The restaurant is brilliant, with two or three course menus that include wonderful choices - smoked duck breast and mango salad, lobster and scallop ragout, roast salmon and prawns with a lime and avocado salsa or roast pork with sage crust and apple sauce. Vegetarian dishes also feature and there is a children's menu. The wine list is exciting. Buffet meals, also including seafood, are served in the cosy cellar bar. There is an attractive conservatory for relaxing while children have their own play area outside. There are twelve charming en suite bedrooms and those at the top of the house have splendid views over the sea. This is Thomas Hardy country and there are famous gardens and historic houses to visit. Chesil Beach and Abbotsbury Swannery are nearby and water sports and country pursuits can be enjoyed. **Directions:** West Bexington is on the B3157, 5 miles east of Bridport, 11 miles from Dorchester and Weymouth. Price guide: Single from £55; double £98–£108.

THE BOARS HEAD

MAIN ROAD, AUST, BRISTOL BS12 3AX
TEL: 01454 632581 FAX: 01454 632278

The delightful, welcoming 16th century Boars Head is situated remotely down a maze of narrow lanes just outside the tiny village of Aust. It is almost too comfortable and special to be an inn. Beautifully decorated and furnished, its interior is broken up with lots of intimate areas which feature soft seating, large sofas and armchairs. The Boars Head is enthusiastically run by Brian Holder and Mary May who say that many visitors apologise after stepping through the front door because they believe they have wandered into someone's private home. There is no public bar, just comfortable armchairs where visitors can relax over their newspapers or a friendly chat. Open fires burn logs resembling small tree trunks during winter months. The inn is a favourite lunchtime venue with business executives from Bristol, Avonmouth, Chepstow and Newport and an evening attraction for the locals. All are drawn by the hospitable atmosphere and excellent traditional food. Tempting dishes include such delights as River Severn salmon, trout from Cirencester and plaice served with Evesham asparagus when in season. A short drive away, at Thornbury, is the unfinished "castle" of the Duke of Buckingham, one of the most imposing Tudor buildings in the west of England. There are no bedrooms. **Directions:** M4 to M48 turn off at Junction 1 and join the A403 to Aust.

THE NEW INN

BADMINTON ROAD, MAYSHILL, NR FRAMPTON COTTRELL, BRISTOL BS36 2NT
TEL: 01454 773161 FAX: 01454 774341

Built as a rest-stop for travellers on the road north from Bristol via Chipping Sodbury, this lovely 17th century inn has a unique rustic charm. It is a superb example of a historic coaching inn and the hospitality afforded to those early passengers and coachmen is just as generous today. It is a delightfully unspoilt tavern. A plaque discovered inserted above the fireplace in an upstairs room bears the date 1655 and it is now displayed in the main bar. Although renovated and sympathetically modernised, many of the fitments and the unevenness of the floors and ceilings ensure that much of the New Inn's 300-year-old character remains. A rotating hook for supporting a baby's cradle away from the fire hangs from the ceiling in the traditionally furnished Says Court Lounge. Popular with locals, the inn's fine range of beers, good homely food and conviviality also attracts visitors from miles around. The shopping and entertainment delights of Bristol are close by. It is worth visiting the 14th century church of St James at Iron Acton to see stained glass from the Middle Ages. Popular daytime excursions also include trips to Dyram Park, a country mansion with extensive parkland overlooking the valley of the Severn. **Directions:** The New Inn is situated a just few miles north of Bristol, off the A342 road to Yate.

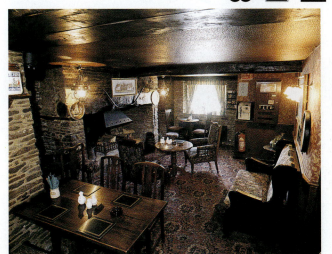

THE BROADWAY HOTEL

THE GREEN, BROADWAY, WORCESTERSHIRE WR12 7AA
TEL: 01386 852401 FAX: 01386 853879 E-MAIL: bookings@cotswold–inns–hotels.co.uk

The delightful Broadway Hotel stands proudly in the centre of the picturesque Cotswold village of Broadway where every stone evokes memories of Elizabethan England. Once used by the Abbots of Pershore, the hotel was formerly a 16th century house, as can be seen by its architecture which combines the half timbers of the Vale of Evesham with the distinctive honey-coloured and grey stone of the Cotswolds. It epitomises a true combination of old world charm and modern day amenities with friendly efficient service. All of the bedrooms provide television, telephone and tea and coffee making facilities. Traditional English dishes and a peaceful ambience are offered in the beamed Courtyard Restaurant. There is an impressive variety of à la carte dishes complemented by a good wine list. The cosy and congenial Jockey Club bar is a pleasant place to relax and enjoy a drink. The inn overlooks the village green at the bottom of the main street where guests can browse through shops offering an array of fine antiques. On a clear day, 13 counties of England and Wales can be viewed from Broadway Tower. Snowhill, Burford, Chipping Campden, Bourton-on-the-Water, Stow-on-the-Wold and Winchcombe as well as larger Cheltenham, Worcester and Stratford are within easy reach. **Directions:** From London M40 to Oxford, A40 to Burford, A429 through Stow-on-the-Wold, then A44 to Broadway. Price guide: Single £68.50–£75; double £110–£125.

THE SNAKECATCHER

LYNDHURST ROAD, BROCKENHURST, HAMPSHIRE SO42 7RL
TEL: 01590 622348 FAX: 01590 624155

The Snakecatcher is one of the New Forest's most delightful inns and incorporates buildings used as stabling for coaching traffic before the arrival of the railway in 1847. Then they were converted into The Railway Inn and in 1983 it was renamed after a local customer, Harry "Brusher" Mills, who roamed the Forest catching adders for payment and brushed the wicket of the nearby cricket pitch. Refurbishment has extended and enhanced The Snakecatcher's facilities but much of the traditional character and features remain, including a skittle alley in Brusher's Bar. The furniture, fittings and décor are in keeping with the inn's history and an excellent range of beers is complemented by good, wholesome, home-cooked food.

There are open fires to comfort winter visitors while during the summer months they can sip refreshments in a charming little garden and, on occasions, enjoy the inn's brass band concerts. There is no smoking at lunchtimes and in some areas during the evenings. Although a lot of the village dates from the railway age there are some 17th century cottages and The Church of St Nicholas is mentioned in the Domesday Book of 1086. It is an ideal base from which to explore the New Forest and for visiting such places as Beaulieu, Broadlands, Salisbury and Winchester. **Directions:** The Snakecatcher is on the A337 between Lyndhurst and Lymington, reached from the M27 via junction 1.

COTSWOLD GATEWAY HOTEL

CHELTENHAM ROAD, BURFORD, OXFORDSHIRE OX18 4HX
TEL: 01993 822695 FAX: 01993 823600 E-MAIL: cotswold.gateway@dialpipex.com.l.c

In the days of horse drawn coaches Cotswold Gateway Hotel was a welcome stopover for travellers visiting Burford. Today, this 18th century inn, which has recently been lavishly renovated, offers its guests every modern comfort and amenity. A friendly and intimate service is offered by the highly trained staff, equal to any found in a family run hotel. All of the bedrooms have been individually designed and furnished and provide a trouser press, alarm clock, television, telephone and tea and coffee making facilities. Deservedly awarded its first AA Rosette, the spacious and pleasantly furnished restaurant has an extensive menu comprising of English and Continental dishes supported by a good wine list.

The bar, where an exciting range of English and continental fare is served, has undergone a complete refurbishment. It is a pleasant place to relax and enjoy a drink, while the coffee shop serves informal meals, tea and refreshments. Adjacent to the hotel is a mews of specialist antique shops offering an array of fine antique pieces. Burford itself has changed little since the end of the 17th century and its streets are lined with exquisite buildings in the honeyed, locally quarried limestone. There are many other pretty Cotswold villages to explore. **Directions:** Burford is on the A40 where it crosses the A361, halfway between Oxford and Cheltenham. Price guide: Single from £65; double from £85.

THE GOLDEN PHEASANT HOTEL & RESTAURANT

THE HIGH STREET, BURFORD, OXFORDSHIRE OX18 4QA
TEL: 01993 823417/823223 FAX: 01993 822621

Much favoured by Queen Elizabeth I, the town of Burford is often referred to as the Gateway to the Cotswolds. At its heart, the Golden Pheasant has an unbroken history as a coaching inn dating back to the 15th century. Unpretentious yet atmospheric, the property is full of character with authentic beams and open log fires. The welcome here is equally warm and families particularly are made to feel at home. Bedroom accommodation is shared between the main building and former outhouses that enclose a rear courtyard; soft furnishings and up-to-date amenities render them both cosy and comfortable. Some of the larger rooms and suites boast traditional four-poster beds and all have en suite bathrooms. Morning coffees, light lunch and afternoon teas are always on offer in the lounge and bar: yet it is the restaurant dinners that are the Golden Pheasant's crowning glory. An extensive à la carte offers modern interpretations of classical fare. Burford is the ideal base for visits to the famous Cotswold villages of Broadway, Bourton and Lower Slaughter and is equally convenient for Oxford and Cheltenham. Nearby places of interest include Blenheim Palace, Gloucester Cathedral and Berkeley Castle. **Directions:** Burford is signposted from A40 Oxford to Cheltenham road at its junction with A361. The Golden Pheasant is in the High Street. Price guide: Single £65; double £85–£105.

THE LAMB INN

SHEEP STREET, BURFORD, OXFORDSHIRE OX18 4LR
TEL: 01993 823155 FAX: 01993 822228

The Lamb Inn, in the small Cotswold town of Burford, is everyone's idea of the archetypal English inn, where it is easy to imagine that time has slipped back to some gentler age. The inn is set in a quiet location with a pretty walled garden. To step inside is to recapture something of the spirit of the 14th century: flagged floors, gleaming copper, brass and silver reflect the flicker of log fires and the well-chosen antiques all enhance the sense of history here. The bedrooms, which have recently been refurbished, offer comfortable accommodation, with oak beams, chintz curtains and soft furnishings. Guests can enjoy the best of British cooking. Dinner, chosen from a three-course table d'hôte menu, is taken in the candlelit pillared dining room and might include such dishes as fresh grilled sardines with lime butter sauce, followed by roast tenderloin of pork wrapped in smoked bacon with a blue cheese cream sauce. Light lunches are served in the bar or in the garden. On Sundays, a traditional three-course lunch is served. Packed lunches and hampers can be provided. The inn is near the heart of the town, where guests can browse through antiques shops or laze by the waters of the River Windrush. Burford is within easy reach of Oxford, Cheltenham, Stow-on-the-Wold and the many attractive Cotswold villages. **Directions:** Sheep Street is off the main street in Burford. Burford is 20m W of Oxford. Price guide: Single £60–£75; double £95–£115.

NEW

THE INN FOR ALL SEASONS

THE BARRINGTONS, BURFORD, OXFORDSHIRE OX18 4TN
TEL: 01451 844324 FAX: 01451 844375 E-MAIL: IFAS@ukgateway.net

This delightful roadside inn is situated just a few miles from the historic Cotswold town of Burford and within a short walk of the peaceful and picturesque unspoiled village of Little Barrington. It has been in chef/patron Matthew Sharp's family for over 13 years and visitors are assured of a very warm and friendly welcome. To step inside is to recapture something of the ambience and spirit of the days when The Inn For All Seasons was a coaching stop. Attractive, open stone walls and flagstone floors envelope guests. Ceilings are low and beamed. There are large open fireplaces, heavy period furniture and muted décor. Mr and Mrs Sharp pride themselves on providing a traditional homely atmosphere complemented by fine cuisine. All ten en suite bedrooms overlook rolling countryside and have been recently refurbished. Attractive soft furnishings and up-to-date amenities render them both cosy and comfortable. Tasty meals and a wide range of real ales and malt whiskies are served in the small, traditional bar and at the rear of the inn is a lawned garden where guests can enjoy relaxing on warm summer days. Horse riding, shooting, fly fishing and a number of golf courses are close by. The inn is also an ideal base for visiting the famous Cotswold villages of Broadway, Bourton and Lower Slaughter. **Directions:** On A40 four miles from Burford. Price guide: Single from £45; double/twin from £83.

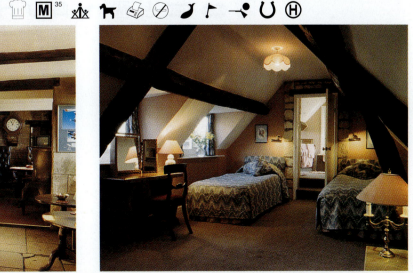

THE HOSTE ARMS HOTEL

THE GREEN, BURNHAM MARKET, NORFOLK PE31 8HD
TEL: 01328 738777 FAX: 01328 730103 E-MAIL: TheHosteArms@compuserve.com

Overlooking the green in the picturesque village of Burnham Market, The Hoste Arms dates back to the 17th century. Deservedly The Hoste has received many awards including Johansens Inn of the Year and the Inn of the Year César Award from the Good Hotel Guide. The en suite bedrooms are individually decorated, some offering views of the village, others of the landscaped garden. Paul Whittome continues his quest constantly to improve and upgrade services and facilities, recently enhancing the enjoyment of his guests with the addition of a very stylish and relaxed lounge and also the new Gallery Restaurant. His wife Jeanne has decorated the rooms throughout the hotel in a simple yet elegant style. A small panelled restaurant offers

scope for private dinner parties and conferences. All the main dining areas are air-conditioned. The excellent menu, created by head chef Stephen David and his team, features an extensive amount of seafood and has British, French and Oriental touches. A selection of well priced wines is offered to guests alongside a private collection of Paul's favourites. The Hoste Arms is well situated to cater for most interests. There are several stately homes in the area such as Holkham Hall, Houghton Hall and Sandringham. For nature lovers there are bird sanctuaries and boat trips. Golf enthusiasts have Hunstanton, Brancaster and Cromer. **Directions:** Burnham Market is 2 miles from A149 on B1155. Price guide: Singles £50–£60; doubles £60–£90.

FENCE GATE INN

WHEATLEY LANE ROAD, FENCE, NR BURNLEY, LANCASHIRE BB12 9EE
TEL: 01282 618101 FAX: 01282 615432

Set within a collection of small villages a short distance from Pendle Hill in the picturesque village of Fence. The Fence Gate was originally a house used as a collection point for cotton delivered by barge and distributed to surrounding cottage dwellers to be spun into cloth. Owner Kevin Berkins has redesigned and refurbished the house into a stylish inn and an extensive banqueting centre for all occasions with two versatile suites and a brasserie. A large, restful conservatory overlooks beautifully landscaped gardens that incorporate waterfalls and fountains. The recently opened Topiary Brasserie, winner of the 1999 Les Routier Plat D'Argent award, offers a unique dining experience with the emphasis on quality and presentation of modern English cuisine. The Topiary boasts a variety of tempting dishes from the extensive à la carte menu, business lunches, a wide selection of vegetarian dishes and a comprehensive range of New World Wines, champagnes and sparkling wines. The restaurant is open seven days a week, from 12 noon to 2.30pm and in the evenings from 6.30pm until 9.30pm. For diners new to the area, there are numerous places to visit, whether it be for shopping at the Boundary Mill Shop or other leisure facilities available nearby. **Directions:** From the M65 exit junction 13, along the Padiham by-pass (A6068) for 1½miles, then follow the brown tourism signs for directions.

THE RED LION

BY THE BRIDGE AT BURNSALL, NEAR SKIPTON, NORTH YORKSHIRE BD23 6BU
TEL: 01756 720204 FAX: 01756 720292 E-MAIL: redlion@daelnet.co.uk

Beamed ceilings, creaky floors and log fires in winter greet you at this former 16th century Ferryman's Inn on the banks of the River Wharfe in the picturesque Yorkshire Dales village of Burnsall. Owned and run by the Grayshon family, it is surrounded by glorious open countryside. Guests can step out for numerous walks straight from the front door. The hotel is actually on the "Dalesway". The 11 bedrooms are all slightly different yet traditionally furnished, many with antiques and most have wonderful views over the village green, river and Burnsall Fell. Large and attractive, it has been awarded an AA Rosette for serving food that is delicious and varied, imaginatively cooked and well-presented. Table d'hôte dishes such as local rabbit braised in ale and served with herb dumplings, or partridge with apricot seasoning and game chips, are complemented by international wines. Special half-board terms and winter warmer breaks are available. Bolton Abbey and Priory, the historic market town of Skipton with its medieval castle and the Settle to Carlisle Railway. The Red Lion has private fishing on the River Wharfe, 7 miles of trout and grayling fishing and offers partridge and pheasant shooting over 3000 acres on the nearby Grimwith Estate. Skipton and Ilkley golf courses are 11 miles away. **Directions:** Burnsall is north of Skipton on B6160 between Grassington and Bolton Abbey. The inn is in the village centre by the bridge. Price guide: Single £45–£75; double £90–£120.

Boar's Head Hotel

LICHFIELD ROAD, SUDBURY, DERBYSHIRE DE6 5GX
TEL: 01283 820344 FAX: 01283 820075

This 17th century house was lost from the famous Vernon estate through a game of cards! It is now a well known local hostelry, having been run by the Crooks family for many years. Guests arriving will be welcomed by the architectural beauty of this very old building. There is a warm bar, with natural brick walls, horse brasses and hunting horns. The residents' lounge looks onto a pretty patio where drinks are served in summer months. Much thought has been given to furnishing the delightful bedrooms which have every possible facility, including teletext and Sky television. Visitors enjoy a choice of real ales and excellent home-cooked dishes with the chef's specials listed on a blackboard. There are two restaurants, the elegant Royal Boar

with an imaginative à la carte menu and the less formal Hunter's Table Carvery and Bistro offering fresh fish, pasta dishes and splendid roasts, both at lunchtime and in the evening. The Royal Boar is closed on Sunday evenings, but is famous for its Sunday lunch. A fascinating wine list covers vineyards worldwide, with 70 entries that include 6 house wines and a selection of 10 half-bottles. Alton Towers and Uttoxeter Racecourse are lively attractions nearby. Other guests will enjoy Chatsworth House, Sudbury Hall, Tutbury Castle and the Bass Museum of brewing. **Directions:** The hotel is on A515, just south of A50 from Stoke on Trent to Derby. Price guide: Single from £39.50; double from £49.50.

YE OLDE DOG & PARTRIDGE

HIGH STREET, TUTBURY, BURTON UPON TRENT, STAFFORDSHIRE DE13 9LS
TEL: 01283 813030 FAX: 01283 813178

Ye Olde Dog & Partridge is a charming half-timbered village inn and hotel offering a delightful blend of modern and traditional touches. The warm welcome and excellent standard of service are reminiscent of the building's 18th century history whilst a modern approach to the cuisine and facilities is clearly evident. The 20 bedrooms are individually decorated with comfortable furnishings and soft fabrics. 14 of the bedrooms are located in the Georgian annexe across the driveway. Each features en suite facilities, colour televisions and thoughtful extras. The new Brasserie is enveloped by an informal ambience and is a popular venue for guests to meet and converse. An imaginative menu comprising classic and modern European food is served and a selection of wines has been chosen to complement the flavours. Those seeking a more traditional dining experience must sample the cuisine at the Carvery Buffet. Freshly cooked meats, fresh seafood and classic roasts are served amidst the tones of the grand piano. Day excursions include trips to the Bass Museum of Brewing, Uttoxeter Racecourse and the many National Trust properties nearby such as Chatsworth House. **Directions:** Leave M1 at junction 23. Take A50 westbound to exit 6 signed Tutbury. Ye Olde Dog & Partridge is on the High Street. Price guide: Single £55; double £80; superior £99.

THE CHEQUERS INN

FROGGATT EDGE, NR CALVER, DERBYSHIRE S30 1ZB
TEL: 01433 630231 FAX: 01433 631072

A Grade II listed building, The Chequers Inn originally comprised four 16th century houses, rebuilt in the 18th century and now extensively refurbished. It is situated on an old pack horse road in the heart of the Peak district National Park. Visitors will see plenty of reminders of the inn's history; a horse-mounting block still stands outside the main building and the old stables house the logs that fuel today's open fires. Behind the inn, acres of unspoiled woodland lead up to Froggatt Edge, with its panoramic views. Each of the six cottage-style bedrooms has its own identity and for an extra touch of romance, one room has a four-poster bed. Local chef Julie Presland creates a wide variety of European and British meals, with several fish dishes and local game in season. The menus are original and healthy and are served in the extended bar areas where quiet corners may be found. Amongst the many regular and popular dishes, Bakewell pudding, the local speciality, is a favourite dessert here – delicious served hot with cream. This is wonderful walking country: you can leave your car and follow the Derwent River or the Peak trails. Organised, guided walks can be arranged for small groups. Chatsworth House, Haddon Hall, the caverns of Castleton and the market town of Bakewell are all close by. **Directions:** The inn is situated on the old pack horse road, now the A625 which links Bakewell and Sheffield, 6 miles from Bakewell on Froggatt Edge. Price guide: Single £48–£55; double £60–£70.

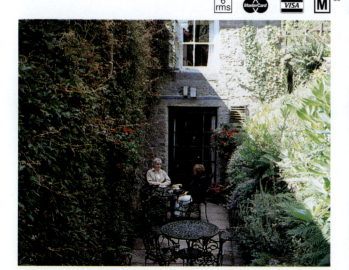

TYACKS HOTEL

27 COMMERCIAL STREET, CAMBORNE, CORNWALL TR14 8LD
TEL: 01209 612424 FAX: 01209 612435

This charming 18th century coaching inn, set in the heart of Camborne, is just three minutes drive from the main A30 road or less than five minutes from the bus or railway stations. The Tyacks is used by business men and women as well as tourists as a base for travelling in the west of Cornwall. Re-opened in 1992, having been totally refurbished to AA and RAC 3 Star standard, the inn has become popular with visitors from all over the world as is reflected in the restaurant's imaginative menus. Adjacent to the restaurant is an attractive lounge bar, ideal for a quiet drink or bar snack. For those who enjoy a lively pub atmosphere there is the Coach Bar. Beside the hotel entrance, opposite the old stables is a

patio and beer garden where drinks and snacks can be enjoyed on a sunny day. The à la carte, table d'hôte and vegetarian menus offer a splendid choice of English and Continental fare using fresh Cornish fish, vegetables and meats. Guests can explore the Tate Gallery at St Ives, Camborne School of Mines and Geology Museum, Tehidy Country Park and Golf Club, Penzance and Lands End. The Engines Museum at Poole, the house of William Murdoch, founder of gaslighting, in Redruth are also worth a visit. **Directions:** From A30 turn off at the sign for Camborne West then follow signs for town centre. Tyacks Hotel is on the left-hand side. Price guide: Single £45; double £60; suite £90.

THE WHITE HORSE INN

HOLLOW HILL, WITHERSFIELD, HAVERHILL, SUFFOLK CB9 7SH
TEL: 01440 706081

The White Horse Inn is the ideal choice of venue for both pleasure and business. Set in the beautiful Suffolk countryside, only 12 miles south of Cambridge, it is just a short drive from East Anglia's many attractions and business centres. Guests are assured of a warm, personal welcome from Bernard and Cherry Lee and their excellent staff. The original character of this charming inn has been carefully retained and with its intimate corners and open fires, there is always somewhere cosy to escape to and relax with a magazine or book. The bedrooms are situated in the renovated Suffolk Cart Lodge, fronted by a pretty garden. Amenities include direct dial telephones. The style is light and airy, with country pine furnishings lending a modern but homely feel to the surroundings. One ground floor room, with its romantic four-poster bed, opens onto its own garden. A growing reputation for superb food means that it is essential for guests to book a table for dinner. The excellent wine list offered here is renowned and the ales are similarly applauded. Small meetings and private functions can be held during the daytime. Among the many places of interest nearby are the university town of Cambridge, Newmarket and Saffron Walden. The inn is ETB 4 Diamonds Highly Commended. **Directions:** From M11, junction 9, take A11 in direction of Newmarket and turn onto A1307. Withersfield is signed after Horse Heath. Price guide: Single £45; double £65; four poster £74.95.

THE TARN END HOUSE HOTEL

TALKIN TARN, BRAMPTON, CUMBRIA CA8 1LS
TEL: 016977 2340 FAX: 016977 2089

The Tarn End House Hotel has idyllic surroundings at any time of year. This former estate farm house is over 100 years old and is set in its own grounds, with lawns running down to the shores of Talkin Tarn. A very warm welcome and traditional hospitality are guaranteed. The nicely furnished bedrooms have every modern facility and offer exceptional views. This is an ideal spot in which to escape from the world and there is a good choice of leisure activities. Long walks can be taken over the surrounding fells, or the more active can take advantage of rowing, wind-surfing or sailing on the Tarn. There are good golf courses nearby and river fishing and rough shooting can be arranged. The inn enjoys a very good reputation for its cuisine. Guests can savour a meal chosen from two menus – à la carte or table d'hôte. Bar snacks are also available at lunchtime. Hadrian's Wall, Lanercost Priory and the City of Carlisle with its historic castle are all nearby. The River Gelt is an ideal place to visit for bird-watchers and the Scottish borders are within easy reach. **Directions:** From M6 junction 43 take A69 to Brampton. From the centre of Brampton take B6413 towards Castle Carrock and Talkin Tarn. Go over the railway and past Brampton Golf Club and take second left to Talkin village – the hotel is on the left. Price guide: Single £40–£55; double £55–£85.

THE FALCON HOTEL

CASTLE ASHBY, NORTHAMPTON, NORTHAMPTONSHIRE NN7 1LF
TEL: 01604 696200 FAX: 01604 696673

Six miles south of Northampton, in the heart of the Marquess of Northampton's estate, The Falcon is a delightful country cottage hotel, secluded and tranquil, minutes away from the rambling acres of Castle Ashby House. The owners have invested energy and enthusiasm into transforming this once modest place into a haven of comfort, excellent food and attentive service. Bedrooms are beautifully furnished, cosy cottage style and the bathrooms have been recently upgraded. Lunch and dinner, which are created where possible from seasonal, home-grown produce, are served in the intimate restaurant which overlooks a lawn with willow trees. The excellent value-for-money cuisine, modern English in flavour, is prepared by chef Neil Helks. A fixed-price menu costs £19.50, including coffee and petits fours. There is also an interesting à la carte selection. The extensive wine list can be studied by guests at their leisure over preprandial drinks by a glowing log fire. Walk in the grounds of Castle Ashby estate. Further afield, visit Woburn, Althorp, Silverstone, Bedford and Stratford. **Directions:** Exit M1 junction 14 northbound or 15 southbound. Follow the signs to A428 where Castle Ashby and The Falcon are clearly signposted, six miles south-east of Northampton. Price guide: Single £75; double £95.

THE CROWN INN

GIDDEA HALL, YATTON KEYNELL, CHIPPENHAM, WILTSHIRE SN14 7ER
TEL: 01249 782229 FAX: 01249 782337

This is a picturesque honey-coloured coaching inn, secluded and tranquil, in a tiny hamlet just a short drive from the attractive market town of Chippenham. Its origins can be traced to the 15th century and renovations and refurbishment reflect the owners' determination to combine history with discreet modernisation, creating an elegant small hostelry. The cosy front bar with an old open hearth fire sets the scene for visitors and the hospitable ambience continues into the interlinking dining areas. The Crown has a reputation for good English food. There are simple bar snacks or more varied and elaborate meals such as breast of pheasant stuffed with paté, wrapped in bacon and finished with sloe gin, casserole of venison in a red wine sauce, or skewered queen scallops and prawns marinated in ginger and lime juice. The Crown's eight adjacent en suite bedrooms have all modern conveniences, are furnished in style and are totally in keeping with expectations for a stay in this beautiful escapists' spot. The Castle Combe golf course and racecourse are nearby. Badminton is only 20 minutes away. Castle Combe, one of the most photographed of Wiltshire's many pretty villages, lies close by. The inn is central to Bath and the West Country. **Directions:** Exit the M4 at Junction 17 for Chippenham (A350), at the third roundabout take A420 Bristol Road, the Crown Inn is 3 miles down on the left hand side. Price guide: Double/twin From £55.

THE CODRINGTON ARMS

WAPLEY ROAD, CODRINGTON, NR CHIPPING SODBURY, BRISTOL BS37 6RY
TEL/FAX: 01454 313145

True West Country hospitality can be enjoyed at this attractive and welcoming old inn situated between historic Bristol and the picturesque Cotswolds. Renovated and modernised over the years it retains a great many of its original period features. The surrounding countryside has been the scene of history making it popular with sightseers who like to explore small villages, hamlets and market towns. Two miles north is the old town of Chipping Sodbury and a short drive east is Regency-style Dodington House whose grounds were landscaped by Capability Brown. Also close by is Badminton House, the Palladian mansion home of the Duke of Beaufort and the venue for the world famous annual horse trials. The Codrington Arms is believed to date back to the 15th century and to have been part of the nearby family estate of John de Codrington (1363–1425), who was Standard Bearer for King Henry V at Agincourt. A warm Cotswold atmosphere prevails throughout the inn's extensive and comfortable bars and dining areas. Fine ales and wines are served as well as an extensive bar menu including good and substantial dishes such as steaks, fresh trout and breaded plaice. The inn has no bedrooms. **Directions:** Leave Bristol on the M32 and join the M4 East to junction 18 and then take the second left.

CHRISTCHURCH (Highcliffe On Sea)

THE LORD BUTE

181/185 LYMINGTON ROAD, HIGHCLIFFE ON SEA, CHRISTCHURCH, DORSET BH23 4JS
TEL: 01425 278884 FAX: 01425 279258 E-MAIL: mail@lordbute.co.uk

This delightful, welcoming new hotel is tucked discreetly behind one of the original lodges of historic Highcliffe Castle whose extensive grounds slope gently down to the cliffs and sands of sweeping Christchurch Bay. Excellently and enthusiastically run by twins Simon and Christopher Denley the hotel opened in 1998 to complement a renowned and award-winning restaurant which had been on the site for ten years. Chef Christopher Denley produces excellent and imaginative two, three and four course menus that include choices such as Atlantic peeled prawns bound with pasta and New Forest venison. With gleaming white exterior walls and tall, slim pillars The Lord Bute has a distinctive and attractive Continental look. The owners have paid great attention to detail and décor throughout and the ten extremely comfortable en suite bedrooms are beautifully furnished and decorated. They offer garden views and every modern amenity, from air conditioning and double glazing to a spa bath, Satellite television, electronic safe and telephone and lap top data ports. Guests have direct access to both the castle and the beach, the edge of the New Forest is only minutes away. Christchurch, Beaulieu, Bournemouth, Lymington and the ferries to Yarmouth are within easy reach. **Directions:** Leave the M27 at junction 1. Take the A35 and then the A337 to the hotel. Price guide: Single £65–£75; double £80–£95.

NEW

THE ELIOT ARMS HOTEL

CLARKS HAY, SOUTH CERNEY, CIRENCESTER, GLOUCESTERSHIRE GL7 2UA
TEL: 01285 860215 FAX: 01285 861121

True friendly and welcoming hospitality can be enjoyed at this attractive old inn situated in the heart of the Cotswold Water Park close to the Roman town of Cirencester. Dating from the 16th century, the Eliot Arms is a typical Cotswold Free House hotel featuring original open fires with York stone surrounds, ceiling beams and small, cosy rooms. The furnishings, drapes and decor are attractive and in character with the inn's historic past. The 12 bedrooms provide individually and tastefully designed accommodation and a full refurbishment is planned for late 1999. A warm atmosphere prevails in the bar and two dining areas. Guests can choose to eat in The Mews, which is non-smoking, or the Dining Room. Chefs Chris Wade and Maggie Chivers have earned a reputation for the quality of her cuisine with menus catering for every taste. Local produce is used whenever possible. The wine list is extensive and there is a good selection of real and cask ales. On summer days these can be enjoyed while relaxing in the garden or on the riverside patio. The Eliot Arms is an ideal base from which to visit Bourton-on-the Water, Stow-in-the-Wold, Burford, Warwick Castle, Stratford, and Cheltenham. The Water Park provides course fishing and a variety of water sports. **Directions:** South Cerney is just off A419 2½miles south of Cirencester. Price guide: Single £41.95; double £54.50; suite £75.

THE NEW INN AT COLN

COLN ST-ALDWYNS, NR CIRENCESTER, GLOUCESTERSHIRE GL7 5AN
TEL: 01285 750651 FAX: 01285 750657 E-MAIL: stay@new–inn.co.uk

In days of yore, when Queen Elizabeth I was giving royal assent to the import of tobacco from the new-found Americas, she was also initiating a travel boom in England, by instigating a network of coaching inns after the pattern already set on the Continent. One of the Cotswold inns that her initiative helped to create was The New Inn at Coln St-Aldwyns on Akeman Street, the old Roman Road, leading North East out of Cirencester. The New Inn, though old in years, is today utterly new in spirit, winning ever fresh awards for food and hospitality – its two Rosettes being in permanent flower as a second Queen Elizabeth reigns and its latest acquisition being the Johansens Most Excellent Traditional Inn 1999. Since Brian and

Sandra-Anne Evans took over in 1992, The New Inn at Coln has blossomed and Stephen Morey's skills in the kitchen have added a gastronomic dimension to the charm and comfort of the ancient but cleverly modernised bedrooms – perfect accommodation for an idyllic week in the Cotswolds, a useful stopover or as a timely resting place after a fine dinner. For the business-minded, there is a charming meeting room. Close to this picturesque Cotswolds base are Stratford-upon-Avon, Bath, Oxford and Cheltenham and within healthy walking distance is Bibury with its photogenic Arlington Row. **Directions:** From Burford (A40), take B4425 to Bibury, turn left after Aldsworth. Price guide: Single £68–£85; double £96–£125.

THE PLOUGH INN

BROCKLEY GREEN, NR HUNDON, SUDBURY, SUFFOLK CO10 8DT
TEL: 01440 786789 FAX: 01440 786710

The Plough is a typical, charming, early 19th century inn commanding superb, panoramic views from its windows over the beautiful Stour Valley and five acres of immaculate grounds. Old beams, exposed soft red brickwork, solid, heavy furniture and comfortable sofas and chairs contribute to the inn's welcoming ambience. There are eleven comfortable, en suite bedrooms, all providing the comforts and quality expected of a hotel awarded four crowns from the English Tourist Board. The intimate, attractive bar is a restful delight offering an imaginative choice of bar meals and a good selection of traditional ales. Simms restaurant is highly regarded locally and serves superb English style cuisine. The Plough's peaceful rural location belies the presence of the many areas of interest within a short distance. Cycles are available for those seeking to explore the delightful picture-postcard villages nearby and landscape immortalised by painter John Constable. Within a 30 minutes drive there is the historic market town of Bury St Edmunds, the medieval wool towns of Lavenham and Long Melford, Constable's birthplace at Sudbury, Cambridge, Ely, Newmarket and the Imperial War Museum at Duxford. **Directions:** Exit the M11 at junction 9. Follow the A604 towards Haverhill. Turn left onto the A143 and after 2 miles turn right to Kedington and follow the signs to Clare. Price guide: Single from £50; double/twin from £70.

THE CRICKETERS

CLAVERING, NR SAFFRON WALDEN, ESSEX CB11 4QT
TEL: 01799 550442 FAX: 01799 550882 E-MAIL: cricketers@lineone.net

This attractive 16th century freehouse in the Essex countryside, just ten minutes from Stansted Airport, has responded to its popularity and reputation for good food by purchasing an adjacent residence to provide increased accommodation for guests. Known as The Pavilion, this new house provides six charming bedrooms, two with four-poster beds and one on the ground floor, ideal for those with mobility problems. All are en suite, colourful and well-appointed. Breakfast is served in the main building. The oak-beamed bar serving real ale and restaurant have cricket memorabilia on the walls. There is a non-smoking area. Guests enjoy the big log fire in the winter and alfresco refreshments in the garden in summer. The Restaurant menu, changing seasonally, has ten appetizing starters and ten succulent main courses, interesting interpretations of classic English cooking and the puddings are of the same calibre. A salad bar pleases slimmers. The wine list is diverse, from house wines through to champagnes, European vineyards alongside many New World names, and many half-bottles. Guests enjoy visiting Audley End with its renowned house and park, going racing at Newmarket, or exploring Cambridge, Saffron Walden and Duxford Air Museum. **Directions:** Leave M11 at junction 8, heading west, then right onto B1383, signed Newport and left at the B1038 to Clavering. Price guide: Single £60; double £80.

CROWN AT HOPTON

HOPTON WAFERS, CLEOBURY MORTIMER, SHROPSHIRE DY14 0NB
TEL: 01299 270372 FAX: 01299 271127

This enticing 16th century inn is situated in a hamlet dating back to the Norman Conquest, surrounded by the lush farmland, tumbling streams and wooded valleys of South Shropshire. Exposed beams and wooden floors characterise the bedrooms, which are decorated in an appropriate cottage style. All are en suite, spacious and most attractive. The bar, which offers a selection of cask- conditioned beers, adjoins an open terrace and like all the rooms, has many original features including an inglenook fireplace. Originally a 15th century smithy, the traditionally furnished restaurant – known as "Poacher's" – makes a fine setting in which to relax over dinner. There is an extensive menu offering a choice of imaginatively cooked dishes prepared from fresh, seasonal ingredients. Fish and game in season, are specialities. The wine list is well compiled and dessert wines are available by the glass. A good selection of ports, cognacs and armagnacs is available. Apart from exploring the beautiful countryside, guests can visit Stokesay Castle, many National Trust properties and historic Ludlow. Another option is to take a romantic trip aboard a steam locomotive on the Severn Valley Railway. Ironbridge Gorge Museum is about 30 minutes drive away. **Directions:** The Crown Inn is by the A4117 between Ludlow and Kidderminster, two miles west of Cleobury Mortimer and 30 minutes from the M5 and M42. Price guide: Single £40–£45; double £64–£75.

THE REDFERN HOTEL

CLEOBURY MORTIMER, SHROPSHIRE DY14 8AA
TEL: 01299 270 395 FAX: 01299 271 011 E-MAIL: jon@red-fern.demon.co.uk

This country town hotel provides good value accommodation and a warm welcome in the heart of England. The Redfern Hotel stands in an attractive setting in Cleobury Mortimer – a market town dating back to the *Domesday Book*. Crisply decorated bedrooms have white-painted walls and floral fabrics, in keeping with the country house style. Draught ale is served in the cosy bar where memorabilia and pictures depicting the town's history are displayed. For parents' peace of mind, a baby-listening service is available. Breakfast is served in the conservatory throughout the morning. Freshly baked home-made bread each day. Redfern's English Kitchen Restaurant has a homely, welcoming atmosphere, with its home-cured hams and cider flagons hanging from the beams. The menu is changed daily to offer a variety of home-cooked dished such as Shropshire chicken stuffed with Shropshire Blue cheese and breadcrumbs, or fillet of pork in orange and ginger sauce. Golf is available at a local course with concessionary green fees. For the more adventurous the Redfern also has its own canal narrowboat for hire. Local attractions include the Ironbridge Gorge Industrial Museum or a scenic trip on the Severn Valley Railway. Other sights close by are Ludlow Castle and the beautiful countryside of the Welsh Marches. **Directions:** Cleobury Mortimer is on A4117 between Kidderminster and Ludlow, 11m from each. Price Guide: Single £53–65; double £80–90.

THE WHITE HART HOTEL & RESTAURANT

MARKET END, COGGESHALL, ESSEX CO6 1NH
TEL: 01376 561654 FAX: 01376 561789

A historic hotel, The White Hart is situated in the Essex town of Coggeshall, where it has played an integral part for many years. In 1489 The White Hart became the town's meeting place when most of the adjoining Guildhall was destroyed by fire. Part of that original Guildhall now forms the residents' lounge, and features magnificent roof timbers hewn from sweet chestnut. Sympathetically restored throughout, the hotel has been comfortably appointed with much attention to detail. All the en suite bedrooms have been decorated with bright fabrics to reflect the hotel's colourful character. Heavily timbered and spacious, the restaurant enjoys a good reputation locally. The table d'hôte and à la carte menus feature a choice of Italian dishes with a particular emphasis on seafood and shellfish. Pasta is freshly made and aromatic sauces and tender cuts of meat figure prominently on the menu. The hotel has recently received merit awards from the RAC for comfort and its restaurant, which already holds 2 AA rosettes and an Egon Ronay recommendation. Coggeshall is noted for its antiques shops. It is also convenient for Colchester and Chelmsford and the ferry ports of Felixstowe and Harwich. **Directions:** Coggeshall is just off the A120 between Colchester and Braintree. From the A12 follow signs through Kelvedon, then take B1024. Price guide: Single £65; double/twin £97.

THE NEW INN

COLEFORD, CREDITON, DEVON EX17 5BZ
TEL: 01363 84242 FAX: 01363 85044 E-MAIL: new–inn@eurobell.co.uk

Those wishing to escape the hectic pace of everyday life will be delighted with this lovely 13th century thatched inn, located in a truly secluded valley beside a bubbling brook. The New Inn, a Grade II listed building of cob, has been tastefully renovated and refurbished over the years. Today it retains the character and ambience of a past era, featuring chintz curtains and interesting pictures and ornaments. A warm welcome is extended to guests from owners Irene and Paul Butt and their talkative parrot, Captain! The resident ghost, Sebastian, is also reputed to be friendly... The accommodation is excellent, with spacious and individually-appointed bedrooms offering every comfort. In the winter months, the lounge is the place to sit and enjoy the cosy warmth of a log fire. Two full-time chefs create memorable dishes, using the best and freshest local ingredients. The menu includes delicious starters, such as sherried kidney tart, cream of Devon crab soup or grilled goats cheese with walnuts and walnut oil salad, and a good selection of speciality dishes, grills, snacks and sweets. An extensive choice of drinks, including four traditional ales, is served in the bars. The wine list has been awarded many accolades for its selection. The cathedral city of Exeter, Dartmoor and Exmoor are all close by. **Directions:** Take the A377 Exeter-Barnstable Road. Coleford is signed two miles from Crediton. Price guide: Single £48–£58; double £63–£73.

THE LITTLE ADMIRAL HOTEL

VICTORIA ROAD, DARTMOUTH, DEVON TQ6 9RT
TEL: 01803 832572 FAX: 01803 835815

The Little Admiral is an elegant town house hotel, situated just 150 yards level walk from the River Dart and famous harbour in Dartmouth. Steeped in naval history, this bustling town is located in an area of outstanding natural beauty and offers a wide range of chic shopping. Truly a unique 'port of call', great attention has been lavished on the 10 bedrooms, creating an environment of both opulence and tranquillity. The same exacting standards are evident in the Residents Lounge which is the essence of comfort. The surrounding area offers a host of restaurants and the attentive staff will recommend and make reservations at the nearby establishments. With the majestic backdrop of The Britannia Royal Naval College, Dartmouth offers a plethora of activities and interests throughout the seasons including walking, sailing, sea fishing and golf. There are pleasant boat trips up the estuary to Totnes and a Steam train. Places of interest within easy reach include Dartmouth Castle, Coleton Fishacre Gardens and the home of the writer Agatha Christie. The magnificent scenery of Dartmouth and the South Hams Coast form an ideal contrast to nearby Dartmoor, home to The Little Admiral's sister country house hotel, Holne Chase. **Directions:** From M5 join A38, leave at A384 signposted to Totnes and follow the signs to Dartmouth. Price guide: Single £45–£60; double £80–£110.

DITCHEAT (Nr Wells)

THE MANOR HOUSE INN

DITCHEAT, SOMERSET BA4 6RB
TEL: 01749 860276 E-MAIL: themanorhouseinn@ukonline.co.uk

Slate floors, natural stone walls, huge oak beams and gas mantle lighting are among the fascinating traditional features of this fine old inn whose history dates back to 1700 when it was known as The White Hart and owned by Edmund Dawe, Lord of the Manor of Ditcheat. It became The Bell in 1734 and took its present name in 1861. Careful restoration, refurbishment and attention to detail has created a warm and distinctive atmosphere and owner Keith Shepherd has invested a tremendous amount of energy and enthusiasm into making it a haven of comfort, excellent food and attentive service. The three bedrooms, which are in a courtyard mews, are charming, beautifully furnished and have super-size, well equipped en suite facilities. Chef Neil Chant produces nicely balanced, value-for-money menus to suit all tastes using the freshest and best of local seasonal produce. Daily blackboard specials also tempt lunchtime and evening diners. There are many National Trust properties and gardens to visit and the racing stables of Paul Nicholls and the Maryland Cheese Factory make interesting excursions. Glastonbury, Wells, the dramatic Cheddar Gorge and Wincanton races are within easy reach. Golf, horse riding and ballooning are nearby. **Directions:** Just off the A371 between Shepton Mallet and Castle Cary. Price guide: Single £45; double £65.

HAMILTON'S RESTAURANT & HOTEL

CARR HOUSE ROAD, DONCASTER, SOUTH YORKSHIRE DN4 5HP
TEL: 01302 760770 FAX: 01302 768101 E-MAIL: ham760770@aol.com

Standing in two acres of walled gardens just 200 yards from Doncaster Racecourse this former home of Lord and Lady Hamilton combines the welcoming ambience of a country residence with the comforts of an elegant, modern hotel. Built in 1856, the lavish refurbishment has resulted in five spacious bedrooms, each individually designed and named after a famous opera. 'Cooking is the art, dining is the experience' is the mission statement at Hamilton's and at meal times, this aim is clearly evident. Talented chef Christopher Randle-Bissell is dedicated to Old English and European cooking and his extensive menus will please the most discerning visitor in the warm ambience of the attractively furnished restaurant. His starter of roasted sea scallops with a sweet ratatouille of vegetables, drizzled with truffle essence, followed by a daube of braised beef wrapped in a crepinette with a new potato mash, roasted shallots and morrel mushrooms is not to be missed. The dining experience is complemented by a well chosen wine list and enhanced by classical service. The private dining room has an atmosphere of grandeur and caters for a maximum of 24 guests. Brodsworth Hall, Conisbrough Castle, the Dome leisure complex and the Earth Centre are all nearby. **Directions:** From M18 and A1 follow signs for Doncaster Race Course and Exhibition Centre. Hamilton's in on the left of the dual carriageway, 200 yards before the racecourse roundabout. Price guide: Single £70; double £90; suite £150.

THE GEORGE HOTEL

HIGH STREET, DORCHESTER-ON-THAMES, OXFORD OX10 7HH
TEL: 01865 340404 FAX: 01865 341620

In the heart of the Thames Valley lies The George. Dating from the 15th century, it is one of the oldest inns in the country. In the days of the stage coach, it provided a welcome haven for many an aristocrat including the first Duchess of Marlborough, Sarah Churchill. However, more recent times have seen famous guests of a different hue such as author DH Lawrence. The buildings of the George Hotel have changed little since their heyday as a coaching inn. It retains all the beauty and charm of those days, whilst offering every modern amenity. All the rooms are en suite and furnished with fine antiques and the owners have created a décor which suits the requirements of modern times whilst maintaining the spirit of the past. The menu changes daily allowing the chef to ensure that only the freshest and finest produce reaches your table. The imaginative cuisine, awarded 2 AA Rosettes, is beautifully presented and delicious. The beamed dining room provides a delightful setting in which to enjoy an excellent meal, served by friendly, professional staff. Dorchester-on-Thames provides easy access to the Cotswolds, Blenheim Palace and Oxford. Stratford-upon-Avon, Henley, Windsor and an inexhaustible source of beautiful walks and cultural and sporting activities. Excellent meeting facilities for up to 36 in the Stable Suite and two smaller rooms each for up to 8 people. **Directions:** On A4074, 9 miles south of Oxford. Price guide: Single £62.50; double £80; four poster £92.50.

THE BLUE LION

EAST WITTON, NR LEYBURN, NORTH YORKSHIRE DL8 4SN
TEL: 01969 624273 FAX: 01969 624189

Heather moorlands, waterfalls, limestone scars and remote valleys surround the picturesque village of East Witton – the gateway to Wensleydale and Coverdale. The Blue Lion, a 19th century coaching inn, has much to entice visitors to its doors – lovely individually furnished bedrooms, welcoming public rooms with original flagstone floors and open fires, plus delicious food. Private functions for up to 45 people can be accommodated. Head Chef, John Dalby, provides an ample selection of well-compiled, innovative dishes with a frequently changing menu. Some interesting choices such as red mullet, monkfish or wild boar served with a rich port wine sauce are regularly available.

The wine list that accompanies the menus offers a vast array of excellent wines from all over the world. The dining room is attractively decorated with candle-light creating an intimate atmosphere. In the bar there is a fine selection of hand-pulled traditional beers as well as an extensive menu of freshly prepared meals served at lunchtime and dinner. The spa towns of Ripon and Harrogate are within easy driving distance and well worth a visit. Jervaulx Abbey and many castles are in the area. There is an all-weather tennis court in the village. **Directions:** A6108, eight miles north of Masham and five miles south of Leyburn. Price guide: Single £50–£75; double £75–£95.

THE GEORGE INN

ECCLESHALL, STAFFORDSHIRE ST21 6DF
TEL: 01785 850300 FAX: 01785 851452

This charming family-run 17th century coaching inn is set in the quaint Staffordshire market town of Eccleshall. Its nine bedrooms have been tastefully decorated in sympathy with the age and character of the building and are equipped with a full range of modern amenities. Freshly made teas and coffees are served throughout the day in the bar. With its oak beams, dried hops and Inglenook fireplace, this is also the place to enjoy fine traditional ales, malt whiskies and a selection of light lunches. The hotel also boasts its own micro brewery, producing four different ales for guests to sample. George's Bistro offers an impressive range of imaginative dishes. Tempt your palate with pan-fried breast of chicken, stuffed with a pork and capsicum mousseline and coated with a cream of onion sauce or maybe try the pot-roasted poussin, marinated in a chillied sweet and sour wild berry sauce. There is also an excellent range of fish, pasta and rice dishes to choose from, as well as various omelettes and mouth-watering grills. Shugborough Hall, Weston Park, Bridgemere Garden World, Wedgwood Visitor centre and Lichfield Cathedral are within easy reach. Alton Towers and Ironbridge are also nearby. **Directions:** From the M6 junction 14 turn left towards Eccleshall on the A5013. From junction 15 turn left towards Stoke, then right towards Eccleshall via the A519. Price guide: Single £55; double £90.

YE OLD CROWN

HIGH STREET, EDENBRIDGE, KENT TN8 5AR
TEL: 01732 867896 FAX: 01732 868316

This remarkably preserved old inn and staging post is unmissable in Edenbridge because it has a unique bridging sign spanning the High Street. Ye Old Crown is steeped in romantic history and tradition, having been host to thirsty and hungry wayfarers since the reign of Edward III (1327-1377). The inn's fascinating interior boasts a wealth of nooks and crannies and even a secret passage used by a notorious 17th century dynasty of smugglers, the Ramsey Gang. Although sympathetically added to, restored, renovated, refurbished and modernised over the centuries the Crown has retained many of its original features. These include a fine crown post, moulded roof plates, smoke blackened rafters and an inglenook fireplace in the bar. The six bedrooms are situated just a few yards from the inn. They are all en suite, beautifully furnished, with every facility to make a stay at the inn as comfortable and possible. Guests can enjoy bar meals or a more extensive and excellent restaurant menu that includes smoked salmon and champagne breakfast. Places of interest nearby include Hever Castle, Penshurst Place, Chiddingstone Castle, Royal Tunbridge Wells and Tonbridge. **Directions:** Exit the M25 at junctions 5 or 6. Take the A 25 to Westerham and then the B2026 south to Edenbridge. Price guide: Single from £54; double/twin from £74.

THE WHEATSHEAF INN

EGTON, NR WHITBY, NORTH YORKSHIRE YO21 1TZ
TEL: 01947 895271 FAX: 01947 895391 E-MAIL: wheatsheaf@talk21.com

This traditional, stone-built inn is situated in a delightful part of North Yorkshire in the small village of Egton, just five miles from the sea. Proprietors of The Wheatsheaf, Susan and Michael Latus, create a welcoming atmosphere. With the emphasis on attentive service, guests receive good hospitality and excellent value for money. In the public rooms, the original character has been maintained and the small, cosy bedrooms, three of which are en suite, have been furnished in keeping with the style of an old country inn. Stone walls, oak beams and attractively laid tables are the setting for dinner. The mouth watering and varied menu is changed regularly using fresh seasonal variations. There is a good selection of starters including seafood choices. Main courses range from country pies to international dishes. There is also an extensive Lunch Menu available. The surrounding North York Moors National Park provides ample scope for walking, fishing, riding, canoeing, sailing and trips on steam trains. Captain Cook's birthplace at Great Ayton, Robin Hood's Bay, Staithes and Whitby, with its abbey, are a short drive away. **Directions:** Egton is close to Whitby. From Pickering, turn off the A169 to Grosmont and Egton in Esk Dale. Price guide: Single £30–£45; double £40–£55.

THE CHRISTOPHER HOTEL

HIGH STREET, ETON, WINDSOR, BERKSHIRE SL4 6AN
TEL: 01753 811677 / 852359 FAX: 01753 830914 E-MAIL: sales@christopher–hotel.co.uk

Halfway between Eton College and Windsor Bridge, in Eton's High Street lies The Christopher Hotel, originally a coaching inn which for many years enjoyed somewhat of a racy reputation. The comfortable and elegantly furnished bedrooms are located in the main building and courtyard. A range of modern amenities includes satellite television, tea/coffee making facilities, hairdryer and direct-dial telephone. Guests may choose between having a continental breakfast served in their room or taking a full traditional English breakfast in the restaurant. Excellent food, which has a good local reputation, can be enjoyed in the relaxed atmosphere of the welcoming restaurant. The cuisine is prepared from the freshest organic produce and complemented by a fine selection of wines to suit all pockets. A traditional ambience and friendly service are the hallmarks of the Victoria Bar, offering a wide variety of food and drinks. The hotel has been awarded 3 AA Stars and 4 Crowns Commended. Windsor Castle, Eton College, Legoland, Thorpe Park and Cliveden are within easy reach. Outdoor attractions include trips on the Thames, golf at Wentworth and the Berkshire, Windsor Royal Horse Show and Driving Championships, Ascot and Windsor races. Guests may browse in the many good shops close by. **Directions:** Exit M4 at Jct5; follow signs to Eton. The hotel is in the High Street with its own car park through a carriage entrance. Price guide: Single from £95; double from £100; family rooms from £110.

ACORN INN

FORE STREET, EVERSHOT, DORSET DT2 0JW
TEL: 01935 83228 FAX: 01935 83707

This beautiful 16th century inn lies in a wonderful part of Dorset that found fame in one of Thomas Hardy's novels. Embedded in the literary mind as the 'Sow and Acorn' from the classic 'Tess of the d'Urbervilles', the owners take great pride in their hospitable approach and believe that offering a first class service and providing excellent value for money are paramount. There is an excellent selection of accommodation and the nine bedrooms are individually appointed with interesting antique furnishings. There is everything from a double bedroom with en suite shower or bathroom to a king sized four poster bed with Jacuzzi bath. The non-smoking restaurant offers an unashamedly British menu created by the talented Gordon Sutherland. Dishes such as wild boar sausages with red cabbage and loin of lamb stuffed with black pudding are complemented by a fine selection of wines. The village of Evershot is a very restful place and with first class English country meals, real ales and a selection of fine wines, guests will find this inn the perfect location for a quiet weekend away in the countryside. Places of interest nearby include Forde Abbey, Parnham House and the picturesque seaside town of Lyme Regis, used as a setting for the film, 'The French Lieutenant's Woman'. **Directions:** Evershot is south of A37 midway between Yeovil and Dorchester. Price guide: Single £55; double/twin £80–£120.

THE NORTHWICK HOTEL

WATERSIDE, EVESHAM, WORCESTERSHIRE WR11 6BT
TEL: 01386 40322 FAX: 01386 41070

Elegantly perched above the river Avon, the Northwick Hotel is a distinguished Georgian style building that has been entirely transformed since its acquisition by Gary Start in 1998. The Northwick Hotel is situated at the heart of the Vale of Evesham, whose moniker The Garden of England is richly deserved. Dotted along the surrounding roads are market garden stalls which visitors and residents find impossible to resist. The 31 bedrooms, one of which features a splendid four-poster bed, are well-appointed. Utilising the freshest of local produce, the British-style fare is imaginatively prepared and is accompanied by a wide-ranging, eclectic selection of wines. Boasting intimate meeting rooms and a function room, the hotel is also ideally suited to the business traveller. Nearby Evesham is a throbbing market town which also offers peaceful riverside walks through languid gardens and meadows. Commemorating his death after the Battle of Evesham in 1265, the Simon de Montfort Memorial in Abbey Park is of particular historical note. The Northwick Hotel is also conveniently placed for day trips to Stratford-upon-Avon, the Cotswolds and the Malvern Hills. **Directions:** Travelling south on the M5 from Birmingham, turn left onto the A44 at junction 7. Take second exit at roundabout with the A435. The Northwick Hotel is on the right. Price guide: Single £62–£75; double £85–£110.

RIVERSIDE RESTAURANT AND HOTEL

THE PARKS, OFFENHAM ROAD, NR EVESHAM, WORCESTERSHIRE WR11 5JP
TEL: 01386 446200 FAX: 01386 40021

The Riverside may not be a big hotel, but it has great style and a superb position, being perched high above the River Avon in the original Evesham Abbey's 15th century deer park. Three cleverly converted 17th century cottages blend with the main house to create an elegant 1920's residence. There are just seven enchanting bedrooms, all thoughtfully appointed. Lovely chintz fabrics and views over the gardens and terrace to the river add to guests' pleasure on arrival. Having a Chef-Patron, the restaurant is extremely important and a designated non-smoking area. The three frequently changing menus are reasonably priced for the exceptional range and style of choices offered. Interesting starters are followed by a selection of traditional and innovative dishes, including fresh monkfish and local pheasant. The tempting dessert list is shorter. The cellar holds 60 wines from £11.50 to £60. The restaurant is closed on Sunday evenings and all day Monday. The bar has big sofas, deep armchairs and large windows overlooking the river, the ambience being that of a country house drawing room. Guests may fish in the Avon, take a small boat out or visit the Royal Worcester Porcelain factory, go to Stratford-upon-Avon, or relax watching county cricket at Worcester. **Directions:** Take M5/junction 7 or M40/junction 16 to Evesham and approach the hotel from the B4510 to Offenham down a private drive through market gardens. Price Guide: Single £60; double £80.

THE ROYAL OAK INN

WINSFORD, EXMOOR NATIONAL PARK, SOMERSET TA24 7JE
TEL: 01643 851455 FAX: 01643 851009 E-MAIL: enquiries@royaloak–somerset

This world-famous picturesque thatched inn, dating from the 12th century, stands in the centre of an ancient riverside village on the edge of Exmoor National Park. Eight of the bedrooms are situated in the inn itself while a further six rooms have been created in the courtyard area. All are furnished to a high standard, some featuring four-posters. For relaxation the three lounges and two bars are all well appointed with open fires, chintz fabrics and oak beams. The inn has won a number of accolades and awards including AA 3 Stars. Dogs can be accommodated at the owner's discretion. In the attractive restaurant, tables set with Wedgwood and fine glassware create an attractive setting for dinner. Only the freshest local produce is used to prepare traditional English country recipes to a consistently high standard. Everything, from hams and pies to pâtés and bread, is home-cooked. Menus are changed daily. A good choice of light bar meals is available. Proprietor Charles Steven can arrange many sporting pastimes for his guests, including riding, fishing, hunting, shooting, golf and adventure walking. The hotel also provides a comprehensive sightseeing list covering Exmoor National Park and beyond. **Directions:** Leave M5 at junction 27 to Tiverton, take A396 Tiverton to Minehead road for 20 miles, then turn left to Winsford village. Price guide: Single from £65 (annexe); double £75–£135.

TRENGILLY WARTHA COUNTRY INN & RESTAURANT

NANCENOY, CONSTANTINE, FALMOUTH, CORNWALL TR11 5RP
TEL: 01326 340332 FAX: 01326 340332 E-MAIL: trengilly@compuserve.com

Trengilly Wartha is in "an area of outstanding natural beauty" near the village of Constantine, close to the Helford River. The location is romantic and famous. Daphne du Maurier's novel 'Frenchman's Creek' could have been written here about the local creek Polpenwith. The ambience is like staying in a private house that happens to be the local inn – there are newspapers in the attractive lounge and the Logan and Maguire families are very hospitable. The 'cottage' bedrooms are pristine, furnished in pine. Trengilly's Bar is cheerful, frequented by the locals. Being a freehouse a good range of real ales is available, together with farm ciders. The Beer Garden overlooks the valley and the vine shaded pergola offers escape from the sun. In winter a big fire blazes! The bar food is delicious. The restaurant has a Gallic theme, both in appearance and having an ever-changing inspired Prix-Fixé menu – local fish included – and the wines are superb (180 listed!) The substantial breakfast is very English. Energetic guests sail, golf, ride or surf off the nearby beaches. Cornish gardens, little harbours, the seal sanctuary, Falmouth harbour and the Lizard Peninsula must be explored. Trengilly Wartha also has a self catering house available nearby. **Directions:** A39 to Falmouth, then head for Constantine on B3291, where the inn is signed. Price guide: Single £40–£45; double £56–£85.

NEW

THE MERRYMOUTH INN

STOW ROAD, NR BURFORD, OXFORDSHIRE OX7 6HR
TEL: 01993 831652 FAX: 01993 830840

Originally a traveller's hospice and looked after by the monks from the local monastery, this beautiful inn has an interesting history dating back to the 13th century. It has also been a brewery owned hostelry but it is now a freehouse, providing a fine and attentive service. Close to the antique centres of Burford and Stow, this charming and cosy 13th century inn offers a welcome that is both warm and genuine. The inn itself is three miles north of Burford and affords staggering views over the Cotswold hills. Guests may start the day with a hearty English breakfast of freshly made sausages, prepared by the local butcher and free-range eggs from the hens next door before exploring the surrounding countryside. The more active guest may wish to enjoy a round of golf at the nearby course or try their hand at shooting and fishing and of course wonderful walks literally on the doorstep. Upon returning to Merrymouth, guests can indulge in the array of appetising dishes, served in the beautiful restaurant. For those who choose to take advantage of the hotel facilities in the converted stables, the comfortable rooms are furnished in a simple yet attractive style and feature televisions, tea and coffee making facilities and en suite facilities. Local attractions include Bourton-on-the-water, Sudeley Castle and Snowshill Manor. **Directions:** Fifield can be found just off A40 at Burford. Price guide: Single £39–£45; double £55–£60.

THE WHITE HART

FORD, CHIPPENHAM, WILTSHIRE SN14 8RP
TEL: 01249 782213 FAX: 01249 783075

Believed to date back to 1553, the White Hart is made of stone and prettily situated alongside the Bybrook River. The terrace overlooking the water is the ideal spot to eat and drink while looking out for kingfishers, herons and wagtails. Despite its rustic character, country lanes and riverside walks, the small village of Ford is within easy reach of the M4, Chippenham and Bath. Four of the bedrooms have four-poster beds and two have half-testers. Whether your room is located in the old stable block or main building, it will be comfortable and well-equipped. The White Hart is renowned for its delicious home cooking: all meals are freshly prepared, carefully presented and offer very good value. In the Riverside Restaurant the extensive à la carte menu typically includes venison casserole, herb-roasted grouse, supreme of chicken with a crab and saffron sauce and rack of lamb with chestnut and leek stuffing. The bar menu includes hearty soups, pies and ploughman's lunches. As well as traditional scrumpy, the bar offers one of Wiltshire's widest selection of real beers. The Good Pub Guide 'Pub of the Year' 1995 and Les Routiers Inn of the Year 1996. There are a number of country walks nearby – you can walk through the Bybrook Valley to Castle Combe. Bath, Bowood House, Corsham Court and Lacock are also close by. **Directions**: Leave the M4 at junction 17 or 18. Ford is situated off the A420 Bristol–Chippenham road. Price guide: Single from £50; double from £75.

THE WOODFALLS INN

THE RIDGE, WOODFALLS, FORDINGBRIDGE, HAMPSHIRE SP5 2LN
TEL: 01725 513222 FAX: 01725 513220 E-MAIL: woodfallsi@aol.com

Standing alongside the old coaching route from the beautiful New Forest to historic Salisbury, The Woodfalls Inn has provided rest and relaxation for travellers since 1870. Its welcome, hospitality, quality of service and traditional English ambience is such that the Inn has been awarded '5 Diamonds' by the English Tourist Board. All the bedrooms, named after flowers of the forest, are en suite, extremely comfortable and are tastefully and individually decorated in typically English fashion. Some have four posters. The inn also has a purpose-built conference and meetings suite with a capacity for up to 150 delegates. The standard of cuisine served in the intimate Lovers' Restaurant will satisfy every palate. Chef Reg Chapman produces excellent French dishes and interesting ethnic touches on his frequently changing table d'hôte and à la carte menus. More informal meals can be enjoyed in the conservatory or bar which has an extensive selection of properly stored cask conditioned ales. Picnic baskets can be arranged. Walking and riding in the enchanting New Forest, sailing on the Solent, golf and Salisbury with its cathedral is within easy reach. **Directions:** From the M27, exit at junction 1. Take the B3079, fork left at Brook onto the B3078, then fork right at Telegraph Corner onto the B3080 for Woodfalls. Price guide: Single £49.95; double £59.90–£90.

THE LEATHERNE BOTTEL RIVERSIDE INN & RESTAURANT

THE BRIDLEWAY, GORING-ON-THAMES, BERKSHIRE RG8 0HS
TEL: 01491 872667 FAX: 01491 875308

Winner of the Johansens 1996 Most Excellent Restaurant Award. The setting is unique, on the banks of the Thames in a nature conservation area, overlooking water meadows and the Berkshire Downs. Self-taught chef-patron Keith Read has become widely acclaimed. The Times has awarded him a six-star rating and includes him among today's most accomplished chefs. Egon Ronay described him as unpretentious and imaginative, relying on fresh, quality produce. In summer, dine in the riverside terrace garden, ablaze with colour and scented with wild herbs. The menu may include sea bass with virgin olive oil, samphire and sweet ginger, or tuna with apple mint and a stew of plum tomatoes and basil. In winter, log fires glow and the smell of simmering game stock fills the air. Local pheasant flavoured with lemon thyme and pancetta, or wood pigeon with red chilli, chick peas and coriander, are among the choices. Puddings are simple and mouth-watering: ginger brandy snap baskets full of summer berries, or steaming cappuccino pudding with Mount Gay sauce. The dining rooms reflect the style and taste of the owner: strong colours, fresh flowers and faultless yet relaxed service. Each table has a view of the river and the bar is filled with cookery books and marble sculptures. **Directions:** Signed off B4009 Goring–Wallingford road. From M4 Jct12: 15 mins; from M40 Jct6: 15 mins. Oxford is 30 mins drive, London 60 mins. Price guide (dinner for two incl. wine): £90–£120.

THE BLACK HORSE INN

GRIMSTHORPE, BOURNE, LINCOLNSHIRE PE10 0LY
TEL: 01778 591247 FAX: 01778 591373 E-MAIL: blackhorseinn@saqnet.co.uk

The Black Horse Inn lies within a short detour off the A1. Skilful restoration work has preserved the charm of the old inn while upgrading the accommodation to a high standard of modern comfort. The traditional character of the bar creates a welcoming area for guests and local residents alike. The original beams, stone walls and open fires all add to the considerable charm of the inn. There is a delightful honeymoon/executive suite with its own small sitting room and a spa bath. Guests can chose between the innovative bar and dining room menus and dine on the 2 AA Rosette award-winning cuisine. A typical choice might be millefeuille of pan-fried foie gras with puy lentils and balsamic vinegar, followed by medallions of monkfish with squid ink and saffron noodles and finishing with bread and butter pudding with Armagnac. There is something to tempt the most discerning of palates – with game and fish as in season – and the dishes are complemented by a very reasonably priced fine wine list. Grimsthorpe Castle, with its attractive park and nature trail around the lake, Burghley House, famous for its horse trials, Belvoir Castle and Belton House all lie close by. Golf, fishing and swimming are all within a 20 minute drive. **Directions:** Leave A1 between Grantham and Stamford, taking A151 at Colsterworth heading towards Bourne. Price guide: Single £50–£55; double £69–£79; suite £95.

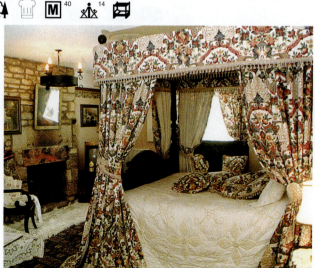

THE MAYNARD ARMS

MAIN ROAD, GRINDLEFORD, DERBYSHIRE S32 2HE
TEL: 01433 630321 FAX: 01433 630445

The owners of this Victorian inn have transformed its ambience and image into a very stylish small hostelry at this superb location overlooking the beautiful Derbyshire Peak National Park. The en suite bedrooms, which include two suites, are charming, comfortable and well equipped. Guests booking Friday and Saturday nights may stay in their room free on the Sunday night (except before Bank Holidays). The excellent restaurant offers a primarily traditional English fare featuring local game when in season, together with a carefully selected wine list. An extensive range of bar food is served at lunchtime and in the evenings in the Longshaw Bar – the busy hub of the inn. The second, quieter, bar is ideal for a drink before dinner and has a big log fire in winter months. There is a peaceful lounge with a view of the pretty gardens and the Dales. Chatsworth, Haddon Hall and Castleton are spectacular reminders of the heritage of the region. The market town of Bakewell is fascinating. Walkers have an endless choice of directions to take. Fishing is on the Derwent. Golf, pony-trekking and even gliding can be arranged locally. Regional theatres abound. **Directions:** Leaving Sheffield take the A625. Continue on this road until it becomes the A6187. Turn left onto the B6521, The Maynard Arms is on the left just as you enter Grindleford. Price guide: Single £67; double £77.

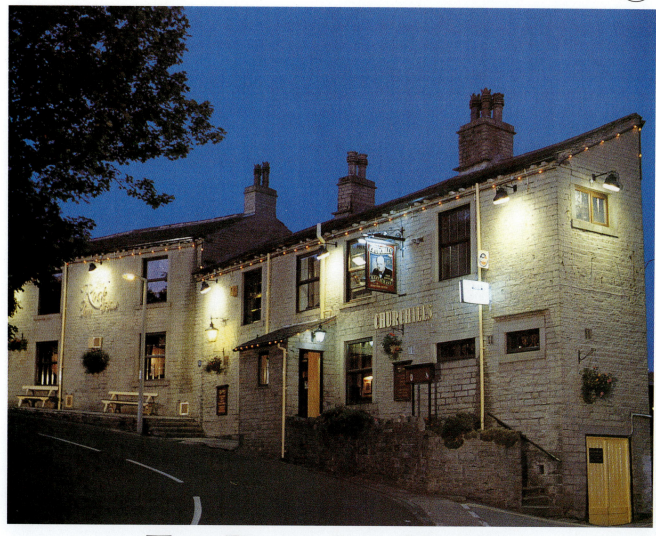

THE ROCK INN HOTEL

HOLYWELL GREEN, HALIFAX, WEST YORKSHIRE HX4 9BS
TEL: 01422 379721 FAX: 01422 379110 E-MAIL: the.rock@dial.pipex.com

Situated in a tranquil valley, yet midway between the commercial centres of Halifax/Huddersfield and Manchester/Leeds, this superb hostelry offers all the attractions of a traditional wayside inn as well as the sophistication of a first-class hotel. Bedrooms are equipped to luxurious standards being en suite with baths and showers, remote-control satellite TV, mini-bar and tea/coffee making facilities. 12 new deluxe bedrooms. The Victorian-style bar serves a range of hand-pulled ales and is open all day, every day, for meals and drinks. Superb conference facilities are available for up to 200 persons. Churchill's is a spacious restaurant, with a dance floor and a light and airy conservatory, opening out on to a large patio, overlooking a delightful rural aspect, where one can dine 'alfresco'. A variety of menus is available all day in any of the dining areas including the two conservatories, ranging from snacks to an 'East meets West' selection and daily blackboard specials. Romantic Brontë country and the spectacular Yorkshire countryside is ideal for rambling. The award-winning Eureka! Museum is a great favourite with families and the immediate area is a golfer's paradise. **Directions:** Leave M62 at Jct24 and follow signs for Blackley for approximately one mile, at the crossroads turn left for Holywell Green. The hotel is ½ mile along on the left. Price guide: Single £45–£110; double £64–£110.

THE CHEQUERS AT SLAUGHAM

SLAUGHAM, NR HANDCROSS, WEST SUSSEX RH17 6AQ
TEL: 01444 400239/400996 FAX: 01444 400400

Situated in the 1996 award-winning Best Kept Village in Sussex, The Chequers at Slaugham is a delightful hostelry offering a good welcome, superior accommodation and acclaimed cooking. All five of the de luxe guest rooms are appointed to a high standard, each with a host of amenities that include remote-control television, trouser press, radio alarm, hairdryer and refreshments. All have four poster beds and some have spa or double baths. The public rooms are given over mainly to dining areas, however, there is a comfortable residents' lounge. The Chequers' culinary reputation has gone from strength to strength. The menu caters for all tastes but it reflects a special emphasis on seafood dishes as proprietor Paul Graham purchases fresh fish from the new Billingsgate Market. Depending upon availability, the menu may include wing of skate, halibut, monkfish, fresh crab, lobster, plaice, lemon sole, scallops, salmon and richly flavoured fish soups. Guests can also dine in the conservatory restaurant with outstanding views of the Sussex countryside. The Chequers is conveniently located just ten minutes from Gatwick and is easily accessible from London. It is also well placed for visiting the stately homes and gardens of Surrey and Sussex. **Directions**: From the main London- Gatwick-Brighton road (A23), exit 2 miles south of Handcross. Price guide: Single £55–£65; double £80–£85.

THE BOAR'S HEAD HOTEL

RIPLEY, HARROGATE, NORTH YORKSHIRE HG3 3AY
TEL: 01423 771888 FAX: 01423 771509 E-MAIL: boarshead@ripleycastle.co.uk

Imagine relaxing in a four star hotel at the centre of a historic private country estate in England's incredibly beautiful North Country. The Ingilby family who have lived in Ripley Castle for 28 generations invite you to enjoy their hospitality at The Boar's Head Hotel. There are 25 luxury bedrooms, individually decorated and furnished, most with king-size beds. The restaurant menu is outstanding, presented by a creative and imaginative kitchen brigade and complemented by a wide selection of reasonably priced, good quality wines. There is a welcoming bar serving traditional ales straight from the wood and popular bar meal selections. When staying at The Boar's Head, guests can enjoy complimentary access to the delightful walled gardens and grounds of Ripley Castle, which include the lakes and a deer park. A conference at Ripley is a different experience – using the idyllic meeting facilities available in the castle, organisers and delegates alike will appreciate the peace and tranquillity of the location which offers opportunities for all types of leisure activity in the Deer Park. **Directions:** Ripley is very accessible, just 10 minutes from the conference town of Harrogate, 20 minutes from the motorway network, and Leeds/Bradford Airport, and 40 minutes from the City of York. Price guide: Single £95–£120; double £115–£140.

THE DOWER HOUSE

BOND END, KNARESBOROUGH, NR HARROGATE, NORTH YORKSHIRE HG5 9AL
TEL: 01423 863302 FAX: 01423 867665

The Dower House, set in the market town of Knaresborough, is a beautiful traditional hotel with features dating back to the Jacobean period. The interior, with its oak beams and comfortable furnishings, is beautifully appointed. The 31 bedrooms, in either the new wing or the main building, vary in size and offer en suite facilities. Those seeking more spacious rooms will favour the older bedrooms in the original house or four-poster bedrooms. A truly convivial atmosphere is created in the cocktail bar, which serves all the favourite drinks alongside some more unusual combinations. The Terrace Restaurant, strictly non-smoking, has daily changing dishes and an inspired brasserie menu. Fitness enthusiasts may take advantage of the hotel's own leisure club, which may be accessed directly from the property. The Corniche Leisure Club has a swimming pool, spa pool, steam room, sauna, fully-equipped gymnasium and a poolside bar serving drinks, light refreshments and snacks. There is a wealth of historic properties within the area and these include Ripley Castle, Harewood House, Newby Hall and Castle Howard. **Directions:** From the A1(M), take the A59 into Knaresborough. Follow signs to Mother Shipton's Cave along the High Street and turn left at the traffic lights. The hotel is on the right. Price guide: Single £60–£87; double £85–£98; suite £100. (Special breaks available).

THE GEORGE & OLIVE'S RESTAURANT

WORMALD GREEN, NR HARROGATE, NORTH YORKSHIRE HG3 3PR
TEL: 01765 677214 FAX: 01765 676201

The George stands just north of the conference and spa town of Harrogate and is a mecca for good food lovers. Essentially a top class dining venue with rooms rather than a hotel, it's reputation for excellent cuisine has spread far beyond North Yorkshire's boundaries. In the George's kitchen is one of the world's leading chefs, Royal Master Chef Graham Newbould, who gained Michelin stars and two AA Rosettes at previous restaurants. Before guests even taste a mouthful of his exquisite cuisine they know that they are in for a culinary experience. At the bar, there is a glass case containing a piece of Prince Charles and Princess Diana's wedding cake, menus of State occasions, a picture of President Ronald Reagan shaking hands with Graham following a Windsor Castle dinner and Christmas cards signed from the late King Hussein of Jordan. Graham was the Queen's chef at Buckingham Palace before joining Prince Charles and Princess Diana and later Inverlochy Castle, Fort William, and then the Calabash in Grenada. With joint patron Steve Lockwood, Graham's ambition is to see their restaurants, Champagne & Olives Brasserie and Newboulds, which opened last autumn following refurbishment of the hotel, unrivalled in the North. The George's five en suite bedrooms are comfortable and offer all modern facilities. **Directions:** On A61 Harrogate-Ripon road. Price guide: Single £50; double £70.

THE LOW HALL HOTEL

RIPON ROAD, KILLINGHALL, HARROGATE, NORTH YORKSHIRE HG3 2AY
TEL: 01423 508598 FAX: 01423 560848

The Low Hall is a lovely Grade II listed building circa 1672, personally owned and run by Richard and Maureen Stokes, with views of seven miles over beautiful Nidderdale. To the rear are lovely spacious gardens. Oak beams, stone walls and open fires all add to The Low Hall's character and cosy atmosphere. The seven bedrooms, created from the mainly Georgian part of this former family home are snug and comfortable, all en suite with modern facilities. A delightful, low ceiling bar/restaurant leads onto a patio and the gardens beyond. The hotel's original coach house is now an attractive, beamed dining area where the accent is on a high standard of cooking, quality and presentation that should please the most discerning palate. Floor-to-ceiling wine racks house a vast variety of choice for guests to consider before sitting down for dinner. The Barn Suite is a large room for parties and meetings for as many as 90 people. Harrogate is only 2 miles away, whilst Ripon is 9 miles. The historic city of York, Skipton and Leeds are within easy reach. There is trout and coarse fishing on the River Nidd, boating, horse-riding, shooting on the moors and several golf courses close by. **Directions:** The Low Hall Hotel is on the edge of the village of Killinghall, two miles north of Harrogate on the A61. Price guide: Single £55–£80; double £65–£95.

THE HATCHGATE

BRAMSHILL, NR HOOK, HAMPSHIRE RG27 0JX
TEL: 01189 326666 FAX: 01189 326608

The Hatchgate is a delightful, white-fronted, traditional roadside inn that has been offering a warm welcome and serving fine beers and wine since the early years of this century. Surrounded by open countryside, it was formerly a cottage believed to have been used as a gate or toll house on the lane side between the great estates of Heckfield Park and Bramshill House, built by Lord Zouch and now the National Police College. The hostess, Gilly Alexander, has invested a great deal of enthusiasm and energy into making The Hatchgate a welcoming haven of comfort, sumptuous food and attentive service. It is full of good humour, atmosphere and character. Gilly herself is a cheerful personality with many interesting stories to tell of her days as a performer with the famous Black and White Minstrels Show. As well as an extensive bar menu of snacks and light meals, appetising and comprehensive à la carte cuisine tempts locals and visitors alike to the inn's restaurant. There is a well-selected wine list featuring affordable vintages. Visitors can enjoy a pre or post drinks stroll through the nearby Bramshill Wood and within easy reach are historic Heckfield Church, Wellington Country Park and Stratfield Saye House. No bedrooms are available for guests. **Directions:** Exit the M3 at junctions 4 or 5. Take the A30 to Hartley Wintney and then the B3011. Bramshill is clearly signposted. Look for the Police College signs.

THE PLOUGH INN

LEADMILL BRIDGE, HATHERSAGE, DERBYSHIRE S30 1BA
TEL: 01433 650319 FAX: 01433 651049

Situated in nine acres of grounds, the 16th century Plough Inn has recently been restored to give visitors every modern facility and comfort. It is in an idyllic position, close to the meandering River Derwent and surrounded by magnificent countryside which is home to many species of wildlife. Cosy and tastefully decorated, The Plough Inn provides an ideal environment in which to unwind and is an ideal base from which to explore the heritage of the Peak District. The adjoining spacious bedrooms, which are reached by an external staircase, are decorated in an attractive and welcoming cottage style and have satellite television, hairdryer and tea and coffee making facilities. All have countryside views. The inn is closed on Christmas Day. The owners have created a welcoming ambience complemented by attentive service. A good value menu offers a splendid choice of dishes. Castleton with its caves and caverns and the ruins of Pevril Castle, Bakewell's 700-year-old arched bridge and 17th century Bath House built for the Duke of Rutland, Haddon Hall and 18th century Chatsworth House, one of the great stately homes of England, the Blue John Mine, Speedwell Cavern and Treak Cliff are all nearby. Potholing, riding, climbing, para-gliding and golf can be enjoyed locally. **Directions:** From M1 exit 29 take A617 west and then via A619 and A623. Shortly after Baslow turn north onto B6001 toward Hathersage. Price guide: Single From £40–£55; double From £60–£75.

RHYDSPENCE INN

WHITNEY-ON-WYE, NR HAY-ON-WYE, HEREFORDSHIRE HR3 6EU
TEL: 01497 831262 FAX: 01497 831751

This 14th century manor house is set in the heart of Kilvert country and features several times in the works of the celebrated diarist. A striking half-timbered building, it has been tastefully extended to create an attractive dining room overlooking a well-kept garden. The bedrooms are individually furnished in time honoured style and all afford scenic views of the Wye Valley and the Black Mountains. The two welcoming bars have exposed beams and open fires typical of traditional inns and both serve draught ale and cider on tap. Closed for two weeks in January. An exceptionally well-balanced à la carte menu offers the best of country fare and international cuisine. Advantage is taken of the abundance of fresh local produce – Hereford beef, Welsh lamb, fresh fish and seasonally available game are among the choices on the frequently changing menu. The sweet trolley offers a delicious array of puddings. Snacks, both the traditional and more unusual, are served in the bar. Private parties can be catered for. The area is a paradise for nature lovers. Riding, pony-trekking, caving, wind-surfing and canoeing on the River Wye are all available and Hay-on-Wye, famous for its second-hand bookshops, is close by. For walkers Offa's Dyke Path passes near to the inn. **Directions:** The Rhydspence stands above and is well protected from the A438 Brecon-Hereford road. OS map reference 243472. Price Guide: Single £32.50–£37.50; double £65–£75.

THE WALTZING WEASEL

NEW MILLS ROAD, BIRCH VALE HIGH PEAK, DERBYSHIRE SK22 1BT
TEL: 01663 743402 FAX: 01663 743402

The Waltzing Weasel is a traditional country inn which, as its distinctive name suggests, offers a welcome alternative to the anonymous urban hotel. It is set within the heart of the Peak District, yet is only 40 minutes from Manchester and its international airport, Sheffield and Stockport. With its log fires, relaxed rustic character and country antiques, this is a civilised retreat for those looking for a restful break, be they tired executives, hardy walkers or confirmed slouches. They are guaranteed no jukeboxes nor fruit-machines here. Individually styled bedrooms offer comfortable accommodation and most of the rooms enjoy lovely views over the surrounding countryside. Acclaimed chef George Benham provides good, honest food in the intimate restaurant which overlooks the garden towards the dramatic landscape of Kinder Scout. Starters such as seafood pancakes, fresh asparagus and gravadlax promise good things to come. Main courses may include poached Scotch salmon, roast duck with figs and chicken cooked to order in white wine, tomatoes, mushrooms and crevettes. Excellent bar meals are served at lunchtime. Shooting, fishing and golfing facilities are within easy reach, as are Chatsworth, Haddon Hall, Castleton, Bakewell and Buxton with its opera house. **Directions:** The Waltzing Weasel is near A624 on the A6015 New Mills-Hayfield road, ½ mile from Hayfield. Price guide: Single £38–£78; double £65–£95.

THE FEATHERS HOTEL

MARKET PLACE, HELMSLEY, NORTH YORKSHIRE YO6 5BH
TEL: 01439 770275 FAX: 01439 771101

This 15th century inn is set in the centre of Helmsley, a beautiful market town lying on the edge of the North Yorkshire Moors National Park. There are three bars: the Pickwick bar with its low beamed ceiling and open fire, the cosy Feversham lounge bar where bar meals are served and the Stables Restaurant cocktail bar. Local Thompson 'Mouse Man' furniture is featured throughout the hotel. Its 14 bedrooms have been recently refurbished and redecorated to a high standard. The hotel has an excellent local reputation for good food and fine ales. The restaurant has an à la carte menu and a carvery and bar meals are served at both lunch-time and in the evening. Delicious main courses include roulade of chicken filled with black pudding and Stilton cheese; pork fillet with a whisky and green peppercorn sauce; poached supreme of salmon set in a pool of lemon and chive butter sauce and home-made steak pie. Leisure activities in the area include golf at the Kirkbymoorside Golf Club, pony-trekking and racing at York. The East Coast resorts, Rievaulx Abbey, Byland Abbey, Duncombe Park and the historic city of York are all within easy reach. **Directions**: The Feathers is in the centre of Helmsley overlooking the Market Place. There is a private car park at the rear of the hotel. Price guide: Single £35–£40; double £60–£70.

THE FEVERSHAM ARMS HOTEL

HELMSLEY , NORTH YORKSHIRE YO6 5AG
TEL: 01439 770766 FAX: 01439 770346

This historic coaching inn, rebuilt in 1855 of mellow Yorkshire stone by the Earl of Feversham, has been owned and managed by the Aragues family since 1967. Set in two acres of walled gardens, The Feversham Arms has been updated to a high standard to offer every modern amenity, while special care has been taken to preserve the character and charm of the older parts of the hostelry. The bedrooms are individually furnished and some have special features such as four-poster beds and de luxe bathrooms. Open fires blaze in the winter months. Dogs can be accommodated by arrangement. The attractive candle-lit Goya Restaurant serves English, French and Spanish cuisine and by relying on fresh local produce, offers seasonal variety. There is a delicious fish and seafood menu. To accompany dinner, an extensive wine list includes a wide selection of Spanish wines and clarets. Situated in the North York Moors National Park and close to many golf courses, this comfortable and welcoming hotel is ideal for sporting pursuits as well as for touring the moors, dales, east coast and the medieval city of York. The ruins of Rievaulx Abbey in Ryedale (2½ miles) should not be missed. Special Bonanza Breaks available, ask for brochure. **Directions**: From the A1 take the A64, then take the York north bypass (A1237) and then the B1363. Alternatively, from A1, take A168 signposted Thirsk, then A170. Price guide: Single £55–£65; double £80–£90.

NEW

THE GROSVENOR ARMS

HINDON, SALISBURY, WILTSHIRE SP3 6DJ
TEL: 01747 820696 FAX: 01747 820869

Recently refurbished to a very high standard, The Grosvenor Arms is a former coaching inn set in the picturesque and historical village of Hindon. Its 18th century tradition of serving travellers between London and the West Country is still maintained today and guests are treated to the attentive service and hospitality reminiscent of bygone days. The seven en suite bedrooms are individually appointed and feature the latest facilities for the modern traveller. Soft fabrics and large towels add to the inviting ambience. Guests may relax in the comfortable lounge or refresh themselves with a pint of real ale in the bar, where stone floors and log fires add to the traditional character. The cuisine is excellent and is prepared in an unusual glass-fronted theatre style kitchen as diners anticipate their meals. The mouth-watering creations include caramelised sautéed Brixham scallops on a Thai flavoured risotto finished with lobster oil and pan fried breast of wood pigeon served with lentils du Puy on killer mash potato. Keen heritage enthusiasts will be pleased with the many historical treasures located nearby such as Stourhead, Longleat house and safari park and the intriguing Stonehenge. **Directions:** Only 1 mile away from the A303 and A350. Follow signs to Hindon, the inn is in the centre of the village. Price guide: Single £55; double £65–£85.

THE LAMB AT HINDON

HIGH STREET, HINDON, SALISBURY, WILTS SP3 6DP
TEL: 01747 820573 FAX: 01747 820605 E-MAIL: the-lamb.demon.co.uk

The Lamb at Hindon is a fine 17th century inn, set in this picturesque Wiltshire village, offering both comfortable accommodation and superb cuisine. The well-appointed, traditionally decorated bedrooms have en suite facilities. Popular with shooting parties and the local villagers, Cora Scott and John Croft have had a long association with the Inn and have recently acquired the freehold. The restaurant prides itself on its use of local produce and game, with seafood from Cornish ports dropped off on its way to the London markets. The friendly staff are both welcoming and professional and ensure an excellent standard of service. The Bar, with its enchanting log fires, has a relaxing ambience and guests may indulge in a variety of drinks including real ales brewed locally or choose from the extensive wine list. Trout fishing, shooting, riding and other outdoor pursuits can be organised locally. Other distractions close by include the superb cathedral at Salisbury and the breath-taking Stonehenge. Historic houses such as Stourhead, Longleat, Old Wardour Castle and Wilton are located nearby. **Directions:** From the A350 Warminster to Shaftsbury road, turn on to the B3089. Price guide: Single £43; double £65.

HOME FARM HOTEL

WILMINGTON, NR HONITON, DEVON EX14 9JR
TEL: 01404 831278 FAX: 01404 831411

Home Farm is an attractive thatched farmhouse, set in four acres of beautiful grounds. A small hotel since 1950, which the owners have tastefully restored to create a charming and relaxing ambience. The staff are friendly and children are made welcome. The public rooms have big bowls of flowers in summer and enchanting log fires in the winter. Value for money is an important criterion. The Residents' Lounge is comfortable and there is a cosy, well-stocked bar serving light meals, draught beer and lager. The restaurant, oak-beamed and with an inglenook fireplace, offers a marvellous à la carte choice as well as a good 'home cooked' table d'hôte menu using local produce. The wine list is extensive. Bedrooms are in the main building or across a cobbled courtyard. All have private bathroom, telephone, colour television, hairdryer, radio alarm and tea/coffee making facilities. Wilmington is in the heart of 25 National Trust properties and there are six golf courses within 15 miles. Riding, water sports and fishing can be arranged. Honiton is known for its lace, as is Axminster for its carpets. **Directions:** Take the A303 to Honiton, join the A35 signposted to Axminster. Wilmington is three miles further on and Home Farm is set back off the main road on the right. Price guide: Single from £35; double £65–£75.

THE WEAVERS SHED RESTAURANT WITH ROOMS

KNOWL ROAD, GOLCAR, HUDDERSFIELD, WEST YORKSHIRE HD7 4AN
TEL: 01484 654284 FAX: 01484 650980 E-MAIL: stephen@weavers–shed.demon.co.uk

Set in the Colne Valley, an area once famous for woollen manufacturing, The Weavers Shed was originally a cloth finishing mill. It was converted to a restaurant 25 years ago and adjoins the Mill Owners residence which comprises fine luxury en suite bedrooms. The fusion of modern and classic influences in the kitchen parallels the blend of styles in the bedrooms. The textile heritage that is omnipresent in West Yorkshire is praised in the accommodation at Weavers Shed as each of the five bedrooms is named after one of the local textile mills. Chef Patron, Stephen Jackson and his team strive to create a welcoming ambience. The excellent menu features Modern British cuisine using predominantly local produce with much of the vegetables, herbs and fruit cultivated in the restaurant's own kitchen garden and orchard. Typical dishes include braised lamb shank with wild mushrooms, mashed roots and parsnip crisps followed by banana tarte tatin with Barbados rum and raisin ice cream. **Directions:** Leave the M62 at junction 23 eastbound and follow the A640 towards Rochdale crossing over the M62. Turn left into Quebec Road and then go into Golcar Village. The Weavers Shed is in the centre of the village on the left hand side of the road. Price guide: Single £30–£45; double £50–£65.

NORTHOVER MANOR

ILCHESTER, SOMERSET BA22 8LD
TEL: 01935 840447 FAX: 01935 840006 E-mail: melhaddigan@compuserve.com

This rambling former 15th century manor house is a welcoming venue for anyone wishing to tour and sample the delights of Somerset. Behind its thickly clad, ivy covered walls is an extremely warm and friendly ambience. Owners Mark and Melanie Haddigan have invested a tremendous amount of energy and enthusiasm in making the hotel into a haven of comfort, excellent food and attentive service. The 12 en suite bedrooms are split evenly between the main house and the coach house. All are enchanting, combining modern needs and requirements with tasteful décor and individual furnishings in cosy cottage style. Tempting à la carte dishes are served in the intimate, heavily beamed restaurant which is warmed in winter months by an open log fire. Snacks and a full menu are also offered in the recently upgraded Village Bar for visitors wanting a more informal setting for lunch or dinner. On summer days and evenings the delightful garden is a favourite relaxation area and there is a play area to keep children amused. The Fleet Air Arm Museum, Haynes Motor Museum, the Main Line Steam Museum and many National Trust properties and gardens, such as Montacute House, are nearby. Glastonbury, Yeovil, Sherborne and Wells are within easy reach. Golf, fishing and horse riding are available locally and can be arranged on request. **Directions:** Ilchester is signed off A303 linking London to the South West. Price guide: Single/double from £58.95.

CLARENDON HOUSE

HIGH STREET, KENILWORTH, WARWICKSHIRE CV8 1LZ
TEL: 01926 857668 FAX: 01926 850669 E-MAIL: ch@nuthurst–grange.co.uk

Set in the heart of England, in the verdant conservation area of Kenilworth, Clarendon House is steeped in a most interesting history. Dating back to 1430, the original timber-framed 'Castle Tavern' is ever present and is still supported by the old oak tree around which it was built. Whilst there has recently been a complete refurbishment of this property, vestiges of the past and traditional features have still been retained, such as the many cottage-style bedrooms. All of the rooms are well-equipped with satellite televisions and modem/fax sockets and furnished in an elegant style. For those seeking an air of romance and sentiment, there are two rooms with four-poster beds and a luxurious suite.

Open day and night, the bar and brasserie form the very heart of this establishment. Offering a deliciously versatile menu, prepared with fresh, seasonal produce, the brasserie serves everything from hearty British meals to delicate seafood platters. A list of carefully chosen fine wines has been compiled with the flavours in mind. With its good function rooms and conference facilities, the hotel is an ideal venue for private dining, business meetings and special occasions such as intimate weddings. Budding thespians will be pleased with the proximity of Stratford-upon-Avon. **Directions:** The nearest motorway is the M40, exit at junction 15. Price guide: Single £49.50–£55; double £75–£90; suite £110.

THE BARN OWL INN

ALLER MILLS, KINGSKERSWELL, DEVON TQ12 5AN
TEL: 01803 872130 FAX: 01803 875279

The Barn Owl Inn has been converted from a farmhouse into a very good value inn. Although the building dates back to the 16th century, it has modern facilities and services, while retaining many original features, including inglenook fireplaces, an ornate plaster ceiling in the largest bar and a sizeable black-leaded range. Handcrafted furniture can be found in the cottage-style bedrooms, where there are complimentary bottles of spring water and toiletries. Selecting ones meal from the fascinating menu is a challenge and the excellent but modestly priced wine list complements the superb dishes. Service is immaculate and the ambience is perfect. There is also a very good bar that serves real ale and excellent food. Torquay is a holiday town par excellence and the neighbouring seaside towns of Paignton and Brixham are in easy reach. Local places of interest include Compton Castle, once the home of Sir Walter Raleigh, Dartmoor and the underground caves in Kent's Cavern. Tennis and riding can be enjoyed locally. **Directions**: Take the M5 to Exeter, then follow the A380 signposted Torquay. Drive one mile past the Penn Inn traffic lights and the inn is on the right, signposted Aller Mills. Price guide: Single from £49; double from £69.

LONGVIEW HOTEL AND RESTAURANT

51/55 MANCHESTER ROAD, KNUTSFORD, CHESHIRE WA16 0LX
TEL: 01565 632119 FAX: 01565 652402 E-MAIL: longview_hotel@compuserve.com

This delightful house, once the home of a Victorian merchant, has been thoughtfully restored by Stephen and Pauline West to create an elegant, small, friendly hotel a few minutes walk from the centre of this little market town, so accessible from Manchester and the airport. The house has been furnished to reflect its era, with well polished antiques, fresh flowers and pleasant chintzes. The pretty bedrooms are decorated in floral cottons and benefit from hairdryers, television and a hot drinks tray, as well as Victorian pin cushions! Ten bedrooms are in the modernised 19th century house next door. There are also six luxury service apartments in a house nearby and all overlook 'The Heath'. There is a well stocked cosy cellar bar where you can relax before being seated in the comfortable period restaurant. Noted for its cuisine throughout the area, guests enjoy delights such as roast beef and Cheshire puddings made with a home-made horseradish mixture, Tatton Estate venison fillet and superb vegetarian dishes. After dinner treats include lovely desserts and delicious home-made ice cream. The wine list is international with very reasonable house wines. Beautiful country house gardens and Tatton Park are nearby whilst Chester is within reasonable driving distance. **Directions:** Leave M6 at Jct19 on A556 westbound towards Chester. Left at lights, left at roundabout in Knutsford and hotel is 300 yards on the right. Price guide: Single £47–£78; double £66–£93. Special breaks available.

FEATHERS HOTEL

HIGH STREET, LEDBURY, HEREFORDSHIRE HR8 1DS
TEL: 01531 635266 FAX: 01531 638955 E-MAIL: feathers@ledbury.kc3ltd.co.uk

The black and white timbered exterior of The Feathers Hotel stands out very clearly in Ledbury's main street. This traditional coaching inn, which dates back to the 1560s, is impressive even by the high standards of the area. The bedrooms retain their quaint character, with beamed walls and ceilings, yet are comfortably appointed. There are two bars and a comfortable lounge area in which to relax, all with log fires. Up to 150 delegates can be seated in the excellent, first floor conference suite which also doubles as an ideal venue for social occasions. The new leisure suite comprises pool with adjacent spa, fitness gym, solarium and steam room. The Feathers' cooking has earned an AA Rosette and a great reputation in the area. The main restaurant offers an à la carte menu with appetising dishes, many of which are prepared simply, to maximise the flavour of the ingredients. More informal meals are served in Fuggles Brasserie where hops hang from the rafters. A range of ales and over 60 international wines are offered, to accompany dishes such as spiced pork tenderlion with saffron, dates and fragrant couscous. Ledbury, with its narrow lanes and cobblestone streets, is ideally placed for the Malvern Hills, Hereford, Worcester and Gloucester. Eastnor Castle and the Falconry Centre at Newent lie nearby. **Directions:** Leave M50 at Jct2 and take A417 towards Hereford. The Feathers Hotel is in Ledbury High Street. Price guide: Single £69.50–£77.50; double £89.50–£145.

THE THREE HORSESHOES INN & RESTAURANT

BUXTON ROAD, BLACKSHAW MOOR, NR LEEK, STAFFORDSHIRE ST13 8TW
TEL: 01538 300296 FAX: 01538 300320

A homely family run hostelry situated in the beautiful Staffordshire Moorlands on the edge of the Peak District National Park, the Three Horseshoes is a traditional farmhouse style inn providing comfortable accommodation and excellent food. It stands in its own large and beautiful garden, with patios, terraces and a children's play area. The six en suite cottage style bedrooms have been recently redecorated and furnished. Affording superb views, Kirk's restaurant serves fine food, fresh vegetables and a choice of over 200 wines. In the evening, candlelight and romantic music combine to create a peaceful and relaxing atmosphere. On Saturday nights, there is a dinner and dance with a cabaret and à la carte menu offering an extensive choice of food. A Bar Carvery provides home-cooked traditional dishes, as well as a roast of the day, accompanied by fresh market vegetables. The inn is closed from Christmas through to the New Year. The area around the inn includes Rudyard Lake for sailing and walks (from which Kipling took his name), Tittesworth Reservoir for fishing, walking and bird watching and the Roaches for climbing and rambling. About 15 minutes away are the Manifold Valley, Dovedale, Berrisford Dale, Hartington, Alstonefield and Butterton. Alton Towers and Chatsworth are just 20 minutes away. **Directions:** Inn is on the A53 road to Buxton, easily reached by M6 via the Potteries and M1 via Derby. Price guide: Single £45; double £55–£65.

THE COUNTRYMEN

THE GREEN, LONG MELFORD, SUFFOLK CO10 9DN
TEL: 01787 312356 FAX: 01787 374557

Overlooking Melford's magnificent green, The Countrymen has received wide acclaim for its superb food and splendid accommodation. Recognised by all major guides, The Countrymen is enjoyed by visitors and locals alike. Stephen and Janet have earned much praise for their enthusiastic and generous hospitality. The bedrooms, individually furnished with country antiques, offer every modern amenity. If you are lucky or ask in advance you could be sleeping in one of the four-posters or in an antique brass bedstead in a room with panoramic views over Melford. The comfortable lounge offers scope to enjoy the many books and games; whilst the attractive restaurant leads out to a picturesque walled courtyard garden, where you can dine alfresco on warm summer nights. Stephen who learned his skills at the Dorchester creates dishes to tempt even the most jaded palate. The Countrymen Dinner menu is complemented by a unique Gastronomic menu with different wine, selected by Janet, to accompany each course. Today, The Countrymen also offers a Bistro Wine Bar where Stephen's specialities, particularly his own pasta, can be enjoyed in relaxed informality. Melford Hall, Kentwell Hall and a plethora of antique shops; Constable country, Gainsborough's birthplace, historic Bury St Edmunds, Lavenham, Newmarket and Cambridge are all close by. **Directions**: On the village green on the A1092 and the A134. Price guide: Single £55–£65; double £70–£105.

THE BATH ARMS

HORNINGSHAM, WARMINSTER, WILTSHIRE BA12 7LY
TEL: 01985 844308 FAX: 01985 844150

Previously known as Lord Weymouth's Arms, this former monastry is surrounded by the largest collection of rare Glastonbury Cockspur Thorn trees in the country. The Bath Arms is ideally located in the charming village of Horningsham, with fantastic rural views across the unspoilt countryside. Inside, polished wood floors, open fires and interesting ornaments add to the character of this lovely inn. The beautifully appointed bedrooms, all of which are en suite, feature an array of modern amenities such as colour televisions and tea and coffee making facilities. A tasty menu is served in the convivial bar and includes salmon and spinach fishcakes. Home-cooked food is prepared in the restaurant and fillet of sea bream, roast saddle of lamb or duck breast coated in honey with caramelised apples and a green peppercorn jus are some of the many mouthwatering dishes that may be enjoyed. The large beer garden is particularly popular during the summer months and is perfect for families with children. Special occasions, business meetings and corporate events may be held at The Bath Arms and country pursuits such as riding, shooting and fishing may be arranged nearby. Longleat stately home and safari park, Stonehenge and the Roman city of Bath are all within easy reach. **Directions:** From Jct17 of M4, go to Chippenham and then Warminster, then take A350 towards Horningsham. Price guide: Single £45–£55; double £65–£80.

THE ANGEL INN

HIGH STREET, LYMINGTON, NEW FOREST, HAMPSHIRE SO41 9AP
TEL: 01590 672050 FAX: 01590 671661

This attractive former 17th century coaching inn, with its resident ghost, can be found on the edge of the New Forest in the beautiful, historic maritime town of Lymington. With the sandy beaches of Bournemouth nearby and the Isle of Wight just a hop away on the ferry, this is a good venue for those wishing to explore the region. The owners of the inn pride themselves on the well-known guests of the past and present, perhaps the most notable being Edward VII. A suite has been named in his honour and visitors will find that it affords the most dazzling views over the Solent. A Thomas Ronaldson Suite can also be found at the inn which features a four-poster bed; perfect for a romantic weekend.

Bedrooms located at the front of the top floor have views over rooftops to the river estuary and the boating activity for which Lymington is famous. The restaurant serves a wide range of menus catering for all tastes, ranging from traditional English to exotic Thai and a menu specially created for children. The Inn provides excellent conference and wedding facilities in the Admiral suite which has recently been refurbished in order to maintain its traditional charm. There is a plethora of opportunities nearby and the local yatching marina is a must. **Directions:** From the M27, exit at junction 1 and then take the A337 to Lymington. Price guide: Single from £30; double/twin from £60.

THE RISING SUN

HARBOURSIDE, LYNMOUTH, DEVON EX35 6EQ
TEL: 01598 753223 FAX: 01598 753480

Recommended in every way, this award-winning 14th century thatched smugglers' inn is perfectly positioned on the picturesque harbour overlooking East Lyn River. The building is steeped in history: Lorna Doone was partly written here and the inn's adjacent cottage – now luxuriously equipped for guests' use and pictured below – was once the honeymoon retreat for the poet Shelley. The best of the inn's medieval character has been preserved: oak panelling, open fires and crooked ceilings, all enhanced by tasteful furnishings and modern comforts. The bedrooms lack nothing and like the terraced gardens, have splendid views. Parking in Lynmouth can be difficult at the height of the season. The food served in the oak-panelled restaurant is of excellent quality. Classic modern cuisine is provided on an à la carte menu, which also features local specialities such as fresh lobster. Good value bar meals are also available. Self catering accommodation and bed and breakfast available at Highercombe-Dulverton. The inn owns a ½m stretch of river for salmon fishing and there are opportunities for sea angling. Exmoor National Park, the North Devon coastline and Doone Valley are nearby. **Directions:** Leave M5 at Jct23 (signed Minehead) and follow A39 to Lynmouth. Or take A361, exit 27 (Tiverton) to South Molton, then B3226 in the direction of Ilfracombe and then A39 at Blackmoor Gate to Lynmouth. Price guide: Single £60; double £110–£150.

RINGLESTONE INN

**'TWIXT HARRIETSHAM AND WORMSHILL, NR MAIDSTONE, KENT ME17 1NX
TEL: 01622 859900 FAX: 01622 859966 E-MAIL: michelle@ringlestone.com**

Truly traditional is the welcome that awaits visitors as they step back in time into this delightfully unspoilt, medieval, lamplit tavern. Built in 1533 as a hospice for monks, the Ringlestone became one of the early Ale Houses around 1615 and little has changed since. Its delights include original brick and flint walls and floors, massive oak beams, inglenooks, old English furniture and eight acres of idyllic gardens. There are three en suite bedrooms and a separate cottage at a charming farmhouse just opposite the inn, all furnished in a style totally in keeping with expectations for a stay in this beautiful escapists' spot. Spacious farmhouse dining and reception rooms are also available for private and corporate functions. Full of character

and candlelight ambience with sturdy, highly polished tables made from the timbers of an 18th century Thames barge, the Ringlestone has a reputation for excellent English cooking and features in many food guides. A help yourself 'hot and cold' buffet lunch offers a seasonal variety of traditional country recipes. The diverse evening menu includes unusual and interesting pies and local trout, complemented by their exclusive house wines imported directly from France and a wide range of English country fruit wines. Leeds Castle is nearby. **Directions:** Leave M20 at Jct8. Head north off A20 through Hollingbourne, turn right at water tower crossroads towards Doddington. Price guide: Single from £69; double/twin from £79.

THE HORSE AND GROOM INN

CHARLTON, NEAR MALMESBURY, WILTSHIRE SN16 9DL
TEL: 01666 823904 FAX: 01666 823390

In the small village of Charlton in the heart of Cotswold country, the Horse & Groom Inn possesses a unique rustic charm. Inside, this 16th century coaching inn has been sensitively reinterpreted, with no loss of its period atmosphere; careful thought and attention has been invested in each of the three bedrooms, resulting in peaceful, relaxing rooms with all modern conveniences (plus extra touches like mineral water, fresh fruit, flowers and bathrobes). Décor is muted, in elegant shades like sage green, jasmine and peach; windows look out over the beautiful Cotswold countryside. A full English breakfast is included in the tariff. Awarded an AA Rosette, The Horse & Groom has a fine reputation for its cuisine, which has attracted the attention (and

recommendation) of food connoisseurs. There are simple bar snacks including jacket potatoes and ploughman's lunches, or more elaborate meals such as roasted fresh guinea fowl with a rich game sauce; red mullet fillets on buttered egg noodles; and wild mushroom and tomato omelette. The Horse & Groom is a free house serving Wiltshire ales and selected great beers. In summer, drinks and meals may be enjoyed in the private garden. In winter, guests choose to relax by log fires crackling in the grates. Bath, the Cotswolds and Malmesbury are nearby. **Directions:** Exit M4 junction 17. The inn is 2 miles east of Malmesbury on B4040. Price guide: Single from £60; double from £80.

THE TALBOT INN AT MELLS

SELWOOD STREET, MELLS, NR BATH, SOMERSET BA11 3PN
TEL: 01373 812254 FAX: 01373 813599 E-MAIL: talbot.inn@lineone.net

This beautiful coaching inn is set in the picturesque village of Mells on the edge of the Mendips. Parts of the building date back to the 15th century and the bedrooms have been individually furnished and decorated in keeping with an old 'traditional style' inn. However, character and charm are combined with every modern amenity to ensure that guests can relax in total comfort. The cobbled courtyard and pretty cottage garden are ideal places to sit and enjoy an early evening drink on a warm summer day or to take an alfresco meal. In the oak-beamed Oxford and Snug bar restaurant guests can enjoy a quick snack or a superb à la carte meal. Freshly prepared dishes include game from the local shoot and fresh fish which is delivered daily. Sample the poached fillet of salmon with linguini pasta, vermouth and fresh herb sauce; oven baked breast of chicken with a fresh sage mousse and port wine sauce; or oven roasted breast of guinea fowl with potato rosti, oyster mushrooms and rosemary cream sauce. An excellent wine list is also available. Nearby are the historic cities and towns of Bath, Wells, Cheddar, Glastonbury and Longleat. **Directions:** Exit M4 at junction 18 to Bath and then take A36 towards Warminster. Turn right onto A361 into Frome and then take A362 towards Radstock. Within ½ mile turn left to Mells and follow signposts. Price guide: Single £45 (including dinner £65); double £65 (including dinner £95); four-poster suite £95 (including dinner £125).

THE SWAN INN

NEWBURY ROAD, GREAT SHEFFORD, HUNGERFORD, BERKSHIRE RG17 7DS
TEL AND FAX: 01488 648271

This charming inn standing on the banks of the River Lambourne is steeped in history dating back to the early 1800's when it was a welcoming stop for coach travellers on the busy routes of the Cotswolds and Thames Valley. Some of its history is depicted in the many prints around the walls, with the low-ceiling lounge bar displaying old photographs of the village as well as those illustrating The Swan's links with horse-racing. The Lambourne Valley is a historic horse-racing area and many of the country's leading trainers have their stables here. Several open their yards for public viewing during summer. The name of the inn was inspired by its beautiful riverside setting while Great

Shefford derived from the words "Old Sheep Ford". The ford was adjacent to The Swan and provided access to an old track leading to the market town of Hungerford. The Swan has character, a very warm, friendly atmosphere and is beautifully and traditionally furnished. The congenial, welcoming bars are well stocked with fine beers and wines, complemented by delicious snacks and an interesting selection of more substantial meals. Dotted throughout the well-known area are numerous ancient burial mounds, some dating back to prehistoric times. **Directions:** Great Shefford is on the A338, a short distance north of junction 14 of the M4.

THE SWAN HOTEL

NEWBY BRIDGE, NR ULVERSTON, CUMBRIA LA12 8NB
TEL: 015395 31681 FAX: 015395 31917 E-MAIL: swanhotel@aol.com

The historic Swan Hotel nestles amid breathtaking scenery on the water's edge at the tip of lovely Lake Windermere at the gateway to the glorious Lakeland National Park. Recent extensive refurbishment and restoration has enhanced the hotel's reputation for quality and traditional charm. Comfort is the declared top priority of the management. The en suite guest rooms are luxurious and have every modern amenity. All have kingsize beds and home-from-home comforts ranging from satellite television to hairdryers. Six superb executive suites each have a relaxing lounge area and business extras such as a fax machine and computer point. Many of the rooms offer magnificent views over the water and surrounding countryside. Diners in the stylish Revells restaurant may also admire these views as they enjoy a split-level experience offering a totally new concept, from a club sandwich to full à la carte meal. The comprehensive menu includes a variety of local dishes such as Cumberland sausages, Esthwaite trout, venison, pheasant and Morecambe Bay shrimps. Good pub food is served in the adjoining 17th century Morgan's Bar. A new leisure complex features a heated pool, fully equipped gym, Jacuzzi, sauna, tennis courts and beauty salon. The Swan has its own fishing rights and boat moorings. **Directions:** From M6, exit at Jct36 and follow A590 to Barrow. The Swan is just across the bridge at Newby Bridge. Price guide: Single £75–£85; double £140; suite £200.

ELDERTON LODGE

GUNTON PARK, THORPE MARKET, NR NORTH WALSHAM, NORFOLK NR11 8TZ
TEL: 01263 833547 FAX: 01263 834673 E-MAIL: elderton@mistral.co.uk

Quietly grazing red deer, proudly strutting pheasants and cooing wood pigeons provide memorable awakening viewing to guests gazing from their bedroom windows over the vast and tranquil Gunton Park that is the scene of this 18th century, Grade II listed hotel. Standing in the heart of unspoiled countryside yet only four miles from the coast, the impressive Elderton Lodge Hotel and Restaurant, with its own six acres of mature gardens, was once the Shooting Lodge and Dower House to Gunton Hall Estate. Gunton Hall, home of the Barons of Suffield, was a favoured retreat for Lillie Langtry, the celebrated Victorian beauty, who according to legend entertained Edward VII here when he was Prince of Wales. Owners Christine and Martin Worby are restoring the hotel to its original country house splendour, complete with gun cupboards and elegant panelling. Bedrooms are attractive and comfortable, the bar informal and welcoming and the excellent cuisine featuring local game and seafood specialities – fit for a King, not only the Prince of Wales. This is an ideal venue for small meetings and conferences. The cathedral city of Norwich, National Trust properties including Blickling Hall, Felbrigg Hall, Sheringham Park and the Heritage Coast and Norfolk Broads National Park are nearby. **Directions:** Leave Norwich on A1151. Join A149 towards Cromer and the hotel is on the left prior to entering Thorpe Market. Price guide: Single £60; double £90–£110.

HOTEL DES CLOS

OLD LENTON LANE, NOTTINGHAM, NOTTINGHAMSHIRE NG7 2SA
TEL: 01159 866566 FAX: 01159 860343

Guests arriving at this Victorian farmhouse conversion sense the welcoming ambience of the property's origins throughout its attractive interior. The buildings have since been converted and the owners, the Ralley Family, ensure that attentive service and warm hospitality is provided throughout your stay. The bedrooms are individually designed and well-equipped with an array of up-to-date amenities. The sumptuous Honeymoon suite is beautifully decorated with a Breton marriage bed as its centrepiece and antique furnishings. Guests must sample the award winning cuisine in the restaurant, presided over by Satwant Bains, the winner of the 1999 Roux Brothers Diners Club Scholar Award. The fine dishes are complemented by a wine list of over 100 bins including many excellent New World vintages. The Hotel Des Clos offers special weekend break packages and with its conference and special function rooms, it is ideal for small intimate weddings. The National Watersports Centre, Trent Bridge Cricket Ground, Nottingham University, a well-equipped tennis centre and a large market are all nearby. Other notable landmarks are Nottingham Castle and Sherwood Forest. **Directions:** Leave M1 at junction 24 and follow A453 signposted Nottingham. As you approach the flyover stay in the middle lane, signposted Lenton Industrial Estate. Turn left at the roundabout and immediately left again. Price guide: Single £80; double £80–£90; suite £125–£150.

OLD HUNSTANTON

THE LODGE HOTEL & RESTAURANT

OLD HUNSTANTON, NORFOLK PE36 6HX
TEL: 01485 532896 FAX: 01485 535007

Dating from the 17th century this unpretentious but extremely comfortable, ivy clad hotel with dower house origins is a favourite with visitors to this delightful north-west corner of Norfolk. Grade II listed it provides a comfortable and friendly atmosphere and is within 300 yards of beautiful, long, sandy beaches on which to enjoy quiet strolls in all seasons. The 22 en suite bedrooms, some of which are in a rear courtyard coach house, are attractive, individually styled and offer every modern amenity from television and direct dial telephone to trouser press and beverage making tray. There is a luxurious honeymoon suite and a four-poster bedroom. Chef Darren Menham uses, whenever possible, fresh local produce to prepare his delicious table d'hôte and à la carte menus for diners in the tastefully furnished restaurant which has a deserved high reputation. Specialities are crab, oyster, mussels and fish from which the chef creates some wonderful dishes, complemented by an extensive wine list. The Lodge is an ideal base for bird watching at the reserves of Snettisham, Holme and Titchwell or for visiting the area's many attractions, including Houghton Hall, Holkham Hall and Sandringham for which the hotel arranges special tours in a chauffeur driven classic Rolls-Royce, complete with smoked salmon and champagne picnic. **Directions:** The Lodge is just beyond Hunstanton town on the A149 Kings Lynn-Cromer road. Price guide: Single £46; double/twin £84.

HOLCOMBE HOTEL

HIGH STREET, DEDDINGTON, NR WOODSTOCK, OXFORDSHIRE OX15 0SL
TEL: 01869 338274 FAX: 01869 337167

Conveniently located a few miles north of the university city of Oxford, this delightful 17th century high quality hotel is family run and set in a pretty Cotswold village. It offers personalised attention and traditional hospitality and has a relaxed and friendly atmosphere. Each of the 17 bedrooms is tastefully appointed and has its own distinctive character. Every amenity, including ionisers, is provided for the comfort of guests. Holcombe Hotel is known locally for its superb French, classical and traditional English cuisine. It is highly recommended and is recognised with an AA Red Rosette and RAC awards. Great care is taken in creating original and beautifully presented food. Real ale and excellent bar meals are served in the oak-beamed cottage bar. The Holcombe has been in the resident ownership of Chedley and Carol Mahfoudh since 1988, during which time they have received 5 awards, including the AA Courtesy and Care Award 1993, one of only 15 hotels out of 4,000. The Cotswolds, Stratford, Woodstock and Oxford and Bicester Shopping Village "Bond Street at a 50% discount" and many National Trust properties are nearby. Golfing arranged at two excellent, 18-hole golf courses. **Directions:** Deddington is on A4260, 6 miles south of Banbury M40 J11. Follow A4260 to Adderbury; hotel is on the right at traffic light. M40 J10: follow A43, then B4100 to Aynho, then B4031 to Deddington Price guide: Single £65–£78; double £92.50–£110.

THE JERSEY ARMS

MIDDLETON STONEY, OXFORDSHIRE OX6 8SE
TEL: 01869 343234 FAX: 01869 343565

Near Oxford, the city of dreaming spires, in the country of sparkling streams and gentle green pastures, The Jersey Arms occupies a site rich in history. As far back as 1241, the inn was listed as providing William Longsword 'for 25 men of Middleton, necessaries as food and drink'. It thrived in the days of coach-and-horse long-distance travel and in 1823 was a key posting house for cross-country traffic. Today, The Jersey Arms has been honed into a retreat of comfort and peace. An informal air is created with old beams, antique flintlocks and simple, elegant furnishings. Bedrooms, all with private access, vary in size, while blending the charm of the past with modern décor. Facilities include hairdryers, colour TV and telephone. Cuisine of exceptional quality is prepared from the freshest local ingredients and the menu is changed according to season. Diners can sit in the Bar or Restaurant or, in fine weather, in the secluded courtyard garden. Relax first with an apéritif in the elegant lounge. Oxford, Woodstock, Blenheim Palace with its gardens, Towcester and Cheltenham racecourses and Silverstone Racetrack. Heathrow airport is an hour away by car. **Directions:** Between junctions 9 & 10 of the M40 on the B430 10 miles north of Oxford. From junction 9 take the Oxford Road, Middleton Stoney is signposted 1 mile down. From junction 10 Middleton Stoney is signposted as you leave the slip road. Price guide: Single £75; double £89.

THE MILL & OLD SWAN

MINSTER LOVELL, NR BURFORD, OXFORDSHIRE OX8 5RN
TEL: 01993 774441 FAX: 01993 702002

The Mill and Old Swan stands in the historic village of Minster Lovell, a small Oxfordshire village lying in the valley of the River Windrush, on the edge of the Cotswolds. According to the Doomsday Book, three mills were at Minster Lovell, two of which existed on the present site and now constitute part of these historic properties. A wealth of oak beams, glowing fires, four-poster beds and antique furnishings welcome you to The Old Swan, which has been carefully restored to luxury standards. King Richard III was a regular visitor to Minster Lovell and The Old Swan – his original crest 'The Sun in Splendour' can be found emblazoned on one of the bedroom walls. The Mill: Adjacent to The Old Swan is The Mill, a conference centre, set in a 60 acre estate by the River Windrush (which was the inspiration for Kenneth Grahame's children's book 'The Wind in the Willows'). It is a charming location for relaxing, walking through the gardens or enjoying a choice of sporting activities including tennis and mountain biking. Fitness enthusiasts will be delighted with the gymnasium and sauna. The Mill was awarded the European Architecture Heritage Award for its design in bringing modern facilities into a historic building. **Directions:** From A40 (Oxford/Burford road), take B4047 signposted to Minster Lovell. Once in the village follow the signs for Minster Lovell Hall. Price guide: Single £50–£80; double £80–£140.

JUBILEE INN

PELYNT, NR LOOE, CORNWALL PL13 2JZ
TEL: 01503 220312 FAX: 01503 220920

The Jubilee has been an inn since the 16th century, changing its name from The Axe in 1887 to mark the 50th anniversary of Queen Victoria's accession. The low beamed ceilings, open hearths and old prints create an air of tradition and charm throughout. The bedrooms are tastefully furnished in a cottage style; three are for families and one is a bridal suite with a spiral staircase designed by the well-known artist, Stuart Armfield. With a residents' lounge, three bars, a beer garden plus a large garden with a children's play area and volley-ball net, there are plenty of places to relax. Barbecues are held in the summer. Special breaks arranged. An impressive à la carte menu and friendly, professional service are offered in the dining room. The inn's speciality is fish and shellfish, which come straight off the boats in nearby Looe. An extensive bar menu and traditional Sunday lunches are also on offer. The Duchy of Cornwall nurseries, several National Trust Properties and Dobwalls Adventure Park and Monkey Sanctuary are a selection of the many interesting places to visit. Bodmin Moor, numerous picturesque villages and beautiful coastline are all to be explored. **Directions:** From Plymouth, cross Tamar Bridge and follow the main road to Looe. Leave Looe on the Polperro road and turn right for Pelynt. Price Guide: Single £32–£38.50; double £52–£65.

THE FOUNTAIN INN & ROOMS

WELLTHORNE LANE, INGBIRCHWORTH, NR PENISTONE, SOUTH YORKSHIRE S36 7GJ
TEL: 01226 763125 FAX: 01226 761336 E-MAIL: reservations@fountain–inn.co.uk

This attractive, historic inn stands peacefully in a quiet country lane just off the main A629 road, midway between Huddersfield and Sheffield. Built in the 17th century as a coaching inn it was bought by the present owner, David Broadbent, ten years ago and has been sympathetically renovated and restored. Over the past year additional bedrooms and a function room have been incorporated. The bedrooms are in an extension overlooking Ingbirchworth Reservoir and the South Yorkshire countryside. All are en suite, are beautifully and comfortably furnished and have a full range of facilities. These include CD players, welcoming decanters of sherry and home-made biscuits and fluffy bathrobes.

The atmosphere in the hotel is busy but friendly with the emphasis on informal eating in stylish surroundings. There is no restaurant but there are sections of the friendly bar for Diners Only, and an extensive menu is available. The Kirklees Light Railway, Holmfirth (Last of the Summer Wine country) and the Peak District are nearby. Barnsley, Huddersfield and Sheffield with its theatres, arena and Meadowhall Shopping Centre are approximately ten miles away. **Directions:** Exit the M1 at junction 37 and take the road to Manchester and Penistone. Then turn right onto the A629. In Ingbirchworth turn left into Wellthorne Lane. Price guide: Single £40–£65; double/twin £50–80.

BADGERS

COULTERSHAW BRIDGE, PETWORTH, WEST SUSSEX GU28 OJF
TEL: 01798 342651 FAX: 01798 343649

This glorious Georgian inn, just outside Chichester in the beautiful countryside from which Turner derived so much inspiration, has a fascinating history. It was built in conjunction with the railway in 1860, with horse and carts from the inn transporting passengers and goods into Petworth. The bore hole dug to provide water is today a trout stream and pond. The interior of the inn is immaculate, the furnishings and decorations appropriate, and the ambience in the bar is wonderfully relaxing, enhanced by open fires in winter. The spacious bedrooms, each different, are exquisite. The beds are king-size, with attractive en suite bathrooms. The stylish restaurant has a fine reputation, the menu a Mediterranean influence. Zarzuela, a Spanish fish casserole, is a house speciality. It also includes delicious interpretations of classical English dishes. The wine list makes good reading. The Inn has a charming secluded sunny cobbled courtyard, perfect for alfresco apéritifs and summer dining. Sporting guests will enjoy golf at Cowdray Park and Goodwood. The former also is famous for polo and the latter for racing. Fly fishing, ballooning and speed festivals are alternatives. Petworth House and Arundel Castle should be visited and Chichester with its sailing harbour and theatre is a 'must'. **Directions:** Badgers is south of Petworth on the A285. Price guide: double £70.

STONEMASON'S INN

NORTH STREET, PETWORTH, WEST SUSSEX GU28 9NL
TEL: 01798 342510 FAX: 01798 342510

Variously named The Vinson's, The Mason's and The Trap, The Stonemason's Inn can probably trace its origins to a row of 15th century cottages, while its present use as an inn of distinction certainly dates from at least 1780. Much effort has gone into preserving parts of its history, as evidenced by the quaintly-named Uncle Jed's Parlour and Mrs Smith's Cottage – both used now as dining areas – where fires glow in their open hearths in winter. Hosts Alan and Sheila Capehorn proudly uphold the inn's fine traditions, providing excellent home-cooked food and comfortable accommodation. A welcoming atmosphere extends throughout the property to an enclosed rear patio that overlooks the colourful, award winning garden. In the Coach House Restaurant fare is both traditional and substantial. Home-made shortcrust pies, steak and kidney pudding and liver with bacon and onion gravy are supplemented on a daily basis by the freshest fish, seafood and other delights. A wide choice for vegetarians and a wine list including the landlord's selection of a dozen choices by the glass show commendable regard for guests' well-being. Nearby are Petworth Park, the town of Petworth, a haven for antique hunters, and Goodwood racecourse. **Directions:** Leave Petworth on A283 for Guildford. The Stonemason's Arms is at the junction with A272 east of the town. Price guide: Single £45; double/twin £58.

PETWORTH (Fittleworth)

THE SWAN INN

LOWER STREET, FITTLEWORTH, NR PETWORTH, WEST SUSSEX RH20 1EN
TEL: 01798 865429 FAX: 01798 865721

Situated in an idyllic Sussex village, this 14th century inn, dating from 1382, houses a captivating ensemble of oil paintings, which is kept in The Picture Room dining area. This wonderful collection dates from the late 1800s when they were given to the innkeeper of the time by a local artist who found much charm and natural beauty in the surrounding area. Visitors today can still find that same outstanding charm and beautiful countryside that has been attracting artists and fishermen alike to this area for over 300 years. The inn is very well situated for business and leisure travellers with Gatwick and Southampton airports both within easy driving distance. Nestling in award-winning gardens in a pretty Sussex village, the inn prides itself on a "first class welcome in an informal atmosphere". This is emphasised by the excellent variety of dishes on offer in the inn's oak-beamed restaurant. The more traditional meals can be found such as the chef's roast of the day, however, for those feeling more adventurous, platters such as Italian chicken are sure to entice. The bedrooms are fully-equipped with everything needed by the independent traveller ranging from tea and coffee making facilities to a trouser press. **Directions:** Fittleworth lies between Petworth and Pulborough on the A283. The Inn is at the centre of the village on the B2130. Price guide: Single £30–£35; double/twin £60–£75.

WHITE HORSE INN

SUTTON, NR PULBOROUGH, WEST SUSSEX RH20 1PS
TEL: 01798 869 221 FAX: 01798 869 291

This privately owned inn has offered rest and comfort to both travellers and locals since 1746. Howard and Susie Macnamara have restored the traditions of the inn by making available six pretty rooms which are comfortably furnished and appointed with modern amenities. The double-bedded rooms have king-size beds and all rooms have well-kept en suite bathrooms. All bedrooms are 'non-smoking' – all have tea and coffee facilities and colour television. There is also an attractive garden cottage; however, unlike the other bedrooms, this does not have a direct-dial telephone. Joss and Val Maude are always on hand to offer a friendly welcome. Deep in the magnificent Sussex countryside, the White Horse is a popular place to eat, both with locals and patrons from further afield. Fresh wholesome food is always featured on the menu. The three-course table d'hôte dinner with coffee is very reasonably priced. Amberley Chalk Pits, horse-racing at Goodwood, the harbour town of Chichester, Arundel Castle, Petworth House, Parham House and Gardens and the Roman Villa at Bignor are nearby. **Directions:** Sutton is a little hamlet situated between A29 (Pulborough to Arundel road) and A285 (Petworth to Chichester road). Look for brown sign to Roman Villa at Bignor – Sutton is a mile further west. Price guide: Single £48; double £58–£68.

THE PORT GAVERNE INN

NR PORT ISAAC, NORTH CORNWALL PL29 3SQ
TEL: 01208 880244 FAX: 01208 880151 E-MAIL: pghotel@telinoc.co.uk

Port Gaverne Inn is situated on the North Cornwall Coastal Path in a secluded cove half a mile from the old fishing village of Port Isaac. Much of the surrounding area is supervised by the National Trust. The 350-year-old inn is owned and managed by Midge Ross and its character owes as much to the skills and materials of local tradesmen as it does to the dedication of its proprietress. Bedrooms are cosy and well-appointed with direct dial telephone and TV. The residents' lounge never fails to woo guests with its old-world personality. At Port Gaverne Inn chef Ian Brodey and his staff have built up an international reputation for fine cuisine with delicious seafood dishes and a vegetarian menu. It was recently awarded an AA Rosette. The inn is also noted for its 'Breather' short breaks and winter and its self-contained 18th century cottages and 2 flats overlooking the sea. Walk the coastal path in either direction for National Trust countryside in abundance. There is safe, sheltered swimming within seconds of the inn door. Delabole Slate Quarry and Tintagel Castle (King Arthur's birthplace) are nearby. **Directions:** Port Gaverne is signposted from the B3314 south of Delabole and is reached along the B3267. Follow the signs for Port Gaverne only (not Port Isaac). Price guide: Single £51–£53; double £102–£106.

YE HORN'S INN

**HORN'S LANE, GOOSNARGH, NR PRESTON, LANCASHIRE PR3 2FJ
TEL: 01772 865230 FAX: 01772 864299 E-MAIL: yehornsinn@msn.com**

A striking black-and-white timbered building standing at a crossroads in lovely rolling countryside, Ye Horn's radiates charm and atmosphere. Built in 1782 as a coaching inn, the hotel has been run by the Woods family for 40 years. Today it is expertly managed by Elizabeth Jones, her brother Mark Woods and his wife Denise, offering first-rate accommodation for both business visitors and the holiday-maker. The 6 spacious bedrooms, all en suite, are in the adjoining barn – a recent conversion – and are stylishly furnished. All offer tea and coffee-making facilities, trouser press and hairdryer. Oak beams, sumptuous carpets and in winter, open fires, combine to create a mood of cosy, relaxed hospitality throughout. The restaurant has earned a fine reputation for its delicious traditional cuisine, prepared wherever possible from fresh, local produce and served in the main dining room or the 'snug' next to it. Specialities include home-made soup, roast duckling, roast pheasant and a truly addictive sticky toffee pudding. Full English or Continental breakfasts are available. Chingle Hall, a haunted house, the Ribble Valley, the Forest of Bowland and Blackpool are all nearby. **Directions:** Exit M6 Jct32, take A6 north to first traffic lights. Turn right onto B5269 signposted Longridge, to just past Goosnargh village shop. Where the road veers sharply right, continue straight ahead into Camforth Hall Lane: the hotel is signed after a few minutes. Price guide: Single £49; double £75.

THE BULL AT STREATLEY

STREATLEY ON THAMES, READING, BERKSHIRE RG8 9JJ
TEL: 01491 872392 FAX: 01491 875231

The Bull is situated in a beautiful setting on the west bank of one of the loveliest stretches of the River Thames. It is overlooked by Streatley Hill from where visitors who complete a 10 minutes climb to the summit can enjoy one of the best upstream views of the Thames Valley. Streatley is an unspoilt town with many fine Georgian houses and a 19th century malt house now used as a village hall. Tasteful and sympathetic refurbishment has complemented the ambience of The Bull whose history dates back to the 15th century. All the bedrooms have been individually designed to a high standard. They have every comfort to make guests feel at home, including colour television, trouser press, hairdryer, alarm clock and tea and coffee-making facilities. Two of the rooms have four-poster beds. The traditional character and atmosphere of the extensive bar and dining area is enhanced by open fires in the winter. The Bull enjoys a reputation locally for its good cooking which is modern English with seasonal and seafood dishes. There is also a vegetarian menu. Reading is within easy reach and events in the locality include Henley Regatta, Ascot and Newbury races. Windsor Castle, Blenheim Palace, Oxford and Reading are easily accessible. **Directions:** The Bull is on the A340, eight miles from junction 12 of the M4. Price guide: Single £60; double/twin £60.

DUKE'S HEAD

GREATBRIDGE, NR ROMSEY, HAMPSHIRE SO51 0HB
TEL: 01794 514450 FAX: 01794 518102

This is a beautiful, fascinating old inn situated close to the ancient market town of Romsey. It is an absolute delight, offering great warmth, hospitality, style and outstanding food. Witty remarks from the great American comic W.C.Fields plus quotations and thought provoking texts from Oscar Wilde adorn the walls. There are a variety of rooms on different levels, all individually themed around dukes, local history, fishing and similar subjects. There has been an inn on the site since 1530 and a peculiar sense of history pervades the Duke's Head. The décor is relaxing and the furniture heavy and extremely comfortable. There are numerous original features and a superb collection of antiques. A notice by the entrance says the food is served with style. It is, and Chef Nigel Collins' dishes are delicious and cooked to perfection. They will satisfy the most discerning palate. Local produce and fresh vegetables are served in abundance, including old English favourites such as rabbit, pheasant and venison. To digest a memorable inn meal visitors may care to stroll around Romsey and take in its 10th century abbey, explore the early 13th century King John's Lodge or visit Broadlands and its beautiful park. **Directions:** Exit the M27 at junctions 2 or 3 and travel north through Romsey. Greatbridge is at the junction of the B3057 and B3084.

THE GOLDEN LION INN OF EASENHALL

EASENHALL, NR RUGBY, WARWICKSHIRE CV23 0JA
TEL: 01788 832265 FAX: 01788 832878 E-MAIL: James.Austin@btinternet.com

The Golden Lion, dating back to the 16th century, is set back from the main road through Easenhall, a delightful English village not far from Rugby and ideal for parents visiting the celebrated boarding school. It has low oak beamed ceilings, narrow doorways and uneven floors which all add to its charm and guests receive a traditional warm welcome. The small bar is proud of its best ales, fine wines and wide range of spirits. Delicious snacks are available both at lunchtime and in the evening. The bedrooms are extremely comfortable and quite spacious, with attractive cottage furniture. The restaurant is divided into two rooms and specialises in country cooking. In summer guests can eat alfresco in the garden and patio, where barbecues are often held, sometimes joined by the pet donkey. Guests can enjoy village cricket or go further afield to Coventry Cathedral, Coombe Abbey or Warwick Castle. The NEC Birmingham and Stoneleigh Agricultural Centre are also in easy reach. There are excellent golf courses in the neighbourhood. **Directions:** Easenhall is reached from the M6 junctions 1/2, taking the B4112 off the A426 for Rugby or the B4027 from the Coventry by-pass. Price guide: Single £45; double £65.

THE GEORGE HOTEL

HIGH STREET, RYE, EAST SUSSEX TN31 7JP
TEL: 01797 222114 FAX: 01797 224065

An imposing pillared entrance way and attractive black and white period façade greet visitors to this 16th century hotel situated at the centre of Rye's picturesque high street. The George was built in 1575 and over the years has been sympathetically and carefully modernised. However, the hotel retains many original features, including oak beams reputedly taken from a galleon which was part of the Spanish Armada. Surrounded by cobbled streets and numerous ancient houses and buildings it has a charming, unique character and offers a comfortable standard of accommodation. The atmosphere is friendly and inviting with the emphasis on total relaxation, cheerful service and value for money. Extensive refurbishment of the hotel is scheduled for completion early in 2000. The Meryons Restaurant specialises in classic English cuisine and a typical menu might include baked mushroom filled with Provençal sauce topped with cheddar cheese, then margert duck with black olives followed by sticky toffee pudding and custard. Light snacks can be enjoyed in the comfortable John Crouch Bar. Rye boasts many art galleries, antique shops and booksellers. Winchelsea, Romney Marsh and Battle Abbey are within easy reach. **Directions:** Take the A21 to Flimwell then take the A268 to Rye. Price guide: Single £55; double/twin £90–£110.

THE OLD BELL INN HOTEL

HUDDERSFIELD ROAD, DELPH, SADDLEWORTH, NR OLDHAM, GREATER MANCHESTER OL3 5EG
TEL: 01457 870130 FAX: 01457 876597

This solid, stone-built, former 18th century coaching inn stands in a delightful little village of old weavers cottages and cobbled side streets on the edge of the Peak District National Park. It is surrounded by moorland and valleys, and by beautiful countryside which is steeped in history and tradition and where brass band contests, Rushcart and Morris dancing festivities prevail. The Old Bell is reputed to have been a centre for hunting, gaming and cock fighting and attracted visitors such as Queen Victoria before her crowning, Charles Dickens and Dick Turpin. The infamous highwayman is alleged to have spent time here, before his untimely end at the gallows of York. The old character, atmosphere and many original features of the inn remain but today's guests also enjoy the sophisticated comforts of attractive en suite bedrooms with all modern amenities in conjunction with old beams, open fires and lead lattice windows in the cosy bar and lounge. The heavily beamed restaurant is a delight to dine in. Menus offer plenty of choice and are both imaginative and adventurous. Less formal meals can be enjoyed in the bar and a separate vegetarian menu is always provided. Places to visit include Castle Shaw Roman Fort, the Huddersfield narrow canal where boat trips can be taken and Doverstones Reservoir with its water sports. **Directions:** Delph is on A62 Oldham-Huddersfield Road. Exit from M62 at junctions 20, 21 or 22. Price guide: Single £37.50–£50; double £55–£75.

THE WHITE HORSE

DOWNTON, SALISBURY, WILTSHIRE SP5 3LY
TEL: 01725 510408 FAX: 01725 511954

Built in 1420 by and for the Bishop of Winchester for a country residence, The White Horse is beautifully situated close to the edge of the New Forest. It is a charming country inn, secluded and tranquil, an ideal spot in which to escape the modern world, take long peaceful walks, and enjoy the nearby River Avon and the delights of picturesque little villages. The hostess, Gilly Alexander, has invested a great deal of energy and enthusiasm into making The White Horse a welcoming haven of comfort, excellent food and attentive service. It is full of good humour, atmosphere and character. Gilly, herself is a cheerful personality with many interesting stories to tell of her days as a performer with the famous Black and White Minstrels Show. As well as an extensive bar menu of snacks and light meals, appetising and comprehensive à la carte cuisine tempts locals and visitors alike to the inn's restaurant. There is well-selected wine list featuring affordable vintages. Just a short drive away are Salisbury, one of Britain's most beautiful cathedral cities, 16th century Longford Castle with its notable collection of paintings and 18th century Trafalgar House at Alderbury, presented by a grateful nation to Lord Nelson's family in 1815. The inn is ideally placed for Salisbury race-goers. **Directions:** Downton is approximately six miles south of Salisbury just off the A338 road to Ringwood.

MANOR HOUSE HOTEL & RESTAURANT

HIGH STREET, OLD DRONFIELD, DERBYSHIRE S18 1PY
TEL: 01246 413971 FAX: 01246 412104 E-MAIL: sales@barrelsandbottles.co.uk

Dating from 1540, the Manor House offers a high standard of luxury for both business and social travellers. All ten en suite bedrooms are individually decorated in keeping with a 450 year old building. There are two spacious luxury suites, one of which is sponsored by a Grande-Marque Champagne house. Both suites feature polished dining tables, crystal glassware and original beamed ceilings, combining the elegance of a bygone era with a luxury expected by today's discerning traveller. The critically acclaimed restaurant offers a tempting selection from both the weekly fixed price menu and the extensive à la carte menus. Locally sourced produce features strongly alongside the superb 120 bin wine list, all of which are available by the glass.

The hotel is ideally located as a business base supplying Sheffield and Chesterfield and for travellers visiting the Derbyshire Peaks, Chatsworth House, Bakewell, Blue John Mines and Dronfield Church. The hotel also operates an in-house Rolls Royce chauffeur service for those travelling by train. **Directions:** Old Dronfield is 5m south of Sheffield; 3m north of Chesterfield on A61 to Bowshaw roundabout, then take B6057 south. First right in the dip, left over bridge on to Wreakes Lane, the hotel is 100yards past the Peel Monument on the right. Price guide (incl extensive breakfast): Single £55; double £75; suite £115.

THE GRANGE HOTEL AND RESTAURANT

OBORNE, NR SHERBORNE, DORSET DT9 4LA
TEL: 01935 813463 FAX: 01935 817464

This 200 year old country house nestles peacefully in formal gardens, situated only 1½ miles from historic Sherborne. The welcome here is both personal and unobtrusive and the attentive hosts, Jonathan and Karen Arthur, are in the process of completing a most splendid transformation and refurbishment. The ten spacious bedrooms are well appointed with a number of modern facilities. Guests may enjoy dinner in a most pleasant ambience, overlooking the attractive floodlit gardens and log fires. The restaurant specialises in both international and traditional British cuisine and has recently been awarded an AA Rosette. For diners with a sweet tooth, the dessert trolley is sure to tempt! For those who are planning a very special occasion, the hotel can provide facilities for up to 100 guests which are also suited to conferences and business meetings alike. This quiet haven is a most ideal escape from city life and guests will be able to unwind whilst horse riding, fishing, enjoying a game of croquet or simply taking in the local scenery. Air enthusiasts will not be left out and they will be pleased to hear that the Fleet Aviation Museum can be found nearby. Keen golfers may use the golf course in close proximity of the hotel. Popular daytime excursions include visits to the abbey at Sherborne or the gardens at Stourhead. **Directions:** Oborne can be found just off the A30 in between Sherborne and Milborne Port. Price guide: Single £55–£59; double £75–£85.

THE HALF MOON INN

HALF MOON STREET, SHERBORNE, DORSET DT9 3LN
TEL: 01935 812017 FAX: 01935 815295

The Half Moon is a splendid, medieval town centre inn overlooked by an imposing, early 8th century abbey which has one of the most graceful fan vaulted roofs in England. Close by is Sherborne School, which incorporates a good deal of the original monastic buildings and was the setting for the film 'Goodbye, Mr Chips'. All around are delightful old inns and 16th and 17th century houses, built in the same golden stone as the abbey and set in curving little streets. The Half Moon exudes charm and character and the warm welcome and hospitality serves as a reminder that this is a classic English inn. The 16 en suite bedrooms, some with showers in preference to baths, are individually decorated and have their own style and ambience. Each has colour television, tea and coffee making facilities and direct dial telephone. All food is fresh and cooked to order and enjoys an excellent reputation for à la carte menus and carvery selections. Less formal dining can be enjoyed in the popular bar. Sherborne is an ideal base from which to explore Hardy's Wessex, dotted with historical houses and gardens and picturesque villages of thatched cottages. Within easy driving distance are Shaftsbury, Dorchester and the remains of ancient trackways and defensive earthworks cut from the shelves of chalk by Dorset's early inhabitants. **Directions:** Exit A30 at its junction with A352 road to Sherborne. Price guide: Single £49; double/twin £69–£89.

WALNUT TREE

WEST CAMEL, NR SHERBORNE, SOMERSET BA22 7QW
TEL: 01935 851292 FAX: 01935 851292

Just over the border from Dorset in a delightful Somerset village with its tranquil setting stands The Walnut Tree. The charming newly renovated en suite bedrooms will satisfy the demanding criteria of today's traveller, with finishing touches of toiletries, hairdryers, trouser-presses, colour television and telephones. Imaginative food is served in the charming candlelit dining room, which has a marvellous ambience. Alternatively, relax and eat in the delightful lounge bar. The Walnut Tree has a fine reputation for its cuisine and has been in the Egon Ronay guide for three successive years, also in the 'Which' guide for inns. For the discerning walker, the 'Leyland Trail' passes through the village of West Camel whilst for the golfer, there are six courses within the area. There are plenty of places to visit locally. The Fleet Air Arm Museum at Yeovilton, Haynes Motor Museum at Sparkford and the historic town of Sherborne and its Abbey Church are within easy reach. Cheddar Gorge, Wookey Hole, Longleat House Safari Park, Glastonbury, Stourhead Gardens, the ancient city of Wells, Montacute House, Stonehenge and Cricket St Thomas' Wildlife Park are also nearby. The Inn is also very convenient for visiting the old Dorset coastal towns of Weymouth and Lyme Regis. **Directions:** From Wincanton follow A303 westward. Cross A359 at Sparkford. West Camel is the next village you come to. Take the first turning left Price guide: Single £47; double £75–£85.

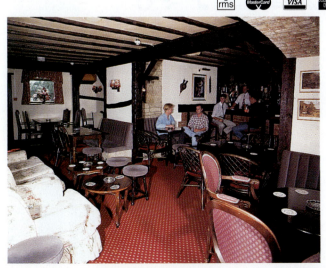

NAUGHTY NELL'S

1 PARK STREET, SHIFNAL, SHROPSHIRE TF11 9BA
TEL: 01952 411412 FAX: 01952 463336

Naughty Nell's is a beautifully restored 16th century coaching inn at the heart of the historic market town of Shifnal, which was described by Charles Dickens in The Old Curiosity Shop. Grade II listed, the inn is surrounded by attractive half-timbered and Georgian houses and close to a Norman church which was one of the few buildings to escape a great fire in 1591 which destroyed most of the town. It was reputedly the home of Nell Gwynn and her legendary bedchamber is now the unique dining, meeting and functions room. Recent extensive and inspired conversions of the interior of the inn have created six low beamed, charming bedrooms which are all en suite and individually decorated and furnished to a very high standard. There is a traditional ale bar where guests may gather and converse over a pint of real ale. The inn has a genuine Mongolian Restaurant which is extremely popular. During most nights of the week there is live entertainment. There are several interesting towns and villages within close proximity and the attractions at Weston Park, the RAF Cosford Museum, Boscobel House and Ironbridge Gorge are close by. **Directions:** Exit the M54 at either junction 3 or 4. Naughty Nell's is situated in the town, on the A464. Price guide Single £55; double/twin £80; four-poster £95.

THE SHAVEN CROWN HOTEL

HIGH STREET, SHIPTON UNDER WYCHWOOD, OXFORDSHIRE OX7 6BA
TEL: 01993 830330 FAX: 01993 832136

Built of honey-coloured stone around an attractive central courtyard, The Shaven Crown Hotel dates back to the 14th century, when it served as a monks' hospice. The proprietors have preserved the inn's many historic features, such as the medieval hall with its ancient timbered roof. This is now the residents' lounge. Each of the bedrooms has en suite facilities and has been sympathetically furnished in a style befitting its own unique character. Rooms of various style and sizes are available, including a huge family room and ground-floor accommodation. Dining in the intimate, candlelit room is an enjoyable experience, with meals served at the tables, beautifully laid with fine accessories. The best ingredients are combined to create original dishes with a cosmopolitan flair. The table d'hôte menu offers a wide and eclectic choice with a daily vegetarian dish among the specialities. An imaginative selection of dishes is offered every lunchtime and evening in the Monk bar. The Shaven Crown is ideal for day trips to the Cotswolds, Oxford, Stratford-upon-Avon and Bath. There are three golf courses and tennis courts close by. Trout fishing and antiques hunting are popular activities in the area. **Directions:** Take the A40 Oxford-Cheltenham road. At Burford follow the A361 towards Chipping Norton. The inn is situated directly opposite the village green in Shipton-under-Wychwood. Price guide: Single £55; double £75–£110.

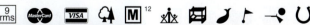

THE ROSE & CROWN

OLD CHURCH ROAD, SNETTISHAM, NORFOLK PE31 7LX
TEL: 01485 541382 FAX: 01485 543172

Dating from the 14th century, this lovely little whitewashed inn is a favourite with visitors to North Norfolk. Tucked away in the delightful village of Snettisham it is an ideal base for bird-watching at the famous reserves of Snettisham, Holme and Titchwell, walking on the wonderful sandy beaches or on the ancient Peddars Way, golf at Hunstanton and Brancaster or visiting the area's many attractions including Sandringham, Houghton Hall and Holkham Hall. The inn has immense charm with its cosy bars, oak beams and log fires and offers excellent food, a wide range of real ales and friendly service. Each of the bedrooms has its own different character and all are decorated in rich glowing colours and fabrics and fully fitted with telephone, television, radio and tea and coffee making facilities as well as having bright and spacious bathrooms. Head chef Martin Lyon uses, wherever possible, fresh local produce to prepare a weekly changing menu of delicious modern British food. Meals may be taken in either the elegant restaurant, bustling bars or, in summer, in the lovely walled garden with its shady willow trees and herbaceous border. **Directions**: From King's Lynn take the A149 towards Hunstanton. Price guide: Single £40; double/twin £60.

TREE TOPS COUNTRY HOUSE RESTAURANT & HOTEL

SOUTHPORT OLD ROAD, FORMBY, NR SOUTHPORT, LANCASHIRE L37 0AB
TEL: 01704 572430 FAX: 01704 572430

The Former Dower House of Formby Hall, Tree Tops, still retains all the elegance of a bygone age, set in five acres of lawns and woods. Over the last 16 years, the Winsland family have restored the house to its true glory and have installed all the modern conveniences sought after by today's visitor. Spacious accommodation is available in well-appointed en suite chalets with all the facilities a discerning guest would expect. An outdoor-heated swimming pool has direct access to the sumptuously decorated Cocktail Lounge. Rich, dark leather seating, oynx-and-gilt tables and subtle lighting all contribute to the overall ambience, complemented by a truly welcoming and friendly staff. Highly polished Regency furnishings, silver tableware and crystal chandeliers set the scene for culinary delights involving only the finest fresh ingredients. The new conservatory restaurant has a totally relaxed atmosphere with a superb new à la carte menu serving modern and interesting dishes together with a special snack selection. Tree Tops is only 7 minutes' drive from Southport with its sweeping sands and 20 minutes from Liverpool. 10 golf courses can be found within a 5 mile radius, including 6 championship courses. **Directions:** From M6 take M58 to Southport to the end of motorway. Follow signs to Southport on A565. Bypass Formby on dual carriageway and as it changes to single carriageway, turn right at traffic lights to Tree Tops. Price guide: Single £53–£68; double £90–£115.

THE DOWER HOUSE

INGESTRE PARK, GREAT HAYWOOD, STAFFORDSHIRE ST18 0RE
TEL: 01889 270707 FAX: 01889 270707

A homely, family-run little hotel surrounded by mature, colourful gardens in the beautiful Royal parkland of Ingestre, The Dower House was formerly owned by the Earl of Shrewsbury and in the 17th century was used as a hunting lodge. It was converted into a Dower House during the 18th century with no expense being spared on the lavish pitch pine staircase and interior woodwork. After generations of farming, the Froggatt family have combined their talents to restore the house to its former Victorian glory and to introduce every modern comfort. There are open fires in the lounge and bar and the beautifully styled bedrooms include a honeymoon suite with four-poster bed. The restaurant, a large, pleasant dining room, serves traditional country food using fresh local produce in season. This is augmented by a good selection of wines. A Sunday lunch with a minimum choice of three roasts is offered and there is an extensive bar menu. Afternoon cream teas and light lunches are available on the garden terrace. Stafford, a charming county town, the old town of Stone with ruins of an ancient priory, 17th century Shugborough Hall and gardens and Cannock Chase, remnant of the vast hunting ground which covered much of Staffordshire in Norman times are all nearby. **Directions:** M6, exit at Jct14 and join A51 north from Stafford. Ingestre Park if off the Great Haywood to Milford Road. Price guide: Single £40–£60; double £75–£140.

NEW

BLACK BULL INN

LOBTHORPE, NR GRANTHAM, LINCOLNSHIRE NG33 5LL
TEL: 01476 860086 FAX: 01476 860796

Set in the Lincolnshire countryside between Grantham and Stamford, this charming former coaching inn, which is surrounded by quiet gardens, is an ideal resting place for business and pleasure travellers alike. Owner Carol Tripp guarantees a friendly, unpretentious atmosphere, with delicious home-cooked meals and special menus available. Dating from the 1730's the inn is of genuine historical interest. Dick Turpin is alleged to have spent time here while in hiding and according to local legend, his escape tunnel has still to be unearthed. Queen Victoria also used the Black Bull Inn as a stopover when travelling to Scotland. A mere two miles away are excellent sporting facilities and at the Rutland Waters, Europe's biggest artificial lake, visitors can fish and sail. Stamford, one of the oldest stone built towns in Europe and the bustling market town of Grantham should not be missed by visitors to the region. Historical Nottingham is a mere 30 miles away, while Grimsthorpe and Belvoir Castles are in the vicinity. The Black Bull Inn is also conveniently located for the East of England show grounds, host to many major showjumping competitions. **Directions:** The Black Bull Inn is situated on the southbound side of the A1, two miles south of the Colsterworth roundabout. It is on the left turn to Lobthorpe. Price guide: Single £37.50; double £50–£65.

THE CROWN HOTEL

ALL SAINTS PLACE, STAMFORD, LINCOLNSHIRE PE9 2AG
TEL: 01780 763136 FAX: 01780 756111 E-MAIL: thecrownhotel@excite.com

Recently acquired by a lively and enthusiastic brother and sister team, The Crown Hotel is being transformed and upgraded. An informal, friendly and comfortable blend of traditional and modern styles is omnipresent. In the public areas, many original features including stone walls have been retained. Open fires, comfortable furnishings and an abudance of fresh flowers, home-grown whenever possible, enhance the interior. Each of the 17 bedrooms have their own individual character yet all display a range of good facilities and spotless white linen. Guests and local patrons alike may sample the appetising menu, offering the best of British traditional dishes, based on fresh local produce and cooked to order. Four real ales including Champion beer of Britain, Timothy Taylor Landlord and a selection of wines by the glass. The hotel is set in the town centre and there are ample facilities for parking. Stamford is an attractive stone built town with most of the properties hailing from the Medieval and Georgian eras and favoured by film makers and producers of costume dramas. Historic properties abound and include Peterborough Cathedral and Burghley House. **Directions:** The town is signed from the A1. Price guide: Single £45; double £60.

THE KINGS HEAD INN & RESTAURANT

THE GREEN, BLEDINGTON, NR KINGHAM, OXFORDSHIRE OX7 6XQ
TEL: 01608 658365 FAX: 01608 658902 E-MAIL: kingshead@btinternet.com

The award-winning Kings Head Inn and Restaurant is peacefully located beside a traditional village green, complete with a babbling brook inhabited by friendly ducks. During the summer months Morris dancers and musicians can regularly be seen in action on the green performing the Bledington Dances. The building has always served as a hostelry and much of its medieval character remains. With its exposed stone walls, original beams, inglenook fireplace and old settles, the Kings Head fulfils everyone's anticipations of a traditional English inn. The attractive timbered bedrooms, are all furnished to complement with full facilities. Activities in the kitchen are supervised by Annette Royce, who has earned the reputation for superbly prepared English and Continental dishes with the 'personal' touch. The carefully compiled à la carte menu is changed daily and is backed up by a selection of fine wines. Excellent inventive bar food is served at lunchtimes and in the evenings together with a changing selection of real ales. The Kings Head Inn is situated in the heart of the Cotswolds, within easy reach of Oxford, Stratford-upon-Avon, Cheltenham and Blenheim. **Directions:** Take the A44 Oxford–Woodstock road to Chipping Norton, then the B4450 to Bledington; or take the Oxford–Burford road to Stow-on-the-Wold and join the B4450. Nearest motorway M40 junction 11. Price guide: Single £45; double £60–£75; suite £90.

THE UNICORN HOTEL

SHEEP STREET, STOW-ON-THE-WOLD, GLOUCESTERSHIRE GL54 1HQ
TEL: 01451 830257 FAX: 01451 831090 E-MAIL: bookings@cotswold–inns–hotels.co.uk

Low oak-beamed ceilings and large stone fireplaces pay tribute to The Unicorn's lengthy past. Over the last 300 years, the inn has changed its standards of accommodation, incorporating the latest modern facilities, yet many vestiges of the former centuries remain. The recently refurbished interior is decorated in a stylish manner featuring Jacobean furniture and antique artefacts whilst log fires abound. Enhanced by floral quilts and comfortable armchairs, the 20 en suite bedrooms are simple yet charming. Fine paintings adorn the walls of the public rooms and the cosy bar offers hand-carved wooden chairs and rich carpets. Modern British cooking is served in the elegant surroundings of the Georgian restaurant from an imaginative à la carte menu. The hotel is well-frequented on Sundays by guests wishing to indulge in the delicious lunchtime roast. Local leisure facilities include horse-riding and the golf course. Shooting and fishing are popular outdoor pursuits. Many historic buildings and castles are within easy reach including the magnificent Blenheim Palace and Warwick Castle. Nature enthusiasts will be delighted with the splendid gardens at Sudeley Castle. **Directions:** The nearest motorway is the M40 junction 10. Then take the A44 or the A436 in the direction of Stow-on-the-Wold. Price guide: Single £60–£70; double/twin £105–£120.

THE COACH HOUSE HOTEL & CELLAR RESTAURANT

16/17 WARWICK ROAD, STRATFORD-UPON-AVON, WARWICKSHIRE CV37 6YW
TEL: 01789 204109 / 299468 FAX: 01789 415916 E-MAIL: kiwiavon@aol.com.uk

For lovers of Shakespeare country the Coach House Hotel is an ideal base from which to explore the Bard's birthplace and the beautiful surrounding countryside. Consisting of two splendid adjacent buildings, one Georgian style dated 1843 and the other Victorian dating from 1857, the Coach House is just a five minutes walk from Stratford town centre and seven minutes from the Royal Shakespeare Theatre. Family owned and run it has a relaxed, friendly atmosphere. Careful thought and attention have been invested in the décor and furnishings of all the rooms. Guests may stay in a beautiful Victorian suite, a luxury Regency four-poster room with whirlpool bath or one of the well-appointed single, double or family rooms, situated either on ground or first floor level. All have a good range of facilities. Guests have complimentary use of the sports and leisure centre nearby. Golf enthusiasts have the choice of four local courses. Special breaks are available throughout the year. The Chef creates superb Continental and English dishes to tempt even the most jaded palate in the intimate Cellar Restaurant beneath the Victorian building. There are two dining areas and a cosy bar. The Royal Shakespeare Theatre and the delights of Stratford-upon-Avon, Warwick Castle, Ragley Hall, Blenheim Palace and the Cotswolds are close by. **Directions:** Five miles from exit 15 of M40, on A439. Price guide: Single £50–£60; double £68–£89; suite £90–£109.

CROWN INN

FRAMPTON MANSELL, STROUD, GLOUCESTERSHIRE GL6 8JG
TEL: 01285 760601 FAX: 01285 760681

This idyllic and historic stone-built inn stands in the very heart of an unspoilt village which is surrounded by gorgeous Cotswolds countryside and wooded slopes of the Golden Valley. Build in 1633, The Crown is one of the oldest buildings in Frampton Mansell and has held a license since they were introduced in the 18th century, at first for the sale of locally produced cider. Traditional character, hospitality and friendliness pervades the whole inn, as attractive and charming inside as it is outside. There are heavily beamed ceilings, open stone walls, large fireplaces, polished wood panelling, solid comfortable furniture and rich window drapes. The bedrooms all have en suite facilities, full modern amenities from direct dial telephone and television to a beverage tray and several thoughtful extras. Each is comfortable and offers superb views over the lawned and rose filled garden and countryside. There are three warm and inviting bars and a cosy, intimate restaurant serving delicious and imaginative country cuisine, including a smoked salmon and champagne breakfast for those wishing to really indulge themselves. Golfers can enjoy a game at the nearby Minchinhampton course, there are fine walks and cycling routes to explore and a gliding club for the adventurous who fancy soaring skywards. **Directions:** Frampton Mansell is signposted off the main A419 Cirencester to Stroud Road. Price guide: Single £44; double £64.

THE BULL HOTEL

HALL STREET, LONG MELFORD, SUDBURY, SUFFOLK CO10 9JG
TEL: 01787 378494 FAX: 01787 880307

Elegance, style and service are the hallmarks of this 15th century hotel standing in the heart of one of Suffolk's prettiest villages and the antiques capital of East Anglia. This is "Lovejoy" country and behind the Bull's magnificent half-timbered façade there is a wealth of ancient delights to please the most ardent enthusiast and collector. From beams, inglenooks and carvings to highly polished brasses, pots and breastplates. There is even an impressive Elizabethan fireplace for lounge guests to relax around. Built in 1450 and an inn since 1570, The Bull has retained much of its original architectural character but has been carefully modernised to cater for today's visitors. Idle relaxation over morning coffee and afternoon tea while reading the newspapers is definitely encouraged. The 25 beautifully furnished, en suite bedrooms have every 20th century facility. Classic English cuisine is served in an intimate, warm restaurant that features open brickwork and solid, heavy furniture, and light snacks can be enjoyed over a drink in the Reeves Bar. Nearby are Melford and Kentwell Halls, Lavenham and Constable country, where Flatford Mill and East Bergholt are still recognisable from the artist's paintings. **Directions:** Exit the M11/A11 at junction 9. Take the A604 then the A1092 following the signs for Long Melford. Price guide: Single £65; double/twin £90–130.

GREYHOUND INN

STAPLE FITZPAINE, NR TAUNTON, SOMERSET TA3 5SP
TEL: 01823 480227 FAX: 01823 481117

Nestling in a delightful small village, guests will be charmed by the warm and inviting atmosphere that envelopes this grade II listed coaching inn. The inn is renowned for its excellent restaurant where a mouthwatering selection of home-cooked foods and traditional ales may be sampled. All the dishes are freshly prepared and cooked to order and include exciting choices such as roast duck breast with orange flavoured noodles and honey glaze and pan-fried pork tenderloin with fried apple slices and Port sauce. The four rooms are an oasis of character and charm and are all excellently furnished with striking fabrics, comfortable décor and first class en suite facilities. Sports enthusiasts will be pleased with the opportunities that this region provides. A golf course can be found nearby, horse riding can be arranged and the Black Down Hills, which overshadow the village of Staple Fitzpaine, are perfect for long walks and taking in the local scenery, and for those who like a little bit of mystery, the 'Sarcen Stones' are sure to intrigue! Staple Manor and the site of Castle Neroche are well worth a visit and for those who are interested in aviation history, Fleet Air Museum is within easy reach. **Directions:** Exit junction 25 off the M5, join the A358 and follow signs to Staple Fitzpaine. Price guide: Single £44; double £64.

NEW

HADLEY PARK HOUSE HOTEL

HADLEY PARK, TELFORD, SHROPSHIRE TF1 4AF
TEL: 01952 677269 FAX: 01952 676938

This converted traditional English manor house, originally built in the late 1700s by Thomas Telford's chief engineer, promises a refined and congenial setting combined with friendly and attentive service. Set in a beautiful 4 acre garden with a picturesque lake, Hadley Park Hotel is at the heart of tranquil Shropshire and beside the thriving town of Telford. The modern bistro-style cuisine is taken in the bright and airy conservatory, decorated in soothing Mediterranean pastel shades. Owners Kevan Downing and Pauline Wilcox pride themselves on the quality of the home-cooked fayre, made with only the freshest of local ingredients. Guests should not miss out on the mouth-watering desserts, or the delicious home-made bread. After

dinner, visitors can relax in the oak-panelled bar and lounge, which has all the convivial charm of a traditional English hostelry. Hadley Park's nine bedrooms are each individually decorated, offering all the modern comforts in traditional surroundings. Hadley Park is ideally situated for trips to the fascinating Ironbridge Gorge Museum, Ludlow Castle and medieval Shropshire. The area is dotted with bustling market towns while the Wrekin, the Long Mynd and the Hawkstone Follies are all nearby. Conveniently placed for Hortonwood Industrial Park, the house is a short drive from Telford's Central Business Parks. **Directions:** Just off A442 north of Telford, see sign post at the Hadley Park roundabout. Price guide: Single £60–£80; double/twin £60–£90.

THE HUNDRED HOUSE HOTEL

BRIDGNORTH ROAD, NORTON, NR SHIFNAL, TELFORD, SHROPSHIRE TF11 9EE
TEL: 01952 730353 FAX: 01952 730355 E-MAIL: hundredhouse@compuserve.com

Character, charm and a warm, friendly atmosphere are guaranteed at this family-run, award-winning inn, situated only 45 minutes' drive from Birmingham International Airport. The bedrooms are attractively furnished with antiques and feature country-style patchwork bed linen and drapes; all guest rooms are fully equipped. There are pretty gardens with a pond, gazebo and herb garden. A special tariff is offered for mid-week and weekend breaks. The inn enjoys a growing reputation for its varied, interesting à la carte and table d'hôte menus. Home-made English fare such as steak pies and game is offered alongside continental dishes and sweets range from delicate sorbets to traditional favourites like treacle tart. Bar meals are served daily, alongside a number of real ales. Early booking is recommended as the restaurant is very popular locally. Awarded Michelin Bib Gourmand 1999. Severn Valley Railway, Midland Motor Museum, Weston Park, Ironbridge Gorge and Telford are within easy reach. Shifnal's cottages inspired Charles Dickens' Old Curiosity Shop. **Directions:** Norton is on the A442 Bridgnorth-Telford road. Price guide: Single £69; double £95–£120.

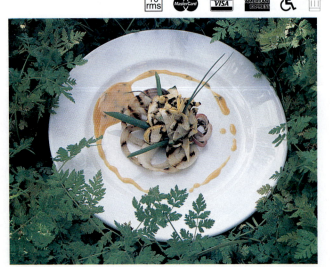

THE WHITE LION HOTEL

THE HIGH STREET, TENTERDEN, KENT TN30 6BD
TEL: 01580 765077 FAX: 01580 764157

The White Lion is a traditional old inn situated at the heart of the wide, green-fringed High Street in the historic market town of Tenterden, an important wool trading centre in medieval times. The inn is surrounded by many attractive, late 15th century buildings and was first mentioned in ancient documents in 1623 as an "Inn near the Market Place". The White Lion offers a warm, friendly welcome and the relaxing atmosphere of a past age. All 15 bedrooms have en suite facilities, are spacious and comfortable. The bar is proud of its best ales, fine wines and wide range of spirits. Delicious meals are available both at lunch time and in the evening and it is well worth looking out for the inn's "signature dishes". Some of these traditional delights include Brewers' Pie, Bangers and Mash, Spatchcock Chicken and Cloutie, Fruit and Ginger Pudding. Tenterden is reputed to be the birthplace of William Caxton, the father of English printing and it is an excellent base for touring the Kent countryside, travelling on the Kent and East Sussex railway and visiting the National Trust properties of Smallhythe Place and Lamb House. Rye and Canterbury are within easy reach. **Directions:** From the M20, exit at junction 9 and take the A28 to Tenterden. Price guide: Single from £54; double/twin £74–£84.

RECORDERS HOUSE RESTAURANT WITH ROOMS

17 TOWN STREET, THAXTED, ESSEX CM6 2LD
TEL: 01371 830438 FAX: 01371 831645 E-MAIL: recordershouse.co.uk

Built early in the 15th century as a royal hunting lodge and used as the Recorders House when the pretty village of Thaxted became a borough. Recently re-opened as a restaurant with rooms, the standard of cuisine is extremely high with the team working towards 3 AA Rosette recognition. A gourmet club is planned and a private room is available for corporate lunches, business meetings, functions and special events. The original part of the building comprises the front of the restaurant and the cosy lounge bar. Many features have been retained including oak beams, fireplaces and carvings. The décor throughout attractively reflects the period charm and blends harmoniously with simple modern elegance and comfort. There is an airy conservatory dining area, overlooking a pretty 'secret' garden. The spacious Recorders bedroom, again a fusion of past and modern styles, has its own little balcony overlooking the garden, whilst the larger Kings room boasts an inglenook fireplace and sitting area, perfect for a romantic break. Activities include watching the horse-racing at Newmarket, walking in Hatfield Forest or practising golf and horse-riding nearby. **Directions:** Leave the M11 at junction 8 and then take the A120 eastbound. Turn off at the exit signed Great Dunmow and then turn left onto the B1184 to Thaxted. Price guide: Single £40–£60; double/twin £60–£75.

CRAB & LOBSTER

ASENBY, THIRSK, NORTH YORKSHIRE YO7 3QL
TEL: 01845 577286 FAX: 01845 577109

Attracting gastronomes and food critics from afar, the Crab and Lobster is the creation of David and Jackie Barnard who bought the Shoulder of Mutton pub ten years ago and have transformed it into this thriving establishment. The inspired and diverse cuisine, made with the finest of ingredients, incorporates flavours from around the world and the exciting menus are prepared by a most talented kitchen team. At lunchtime, the set menu offers choices such as smoked haddock and courgette risotto, followed by roast suckling pig, apricot and apple compote and sage gravy. Echoing the restaurant's name, the dinner menu provides a wonderful mélange of seafood platters such as lobster and king scallops with a gruyère glaze or blue lobster and halibut Thai curry. During the summer, there are garden jazz barbecues and throughout the year, Crab and Lobster hosts an array of gastronomic extravaganzas including the popular Blues suppers. Diners may stay in Crab Manor, the adjacent Georgian Manor House. Set in seven acres of landscaped gardens, the house comprises eleven opulent bedrooms each bedecked with sumptuous fabrics and replicating the style of a world-famous hotel, such as the Le Touessroc in Mauritius. **Directions:** Located on the outskirts of Asenby, which is signposted off A168 (A19) north of the intersection with A1(M). Price guide: Single £70–£90; double/twin £90–£110.

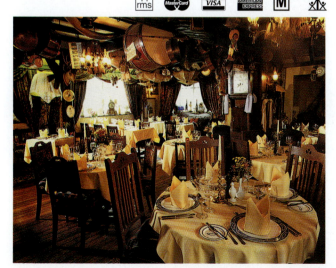

THE LIFEBOAT INN

SHIP LANE, THORNHAM, NORFOLK PE36 6LT
TEL: 01485 512236 FAX: 01485 512323 E-MAIL: lifeboatinn@btconnect.com

The Lifeboat Inn has been a welcome sight for travellers for centuries, offering roaring open fires on a frosty night, real ales and hearty meals. The summer brings its own charm with scenic views over open meadows to the harbour and rolling white horses breaking on Thornham's sandy beach. The original character of this former 16th century smugglers' ale house has been sympathetically restored and modernised. Sitting in the cosy Smugglers' Bar under the warm glow of the hanging paraffin lamps it is easy to drift back through the years. The old English game of "Pennies" is still played here regularly. A vine-hung conservatory backs onto a delightful walled patio garden which is a perfect suntrap. The en suite bedrooms have tea and coffee-making facilities, television, telephone and hairdryer. Most of them have sea views. Awarded an AA Rosette, the cuisine comprises a splendid choice of innovative and traditional dishes, created by Chef Simon Reynolds using local produce, game, fish and meat. The bar menu is enhanced by daily specials to bring the best from each catch or shoot. Holkham Hall, Sandringham House and Nelson's birthplace at Burnham Thorpe are all nearby. There are six nature reserves, beach, clifftop and woodland walks, sailing and windsurfing. Golfers have the choice of five courses. **Directions:** Thornham is approx. 4m NE of Hunstanton on A149 coast road to Wells-next-the-Sea. Price guide: Single £35–£60; double £55–£80. Bargain breaks available.

Green Farm Restaurant And Hotel

NORTH WALSHAM ROAD, THORPE MARKET, NORFOLK NR11 8TH
TEL: 01263 833602 FAX: 01263 833163 E-MAIL: grfarmh@aol.com

Green Farm is a delightful 16th Century Farmhouse Inn. A warm, friendly welcome awaits all guests, be it business or pleasure, from proprietors Philip and Dee Dee Lomax and their staff. All rooms are fully en suite with television, tea and coffee facilities, fresh fruit, flowers and home-made chocolates. Some of the rooms are on ground floor level and are ideal for elderly and less able bodied guests. The Restaurant and Bar are open 7 days a week and the Chef-patron Philip and Head Chef Jonathan Griffin have built up an excellent reputation for the food which is all home-made, and uses local produce such as Cromer crab, shellfish, sea trout and Holkham venison when in season. Many of the dishes are unique to Green Farm; subtle variations on well-loved themes. Try the brie wrapped in filo pastry, served with apple and peppercorn sauce, the Norfolk duckling with rhubarb compote followed by the Pillow of pear on a raspberry coulis. The terraced Marquee offers an ideal location for a wedding or family function. Midweek and weekend breaks are available and special rates for Winter House parties available on request. Green Farm is an excellent base for the Coast, Broads National Trust Properties and Historical Norwich. Ideal for those interested in walking, cycling, golf and bird-watching. **Directions:** On the A149, 4 miles from Cromer and North Walsham. Price guide: Single £52.50–£55; double £60–£85. Bargain breaks throughout the year.

THE PORT WILLIAM

TREBARWITH STRAND, NR TINTAGEL, CORNWALL PL34 0HB
TEL: 01840 770230 FAX: 01840 770936 E-MAIL: william@eurobell.co.uk

The Port William is a delightful old inn, romantically situated 50 yards from the sea overlooking the beach and cliffs at Trebarwith Strand. The small but charming bedrooms have recently been refurbished and offer every modern amenity, including baths with showers, colour TVs, hair dryers and hospitality trays. Each bedroom is positioned so that guests can enjoy spectacular views during the day and dramatic sunsets over the sea in the evening. Well behaved children and dogs are welcome! All the bedrooms are non-smoking. Restaurant: The Inn enjoys an excellent local reputation for the quality of its food. An extensive breakfast menu and lunches and dinners are prepared using only the freshest produce, with home-cooked dishes and a range of superb fish courses and seafood among the specialities. A good selection of vegetarian food is always available. Service is friendly and informal. Proprietory brands and local Cornish ales are available. The unique and stunning display of seahorses and other marine species are guaranteed to relax the most stressed of travellers. In this area, noted for its outstanding beauty, there is no shortage of leisure activities. Apart from magnificent walks, there are plenty of opportunities for surfing, sea-fishing and golf. Nearby: Tintagel Castle, King Arthur's Great Halls and a host of National Trust properties. **Directions:** Follow B3263 from Camelford to Tintagel, then south to Trebarwith via Treknow. Price guide: Single £45–£65; double £60–£90.

THE SEA TROUT INN

STAVERTON, NR TOTNES, DEVON TQ9 6PA
TEL: 01803 762274 FAX: 01803 762506

Runner-up for Johansens Most Excellent Service Award 1996, The Sea Trout Inn dates from the 15th century. It was named by a previous landlord who caught such a fish in the nearby River Dart. Several specimens of the prize fish now adorn the inn in showcases. The two bars retain much of their period charm, with uneven floors, exposed oak beams, brass fittings and log fires. The bedrooms are decorated in an attractive cottage style, while the public rooms are cosy and inviting. Angling permits for trout, sea trout and salmon are available and the inn offers special fishing breaks with tuition. The inn's two Red Rosettes restaurant is highly popular locally and has been acclaimed in several guides. Chef Kim Olsen finely balanced menus are based on the best seasonal produce from local suppliers. Both table d'hôte (£15.50 for two courses or £18.75 for three courses) and à la carte menus are available. Dartmoor is excellent for walking, fishing and pony-trekking. Local attractions include the Devon coast, the Dart Valley Railway, Buckfast Abbey and Dartington Hall. **Directions:** Turn off the A38 on to the A384 at Buckfastleigh (Dartbridge) and follow the signs to Staverton. Price guide: Single £42.50–£46; double £60–£70.

THE WATERMAN'S ARMS

BOW BRIDGE, ASHPRINGTON, NR TOTNES, SOUTH DEVON TQ9 7EG
TEL: 01803 732214 FAX: 01803 732314

The Waterman's Arms boasts an idyllic setting on the bank of the River Harbourne, just two miles from the Elizabethan town of Totnes. The warm and welcoming atmosphere of today's inn is a far cry from Napoleon's era, when it was a prison and a favourite haunt of the feared press gangs! The nicely-appointed bedrooms, which vary in size, all offer the comfort and luxury associated with a first class hostelry. Tastefully decorated and featuring fine hand-crafted furniture, they include every modern convenience. The bar, with its natural stone walls and wealth of beams, is the perfect place to enjoy a quiet drink before moving on to the candlelit restaurant. Here guests are offered an excellent choice of cuisine, complemented by a good wine list. Bar meals – available at lunchtime and in the evenings – can be eaten by log fires or in the inn's lovely gardens, according to the season. Bow Bridge and its surrounding area offers a host of leisure activities. Bird lovers, in particular, will find this an ideal location – a Kingfisher with its young is one sight that spring visitors can hope to glimpse. Totnes is packed with interesting and unusual shops and places to visit, while Dartmoor with its ponies and fabulous walks, is only a short drive away. **Directions:** From A38 follow signs to Totnes. Join the A381 towards Dartmouth and pick up Ashprington to Bow Bridge signs. Price guide: Single from £49; double/twin from £69.

THE MORTAL MAN HOTEL

TROUTBECK, NR WINDERMERE, CUMBRIA LA23 1PL
TEL: 015394 33193 FAX: 015394 31261 E-MAIL: the–mortalman@btinternet.com

Few country inns can match the spectacular Lakeland position of this 300 year old hostelry. Lake Windermere is in view at the foot of the Troutbeck Valley, while Grasmere, the home of Wordsworth, and Coniston, where Ruskin lived, are just slightly further away. The inn is an ideal retreat, offering old-fashioned, friendly service in highly traditional surroundings. The interiors have an abundance of beautiful oak beams, panelling, open fires and solid furniture. All of the bedrooms have stunning views of the surrounding countryside and are equipped with every convenience, including hairdryers and trouser presses. An à la carte menu is presented in the inn's dining room, with its wonderful views of the valley. The dishes are all freshly prepared, accompanied by a variety of sauces and garnishes. The menu is supported by a well-chosen wine list. Bar snacks available all day in the bar, which has a warm, inviting atmosphere. The area is a paradise for country lovers, with fells and mountains to explore. Golf, sailing and pony-trekking facilities are available close by. **Directions:** Take the A592 Windermere-Ullswater road. From the roundabout drive for 2½ miles, then turn left to Troutbeck and right at the T-junction. The hotel is on the right. Price guide: Room rate £80–£90.

THE WHITE LION HOTEL

HIGH STREET, UPTON-UPON-SEVERN, NR MALVERN, WORCESTERSHIRE WR8 0HJ
TEL: 01684 592551 FAX: 01684 593333 E-MAIL: reservations@whitelionhotel.demon.co.uk

Henry Fielding wrote part of his novel "The History of Tom Jones" way back in 1749 where he described the Hotel as "the fairest Inn on the street" and "a house of exceedingly good repute". The owners Jon and Chris Lear have committed themselves to upholding this tradition with good old fashioned hospitality along with examples of the finest cuisine in the area cooked for the popular Pepperpot Brasserie. Using only the finest ingredients Jon and his team produce an imaginative menu served with flair – and home-made breads – which have attracted the attention of a discriminating local clientele and the AA who awarded a Rosette in under one year of ownership. A lunch time menu with lighter meals may be enjoyed in the lounge or in the congenial bar. All ten bedrooms are from varying periods dating from 1510, the Rose Room and the Wild Goose Room at the White Lion are named in Fielding book. The White Lion is central for visiting The Malvern Hills, The Three Counties Show Ground, the market town of Ledbury, Tewksbury's Norman Abbey, Worcester, Cheltenham and Gloucester. The Cotswolds, Black mountains and Shakespeare's Stratford-Upon-Avon are all within an easy drive from this popular town. **Directions:** From M5 Jct8 follow M50. Exit at Jct1 on to A38 north. After 3 miles turn left on to A4104. Go over the bridge, turn left, then right. Parking is at the rear of the hotel. Price guide: Single £53; double £77.

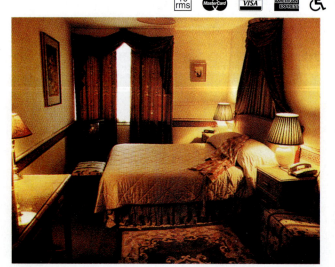

THE ANGEL INN

UPTON SCUDAMORE, WARMINSTER, WILTSHIRE BA12 0AG
TEL: 01985 213225 FAX: 01985 218182

This is a recently restored 16th century coaching inn situated in a small Wiltshire village close to the old wool and corn market town of Warminster, now well-known for its antique shops. Guests enter the pub through an attractive south-west facing walled garden into a warm and welcoming interior with wood floors and open fires. The refurbishment has brought modern facilities and home comforts. The five individually appointed, en suite bedrooms are spacious and comfortable. They are delightfully furnished and offer every facility from direct dial telephone to a mini-stack CD system. Attention to detail is uppermost for owner Charles Barkshire and his appointment of award winning chef Eamonn Redden has made The Angel a Mecca for food lovers. Eamonn, who was Young Chef of the Year 1986, produces excellent and imaginative cuisine. On quiet evenings a table for two can be laid in the kitchen and a specially prepared three course dinner served while watching Eamonn work. His rack of lamb with a minted crust and caramelised shallot sauce is highly recommended. Longleat House, Wilton House, Stourhead, Stonehenge and Bath are within easy reach. **Directions:** From A36, take A350 and follow signs to Warminster and Upper Scudamore. Price guide: Single £45; double £65.

THE MARKET PLACE

WELLS, SOMERSET BA5 2RW

TEL: 01749 672616 FAX: 01749 679670 E-MAIL: marketplace@heritagehotels.co.uk

Located in the very heart of the historic city of Wells, The Market Place is set in the lee of the cathedral. Built over 500 years ago by Bishop Bekynton, an air of medieval charm is present throughout this unusual property which offers superb comforts and up-to-date standards whilst retaining many original features. Guests may enjoy morning coffee in the comfortable first floor lounge area, before relaxing in one of the individual 34 bedrooms. The rooms are furnished in a contemporary style and feature en suite bathrooms and every facility required by today's discerning traveller. Food is an important criterion at The Market Place and awards received such as the two AA Rosettes are a fine testimony to the excellent standards of both cuisine and service. Modern British dishes prepared with a Mediterranean influence are prepared by the talented kitchen team and served alongside a diverse selection of European and New World wines. Alfresco dining may be savoured in the sheltered courtyard garden, beside the bar. Places of interest nearby include the magnificent 12th century cathedral and the Bishop's Palace, where the springs rise, from which Wells takes its name. **Directions:** Leave the M5 at junction 23, follow signs to Glastonbury and Wells. The Market Place is in the town centre. Price guide: Single £69.50–£85; double £79.50–£95; suite £89–£105.

THE SALUTATION INN

MARKET PITCH, WEOBLEY, HEREFORDSHIRE HR4 8SJ
TEL: 01544 318443 FAX: 01544 318216

This black and white timbered inn, an inspired conversion of an ale and cider house and a cottage, over 500 years old, is in the centre of Weobley village. The spire of the 900 year old church is a landmark in the green Herefordshire countryside, as yet undiscovered by tourists. The bedrooms are so individual, with delightful chintz or patchwork quilts, that returning guests demand their favourite, perhaps one with traditional brass bedsteads or a four-poster. Smoking is not allowed in the bedrooms, but is forgiven in the elegant residents' lounge, with its antiques and big, comfortable furniture. Guests will enjoy the well-equipped fitness room. The owners have achieved many accolades in their twelve years here. A non-smoking room, the Oak Room restaurant plays an important role in the inn and has been awarded 2 AA Rosettes. Talented chefs prepare sophisticated and aromatic dishes to order, ensuring they arrive fresh at the table. English with a continental accent describes the menu, which refers to puddings as 'the finishing touch'. There is a very well stocked cellar from which to select fine wines. Informal meals are served in the traditional bar. Nearby attractions include Hereford Cathedral, Hay-on-Wye with its antique books, open air Shakespeare at Ludlow Castle, pony-trekking in the Black Mountains and golf. **Directions:** Leave Hereford on A438 Brecon, taking A480 signed Weobley/Credenhill. Price guide: Single £42–£47; double £67–£72.

THE MANOR HOUSE HOTEL & COUNTRY CLUB

THE GREEN, WEST AUCKLAND, COUNTY DURHAM DL14 9HW
TEL: 01388 834834 FAX: 01388 833566

This recently refurbished, exquisite 14th century style manor house lies within perfectly landscaped grounds. Once a hunting lodge for Henry VIII and home to the Eden family, the Manor House Hotel offers a welcome that is both personal and genuine. With a health club providing full fitness facilities such as an indoor swimming pool with spa bath and a sauna and staff that can provide a personal fitness assessment programme for their guests, this is the perfect venue for those wishing to realise their individual fitness goals. After working up an appetite, diners may choose between the Manor House Beehive Bar in the old Kitchens which offers a cosy and informal place to spend an evening in Juniper's Restaurant or Brasserie, both serving an excellent selection of cuisine for great value for money. This hotel provides conference and wedding facilities and is very sensitive to individual needs when it comes to that very special occasion. Families will like Hamsterley forest with its wonderful wild life. For the walkers, Pennine Way is sure to prove a challenge! There is an open air museum nearby and Barnard Castle, Hadrian's Wall and Durham Cathedral are only a stone's throw away. **Directions:** The Manor House Hotel and Country Club can be found along the A68 just off the A1(M). Price guide: Single £55–£75; double £75–£98.

THE WENSLEYDALE HEIFER INN

WEST WITTON, WENSLEYDALE, NORTH YORKSHIRE DL8 4LS
TEL: 01969 622322 FAX: 01969 624183 E-MAIL: heifer@daelnet.co.uk

Few inns can claim such a beautiful setting as that of The Wensleydale Heifer. This typical Dales inn, dating from 1631, is situated in the tranquil village of West Witton, in the heart of Wensleydale and set against the backdrop of the Yorkshire Dales National Park. The oak-beamed rooms are furnished in chintz, with antiques and log fires to retain the ancient charm of the building. The quaint bedrooms are located in the inn itself and across the road in The Old Reading Room – they have all been recently refurbished and 2 have ground floor access. There are 3 with four-poster beds. A private room can be hired for small meetings of up to 14 people. Both the informal bistro and the beamed restaurant offer rustic country cooking. Extensive menus include fresh fish, shellfish and seafood from the North-East Coast and Scotland, complemented by a good selection of wines. Local produce appears frequently including Dales lamb, Aberdeen Angus beef, game and fresh herbs from their own garden. Recent awards include AA Red Rosette, and RAC Merit Award. The Heifer is situated in the Yorkshire Dales National Park and is ideally placed for undiscovered country walks, Yorkshire abbeys, castles, gardens and racecourses. **Directions:** The inn is on A684 trans-Pennine road between Leyburn and Hawes. Price guide: Single £60; double £72–£98. Special breaks available.

THE INN AT WHITEWELL

FOREST OF BOWLAND, CLITHEROE, LANCASHIRE BB7 3AT
TEL: 01200 448222 FAX: 01200 448298

An art gallery and wine merchant all share the premises of this friendly, welcoming inn, the earliest parts of which date back to the 14th century. It was at one time inhabited by the Keeper of the 'Forêt' – the Royal hunting ground and nowadays it is not uncommon for distinguished shooting parties to drop in for lunch. Set within grounds of 3 acres, the inn has a splendid outlook across the dramatically undulating Trough of Bowland. Each bedroom, including the four new luxury rooms in the coach house, has been attractively furnished with antiques and quality fabrics. All rooms have hi-tech stereo systems and most have videos. Head chef Breda Murphy from Ballymaloe creates cooking of a consistently high quality. The à la carte menu features predominately English country recipes such as seasonal roast game, home-made puddings and farmhouse cheeses. Good bar meals and garden lunches are also offered. 8 miles of water is available to residents only from the banks of the River Hodder, where brown trout, sea trout, salmon and grayling can be caught. Other country sports can be arranged locally. Browsholme Hall and Clitheroe Castle are close by and across the river there are neolithic cave dwellings. **Directions:** From M6 take Jct32; follow A6 towards Garstang for ¼ mile. Turn right at first traffic lights towards Longridge, then left at roundabout, then follow signs to Whitewell and Trough of Bowland. Price guide: Single £55–£70; double £78–£98; suite £110.

THE BIRD IN HAND

HAILEY, WITNEY, OXFORDSHIRE OX8 5XP
TEL: 01993 868321 FAX: 01993 868702

This archetypal English country inn is situated midway between the old blanket-making town of Witney and historic Charlbury. With a history dating from the 17th century it is surrounded by all the charm of the Cotswolds, sleepy villages clad in grey limestone or golden ironstone, ridges grazed by sheep, undulating wolds and gentle streams. The Bird in Hand is a superb inn, spotless and excellent in every way, a place where it is easy to imagine that time has slipped back to some gentler age. Visitors eat, drink and relax in elegant style within heavily beamed rooms which each have their own character and are warmed in winter months by a huge log fire. Sturdy wood furniture, colourful furnishings, antiques and pictures abound.

Sixteen spacious, cottage-style bedrooms surround a quiet grassy courtyard. Each has en suite bathroom and shower and features every home comfort. Two of the bedrooms are equipped for partially disabled guests. The inn's menu is designed to suit all tastes and diets, but is predominately English. Hailey is the ideal base for visiting the famous Cotswold villages of Burford, Broadway, Bibury, Bourton and Lower Slaughter and is equally convenient for Oxford, Stratford and Cheltenham. Nearby places of interest include Blenheim Palace, Gloucester Cathedral and the Oxford colleges. **Directions:** From Oxford take the A40 to Witney and then the B4022 Charlbury Road to Hailey. Price guide: Single £47.50; double/twin £65.50.

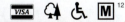

THE TANKERVILLE ARMS HOTEL

WOOLER, NORTHUMBERLAND NE71 6AD
TEL: 01668 281581 FAX: 01668 281387 E-MAIL: enquiries@tankervillehotel.co.uk

Set in the beautiful village of Wooler, Tankerville Arms Hotel has been frequented by travellers to Northumbria since the 17th century and is no less popular today. Comfort and convenience are key qualities of the en suite bedrooms, which are equipped with colour television, hairdryer, direct-dial telephone and several modern facilities. The Cheviot Restaurant affords pleasant views across the attractive gardens and is enveloped by a tranquil ambience, making it the perfect place to enjoy the very best of local fayre. An excellent menu includes over a dozen main courses, including several vegetarian options. There is a variety of wines available to complement any meal. Delicious sweets, such as sticky toffee pudding, banoffee roulade and english trifle can be walked off in the surrounding countryside. The finest of local beer and real ales is served in The Copper Bar, dominated by an imposing log fire. This 17th century coaching inn has been awarded many accolades and is 4 Crown Highly Commended. The area offers visitors the chance to play golf, fish or go horse-riding, as well as enjoying coastal walks and admiring the superb scenery. There are also many magnificent castles within easy reach. The hotel is located in the charming town of Wooler, within easy driving distance of Newcastle and Edinburgh. **Directions:** In the village of Wooler on A697 between Coldstream and Morpeth. Price guide: Single £45–£48; double £80–£85.

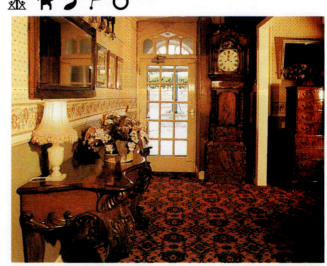

THE OLD TOLLGATE RESTAURANT AND HOTEL

THE STREET, BRAMBER, STEYNING, WEST SUSSEX BN44 3WE
TEL: 01903 879494 FAX: 01903 813399 E-MAIL: otr@fastnet.co.uk

An original Tollhouse centuries ago, travellers now look forward to stopping here and paying their dues for wonderful hospitality. Part of the old building is still in evidence with newer additions attractively blending. There are some splendid suites, even a four-poster, which are excellent value and delightful bedrooms, some of which are reached across the courtyard. The hotel is a popular meeting place for visitors and locals alike, with friendly staff adding to the welcoming ambience. The restaurant has built up a fine reputation, extending far beyond Sussex. It has a magnificent award-winning carvery and sumptuous cold table. Breakfast, lunch and dinner are all catered for at various price structures according to the number of courses consumed. Soups and broths, fresh and smoked fish, roasts and casseroles, pies and puddings and vegetarian dishes are in abundance. Bramber is famous for its Norman Castle and spectacular views over the South Downs. Brighton, with its shops, beach and Pavilion is an easy drive away, as is Worthing. Sporting activities nearby include riding, golf and fishing. **Directions:** Bramber is off the A283 between Brighton and Worthing, easily accessed from the A24 or A27. Price guide (room only): Single £68; double £68–£91; suite £91.

THE BARTON ANGLER COUNTRY INN

IRSTEAD ROAD, NEATISHEAD, NR WROXHAM, NORFOLK NR12 8XP
TEL: 01692 630740 FAX: 01692 631122

While learning to sail on the Norfolk Broads, the young Lord Nelson stayed at this unspoiled hostelry that dates back some 450 years. Set in large gardens, it previously catered exclusively for fishing clubs; but now provides excellent accommodation for anyone wishing to explore North Norfolk. The individually styled bedrooms are pleasantly furnished and some have fine locally crafted four-poster beds. Open fires, exposed beams and antiques feature in the reception rooms; all adding to the interesting character of this attractive building. Special week or weekend breaks are available during winter months. The kitchens are under the supervision of the chef, Timothy and all meals are prepared in the hotel. Bar meals are provided on a first come first served basis. In the Restaurant tables can be reserved – at popular times of the year it is essential to book in advance. Owned by English Heritage, Barton Broad, which is now within Broadlands National Park, offers plenty of opportunities for bird-watching, fishing, sailing and cruising. Boats can be hired for guests. The coast and many historic churches and houses are nearby. **Directions:** A1151 north from Norwich, turn right one mile beyond Wroxham. The inn lies midway between the villages of Neatishead and Irstead. Price guide: Single £35; double £60–£85.

THE GEORGE AT EASINGWOLD

MARKET PLACE, EASINGWOLD, YORK, NORTH YORKSHIRE YO6 3AD
TEL: 01347 821698 FAX: 01347 823448 E-MAIL: georgehotel.easingwold@tesco.net

The George at Easingwold is an 18th century coaching inn standing in the old cobbled square of the pretty Georgian market town of Easingwold. Open fires, a wealth of beams and horse brasses all add to its character and cosy atmosphere. The bedrooms vary in style - some are traditionally furnished while others are more modern - but all have a high level of comfort in common. A large inter-connected bar serves a fine selection of real cask ales, including locally brewed beers pulled straight from the cask and coffee is provided in the relaxing atmosphere of the lounge. The inn's original open courtyard is now an attractive candlelit area where a wide selection of freshly prepared bar meals are served. The 'chef's specials' board changes daily. A choice of à la carte or table d'hôte menus is provided in the cosy oak-beamed lamplit restaurant which overlooks the market square, while on Sundays, a traditional two or three course Sunday lunch is offered. The historic city of York is just 10 miles away and Castle Howard and the Howardian hills are also close by. The George is an ideal base for touring the North York Moors and the National Park. **Directions:** The George is in the centre of the town of Easingwold which is off the A19 midway between York and Thirsk. Price guide: Single £45–£55; double £53–£75.

Johansens Recommended Traditional Inns, Hotels and Restaurants
Wales

Breathtaking scenery, a rich variety of natural, cultural and modern leisure attractions, and the very best accommodation awaits the Johansens visitor in Wales.

Harlech Castle

What's new in Wales?

• Llangollen International Musical Eisteddfod – the 54th International Musical Eisteddfod held at the Royal International Pavilion, Llangollen, between 4th and 9th July 2000. Participants from around 50 countries are drawn together by their love of music, song and dance. A unique cultural festival to be enjoyed by all.
Tel: 01978 860236

• Royal Welsh Show – exhibition of livestock, cattle, horses, machinery, handicrafts, tradestands, sheepdog trials, tug of war plus much more. Held at the Royal Welsh Showground between 24th and 27th July 2000.
Tel: 01982 553683

• Ladies Home International Matches – Golf – annual competition between ladies golf teams from England, Ireland, Scotland & Wales. Held between 13th and 15th September 2000 at the Royal St David's Golf Club.
Tel: 01334 475811

• Welsh International Film Festival – premier welsh film event celebrating the industry in an international context. Held at various venues in Cardiff between 10th and 19th November 2000.
Tel: 01970 617995

For more information please contact:-

Wales Tourist Board
Dept GN
PO Box 1
Cardiff CF1 2XN
Tel: 01222 475226

North Wales Tourism
Tel: 01492 531731

Mid Wales Tourism
Tel: 0800 273747

Tourism South & West Wales
Tel: 01792 781212

THE CASTLE VIEW HOTEL

16 BRIDGE STREET, CHEPSTOW, MONMOUTHSHIRE NP6 5EZ
TEL: 01291 620349 FAX: 01291 627397 E-MAIL: mart@castview.demon.co.uk

This historic 17th century, ivy-clad hotel is set in a prime location opposite Britain's oldest stone castle, begun in the reign of William the Conqueror. It is a friendly, family-owned hostelry, which offers good value accommodation, with Sky television. All rooms have recently been refurbished and many still have original features. There is a hand-turned oak staircase leading to comfortable bedrooms. Some of these have 200-year-old wall paintings and many have views of the castle. There is also a secluded garden which is ablaze with colour during the summer. The kitchen is Michelin 'Fork and Pitcher' Commended and serves imaginative home-cooked meals. Wye salmon and Welsh lamb often appear on the seasonally changing menu, which always offers fresh vegetables, plus many delicious home-made puddings. There is also an interesting range of bar snacks, real ales, a varied wine list and a few good malts. Chepstow is on the edge of the Wye Valley and Forest of Dean. It is well situated for international rugby in Cardiff, racing at Chepstow, golf at St Pierre and visits to Tintern Abbey. **Directions:** Leave M48 at junction 2, follow signs to Chepstow (A48), then follow signs to the Castle. Price guide: Single £46–£51; double £64–£71; suite £76.

THE WEST ARMS HOTEL

LLANARMON D C, NR LLANGOLLEN, DENBIGHSHIRE LL20 7LD
TEL: 01691 600665 FAX: 01691 600622 E-MAIL: gowestarms@aol.com

Originally a 16th century farmhouse, the character of this charming old inn is evident throughout, with log fires, inglenooks, beams and flagstone floors. Its cosy lounges, furnished with chintz-covered sofas and armchairs, are an invitation to relaxation, aided by the warm hospitality of Geoff and Gill Leigh-Ford. The bedrooms are well-furnished, spacious yet cosy with impressive brass bedsteads: all share a view of the surrounding hills. With formal rose gardens and lawns running down to the river, the setting is idyllic. Dogs by prior arrangement. Locally reared lamb, venison and game in season and Ceiriog trout comprise the cuisine, awarded an AA Rosette. Imaginative vegetables and delicious desserts display equal care in cooking and presentation. Dinner served in the beamed, candlelit dining room is complemented by a well chosen list of classic and New World wines and the hearty Welsh breakfast is a perfect start to the day. The hotel can be hired exclusively for weddings and residential conferences. The inn can offer free private fishing on a 2 mile stretch of the Ceiriog river. The Berwyn Mountains provide walking and pony-trekking opportunities. Local attractions include Chirk Castle, the house of the 'Ladies of Llangollen', Erddig Hall and the Roman city of Chester. **Directions:** Take A5 to Chirk, then B4500 for 11 miles to Llanarmon DC. Once over bridge, the inn is on the right. Price guide: Single £44.50–£62.50; double £79–£115; suite £99–£115.

THE PLOUGH INN

RHOSMAEN, LLANDEILO, CARMARTHENSHIRE SA19 6NP
TEL: 01558 823431 FAX: 01558 823969 E-MAIL: theploughinn@rhosmaen.demon.co.uk

Originally a farmhouse, The Plough Inn has been elegantly converted and extended to provide good food and accommodation in the rural market town of Llandeilo. In the older part of the building guests will find a public bar, adjoining which is the cosy and intimate Towy Lounge. The 12 en suite bedrooms enjoy glorious views over surrounding countryside and are all well appointed for your comfort. A gym and sauna provide an added dimension to your stay – why not start the day with an invigorating work-out in the gym or unwind in the sauna before a comfortable night's sleep? A conference suite can cater for business meetings: a comprehensive range of audiovisual aids is available for hire. Closed Christmas. Guests may dine in style and comfort in the à la carte restaurant. Local salmon and sewin, venison, Welsh lamb and beef, cooked simply or in continental recipes, all feature on the menus. An extensive choice of bar meals can be enjoyed in the Towy Lounge. One of the inn's specialities is its tradition for Welsh afternoon teas. These are served in the elegant, chandeliered Penlan Lounge. The Plough Inn is an ideal point of departure for touring the beautiful Towy Valley and surrounding Dinefwr countryside, including the new National Botanic Gardens of Wales (opens in year 2000) just 15 mins drive away. **Directions:** A mile from Llandeilo on A40, towards Llandovery. The inn is 14 miles from exit 49 on M4. Price guide: Single £47.50; double £65–£70.

THE WYNNSTAY

MAENGWYN STREET, MACHYNLLETH, POWYS, WALES SY20 8AE
TEL: 01654 702941 FAX: 01654 703884 E-MAIL: reception@wynnstay-hotel.com

This delightful 18th century inn lies in the heart of the bustling town of Machynlleth at the southern edge of the Snowdonia National Park. With origins dating back to 1780, The Wynnstay is under new ownership and with its recent additions it is a delightfully rambling property whose popular bars are a focal point for the local community. The bar food is ideal for those preferring a less formal bite to eat, whilst the restaurant offers an excellent selection of European specialities freshly prepared using the local Welsh produce. Fine dining is supplemented by a well-chosen wine list that features many unusual Italian vintages. Individually styled bedrooms, of which the pick are the Heritage

Rooms, are spacious and comfortable with up-to-date amenities and smartly tiled en suite bathrooms. The hotel is very well suited for corporate events with meeting rooms, galleries and arts centres available in the town. Outdoor activities abound and include quad bike trekking, white water rafting, mountain biking, climbing and abseiling to name but a few. Kennelling is available for dogs. Machynlleth is a thriving market town with street markets on Wednesdays and an abundance of specialist shopping. **Directions:** At junction of A487 Aberystwyth– Dolgellau and A489 from Newtown. The hotel is in the town centre on the main street Price guide: Single £38–£45; double £60–£96.

NEW

THE RADNORSHIRE ARMS

HIGH STREET, PRESTEIGNE, POWYS, WALES LD8 2BE
TEL: 01544 267406 FAX: 01544 260418

This charming 17th century Elizabethan style house is situated in the heart of the town of Presteigne in Wales. Families with children of all ages are welcomed here and many guests will find the garden lodges, sleeping up to four people, a very suitable spot for a relaxing weekend or break. There are eight bedrooms in the main house, all of which are en suite and decorated and furnished to a very high standard. For diners, there is a choice between the Hatton's restaurant or the bar for an evening meal. Both provide excellent cuisine, with traditional fayre in the restaurant and a less formal atmosphere in the bar, ideal for those just wanting a quick bite to eat or a taste of real ale. There is a lounge on the first floor that overlooks the garden and is popular with guests wishing to unwind and relax. There is plenty to see and do nearby. In the actual town of Presteigne there is an 11th century Norman castle housing a magnificent Norman tapestry. For golf fanatics, the highest golf course in England is just seven miles away in Kington and for those who are interested in wild life and ornithology, this is an excellent area for walking and bird watching. **Directions:** From the M5, junction 3, follow the A456, via Kidderminster and Tenbury Wells then take the B4362 from Woofferton. Price guide: Single £60; double £65–£90.

As recommended

TALISKER.
A PLACE WHERE THE THUNDER ROLLS OVER YOUR TONGUE.

Of all the islands that defend Scotland's west coast from the Atlantic, Skye is the most dramatic. How fitting then that this is the home of the fiery Talisker. Standing on Skye's western shore, the distillery lies in the shadow of The Cuillins. Jagged mountains that rise out of the sea to skewer the clouds for a thunderous retort. In the shadow of these peaks, next to a fearsome sea, Talisker takes its first breath and draws it all in. Skye's explosive fervour captured forever in its only single malt. That Talisker is not a whisky for the faint-hearted is beyond dispute. Indeed even when one seasoned whisky taster once went as far as calling it "The lava of The Cuillins",

no one disagreed.

CLASSIC MALTS OF SCOTLAND

Johansens Recommended Traditional Inns, Hotels and Restaurants
Scotland

Myths and mountains, lochs and legends – Scotland's scenic splendour acts as a magnet for visitors from all over the globe. Superb as it is, Scotland's charismatic charm is more than just visual.

Dunrobin Castle

What's new in Scotland?

• The Big Idea – aiming to be open in the spring of 2000, a state-of-the-art permanent exhibition will be launched on the west coast of Scotland on the Ardeer peninsula. This is a visitor experience, not a science museum, nor an exploratorium but a gigantic workshop where visitors are encouraged to have their own big ideas.

•Scottish Seabird Centre – expected to open in May 2000 in North Berwick, offers visitors an amazing insight into the some of the largest seabird colonies in Europe.

•Our Dynamic Earth – this new visitor attraction opened in July 1999 directly opposite the site of the new Scottish parliament and close to the Palace of Holyroodhouse and tells the story of our planet. Using dramatic special effects this attraction takes the visitor through the fascinating journey from the Earth's creation through to the future (whatever it may be!) Travel through time and step aboard a spaceship and see the creation of earth and the splendour of the natural world.

For further information, please contact:-

The Scottish Tourist Board
23 Ravelston Terrace
Edinburgh
EH4 3TP

Tel: 0131 332 2433

GLENDEVON (South Perthshire)

TORMAUKIN HOTEL

GLENDEVON, BY DOLLAR, SOUTH PERTHSHIRE FK14 7JY
TEL: 01259 781252 FAX: 01259 781526 E-MAIL: reservations@tormaukin-hotel.demon.co.uk

Located in 'The Hidden Glen', amidst the beautiful Ochil Hills, this former drover's inn has a long history of welcoming hospitality. Built in the 18th century, the Tormaukin has, over the years, been sympathetically restored and refurbished whilst retaining the old beams, natural stone walls and large open fireplaces, so preserving the old historical character. Four of the ten bedrooms are on the ground floor. Each bedroom is individually decorated with pine furniture, co-ordinating fabrics and offers the latest amenities. The restaurant has a relaxed atmosphere and has established a reputation for its innovative treatment of Scottish recipes and interesting choice of international dishes. A wide selection of Scottish cheese is offered along with a wine list of over 90 labels. Bar lunches and suppers can be enjoyed in the cosy lounge bars or in the Glendevon Room, where the same relaxed atmosphere and large choice of imaginative dishes prepared by the team of six chefs may be found. There are opportunities for hill-walking, trout fishing, shooting and golf, with Gleneagles only six miles away. Art courses can also be arranged locally. Closed for four days in January. **Directions:** Southbound, leave M90 at junction 7; northbound leave at junction 6. On A9 follow signs to Glendevon, which is on A823, south of Gleneagles. Price guide: Single £50–£55; double £80.

GROUSE AND TROUT

FLICHITY, BY FARR/LOCHNESS, INVERNESS, SCOTLAND IV2 6XD
TEL/FAX: 01808 521314 E-MAIL: reservations@grouse–and–trout.com

Original farm steading from 1860 forms part of the original Flichity Hotel, which has been carefully converted and refurbished whilst preserving much of the traditional features. The result is a charming hotel adorned with timber beams and stonework, set amidst the superb landscape of lochs and heather fields. The five bedrooms in house enjoy glorious views over the magnificent hills of Strathnairn and Loch Flichity adjacent to the famous nature reserve. Kept in simple country house style, they are all en suite with television and tea/coffee making facilities. The menu comprises hearty bar meals, prepared by the chef for lunch and dinner. A warm welcome is extended to all guests in the friendly Lounge and Restaurant, where the range of single malts and extensive wine list complement the convivial atmosphere. Loch fishing, grouse shooting, stalking and horse riding are some of the many outdoor activities available within the locality. The hotel itself offers a hard tennis court and bicycle hire for guests. Other pursuits include the many nearby golf courses, clay pigeon shooting, cruises on the Loch Ness or simply enjoying the beautiful countryside. Places of interest include Culloden Battlefield, Cawdor Castle and Fort Augustus Abbey. **Directions:** From the A9 South of Inverness, take the B851 (Fort Augustus) for 7 miles. Price guide: Single £49; double/twin £90.

HOTEL EILEAN IARMAIN

SLEAT, ISLE OF SKYE IV43 8QR
TEL: 01471 833332 FAX: 01471 833275

Hotel Eilean Iarmain stands on the small bay of Isle Ornsay in the South of Skye with expansive views over the Sound of Sleat and has always meant 'failte is furan' a warmth of welcomes. The hotel prides itself on its log fires, inventive cooking and friendly Gaelic-speaking staff. 1997/8 accolades include the RAC Restaurant Award, RAC Merit Award for Hospitality, Comfort and Restaurant, AA Rosette for Restaurant, AA Romantic Hotel of Great Britain and Ireland Award, Les Routiers Corps d'Elite Wine Award and Macallan Taste of Scotland, runner-up Hotel of the Year Award. The 16 bedrooms are all different, with 6 of them in the Garden House with special views of sea and hills. Original features, period furniture, pretty fabrics and pictures create a cosy atmosphere. Every evening the menu features game in season and guests enjoy fresh seafood landed at the pier. The extensive wine list includes premier cru clarets. A large selection of malt whiskies includes local Poit Dhubh and Talisker, highly regarded by connoisseurs. The bar offers lunchtime meals and in the evening is a haunt of yachtsmen, often the scene of ceilidhs. Clan MacDonald Centre, Armadale Castle and Talisker Distillery are close by. Sports include sea-fishing, stalking, shooting and walking. **Directions:** The hotel is in Sleat, between Broadford and Armadale on A851. 20 mins from Skye Bridge; 15 mins from Mallaig Armadale Ferry and Lochalsh railway station. Price guide: Single £85; double £110–£135.

UIG HOTEL

UIG, ISLE OF SKYE, ISLE OF SKYE IV51 9YE
TEL: 01470 542205 FAX: 01470 542308

A warm Scottish welcome greets visitors to this delightful old coaching hostelry standing in three acres of hillside grounds overlooking beautiful Uig Bay and Loch Snizort in a traditional crofting community. The hotel was awarded the 1999 Les Routiers hospitality award for a genuine welcome and warm friendly ambience. The en suite bedrooms have been individually decorated and offer all modern facilities. Pretty fabrics and well chosen water-colours create a cosy atmosphere and a relaxing sun lounge overlooks the bay. The AA Rosetted restaurant is comfortable and welcoming with chef patron Bruce Skelton providing a good choice of menus featuring fresh locally landed seafood and lamb from the hotel's own flock of Island Blackface

sheep. Appetites are sure to be tempted by dishes such as a trellis of salmon and sole presented on a pool of ginger scented tomato sauce, or maybe pan seared breast of duck served on stir fried leeks. Guests enjoy pony trekking from the hotel's Native Pony Centre in magnificent coastal scenery. The hotel has fishing rights to local rivers for salmon and trout. The Trotternish Peninsula, Quiraing, Storr, Fairy Glen and Duntulm Castle are nearby. 1 mile from the ferry sailing to the Outer Hebridean Isles of Harris, Lewis and the Uists, day trips in summer. **Directions:** Skye is reached by road bridge via A87 or ferry via A830. Approaching Uig from Portree, hotel is on right, beside a white church. Price guide (incl. 4 course dinner): Single £59–£75; double £110–£178.

KYLESKU HOTEL

KYLESKU, SUTHERLAND IV27 4HW
TEL: 01971 502231/200 FAX: 01971 502313

This low, sprawling white and grey slate roofed hotel is a haven of tranquillity at the base of some of the most breathtaking mountains in Scotland. Sullivan, Quinaig, Bern More Assynt, among others, provide challenges for serious climbers, while their foothills offer easier walks for the less adventurous. All around is the scenic splendour of unspoilt terrain which is home to a variety of wildlife from deer and badgers to pinemartins and wild cats. Hand Island, a birdwatchers paradise, is just a ten minutes drive away and the 658 feet 'Eas Coul Aulin', Britain's highest waterfall, is within easy reach. Kylesku is a delightfully quite village and the hotel is an ideal base from which to explore the dramatic surroundings. It is warm, relaxing and friendly. All bedrooms are en suite, centrally heated and equipped with every home comfort. The food is excellent. Both the restaurant and the bar menus specialise in locally caught seafood and venison - in season. The Chef/patron has worked in several European hotels before moving to Kylesku and ensures that the cuisine is unequalled for quality and value. The hotel has the fishing rights to several local lochs and also maintains a boat for sea fishing. There are boat trips to the seal islands and for guests who like touring, Cape Wrath, Durness and Smoo Cave are short drives away. Closed November-March. **Directions:** From Ullapool take A835, A837 and then A894 north to Kylesku. Price guide: Single £35; double £65.

ACHRAY HOUSE ON LOCH EARN

LOCH EARN, ST FILLANS, PERTHSHIRE PH6 2NF
TEL: 01764 685231 FAX: 01764 685320 E-MAIL: achrayhotelsltd@btinternet.com

Overlooking the attractive Loch Earn, Achray House is enveloped by the surrounding southern central Highlands and offers a superb standard of accommodation and service. The bedrooms, all of which are en suite, are well-appointed with a range of modern amenities including tea and coffee making facilities, colour television and direct dial telephone. The hotel has gained an excellent reputation for its cuisine and is popular with both the local residents and guests. The bar menus offer a choice of traditional dishes for lunch and dinner whilst in the restaurant, the specialities include oven baked Scottish salmon on a bed of buttered leeks with roasted cherry tomatoes. Achray House has its own jetty and foreshore and with the proximity of the Loch, opportunities for water sports abound. Trout fishing, sailing and windsurfing may be practised and for golfers, there are 14 courses within easy driving distance including the attractive St. Fillans. Ramblers will also be pleased to explore this designated 'area of outstanding natural beauty' with its plethora of gardens and glens. Heritage enthusiasts will notice the number of historic properties nearby such as Blair, Glamis and Stirling castles. **Directions:** Travelling northwest from Stirling, take the A84 towards Crianlarich. At Loch Earn take the A85 to Perth for six miles, following Lochside to St. Fillans. Price guide: Double £36–£69.

ANNANDALE ARMS HOTEL

HIGH STREET, MOFFAT, DUMFRIESSHIRE DG10 9HF
TEL: 01683 220013 FAX: 01683 221395

True Scottish hospitality can be enjoyed at this welcoming, 200-year-old coaching inn which offers attractive accommodation and excellent value for money. The Annandale Arms stands in the centre of the pretty Southern Upland Hill town of Moffat, where Robert Burns, Sir Walter Scott and John Buchanan found inspiration for many of their works. The area thrives as a sheep farming centre, symbolised by a statue of a ram in the wide High Street. The beautiful surrounding countryside, which looks much like the English Lake District, is steeped in history, making it popular with sightseers, sports enthusiasts and hill climbers. The panelled bar also draws locals and visitors as it serves a wide selection of malt whiskies. All 15 bedrooms are charming and provide full modern comforts. The extensive menu makes good use of local produce. The Annandale Arms is an ideal base for visiting many historic castles and National Trust properties. North of the town is the Devil's Beef Tub, a sheer-sided hollow in the hills, White Coomb (2,696ft) and Grey Mare's Tail, one of Scotland's highest waterfalls. Immediate activities include fishing, golf, shooting, sailing, riding and bird-watching. **Directions:** Moffat is 2 miles off A74M on A 701 road from Dumfries. Price Guide: Single £45; double £70.

THE MOULIN HOTEL

MOULIN, BY PITLOCHRY, PERTHSHIRE PH16 5EW
TEL: 01796 472196 FAX: 01796 474098 E-MAIL: hotel@moulin.u-net.com

The Moulin Hotel stands pristine white against a towering mountain backdrop of deep blues and greens capped by scudding clouds racing to and from the Highlands. Behind its attractive black framed windows is a welcoming world of peace, tranquillity and Scottish homeliness. Opened as an inn in 1695, The Moulin Hotel stands proudly in the village square just three-quarters of a mile from the bustling town of Pitlochry, gateway to the Highlands. All 12 bedrooms have been recently refurbished to include every modern amenity. The comfortable lounge and lounge bar overlook the hotel's garden and Moulin Burn, where the cooing of doves and water babbling over stones is calming music to the ears of visitors wearied by a day's walking, exploring or sightseeing. The chefs serve a varied choice of imaginatively prepared dishes in the spacious and charmingly furnished restaurant. Begin with haggis wrapped in filo pastry on an onion cream, followed by salmon wrapped in lemon sole on a prawn sauce and then a dessert of highland cranachan with local berries before enjoying an after-dinner coffee and malt. Many walks and gentle climbs are close by such as the 2,759 foot summit of Ben-y-Vrackie. Golf, fishing, riding, Pitlochry Theatre, Blair Castle, Scone Palace and numerous historical sites abound. **Directions:** From Perth, take A9 to Pitlochry then turn right onto A924 for Moulin. Price guide: Single £55–£65; double £60–£70 per room.

THE PLOCKTON HOTEL AND GARDEN RESTAURANT

HARBOUR STREET, PLOCKTON, WESTER ROSS IV52 8TN
TEL: 01599 544274 FAX: 01599 544475

With its sheltered harbour fringed by tall palm trees the picturesque village of Plockton, at the mouth of Loch Carron, is a favourite with film makers. Over the years this 18th century waterside hotel has been host to a succession of actors and actresses attracted by its beamed charm, ambience, good food and the scenic splendour of the Applecross Mountains viewed from its windows. It is as far from city life as you can imagine and an ideal centre for visiting Skye or touring north to Applecross, Torridon or Ullapool. Tom and Dorothy Pearson offer a particularly friendly welcome to their antique-furnished hotel with its pretty little garden. They have recently invested in extensive refurbishment and additions which have increased the number of comfortable, en suite bedrooms and introduced a garden restaurant. The food produced by chefs Lorna Murray and Jane Stewart assisted by Una Ferguson is superb and has earned a beer glass and fork symbol award in the prestigious 1998 Michelin Hotel and Restaurant Guide. Particularly renowned are their fresh fish and Plockton prawns dishes There are attractive gardens and National Trust properties nearby, sailing on the loch, swimming from small coral beaches, golf, sea and hill loch fishing. **Directions**: Take the A87 to Kyle of Lochalsh. Plockton is five miles north. Price guide: Single £30–£33; double/twin £60–£65.

POOL HOUSE HOTEL

POOLEWE, ACHNASHEEN, WESTER ROSS IV22 2LD
TEL: 01445 781272 FAX: 01445 781403 E-MAIL: Poolhouse@inverewe.co.uk

The scenic splendour of Wester Ross, with its majestic mountains and spectacular sunsets, makes a perfect backdrop for Pool House. The hotel stands on the shores of Loch Ewe, just across the bay from the world-famous, subtropical Inverewe Gardens and is the former residence of their founder, Osgood Mackenzie. All the bedrooms are nicely decorated and furnished and most benefit from lovely views of the loch or river. They are also strictly non-smoking. There are future plans for a ten bedroom extension with disabled and conference facilities. On view from the ideally-situated lounge is an abundance of wildlife, including seals, cormorants, herons and even occasionally a family of otters. Excellent food and wine is a well-noted feature of the hotel, which has won several prestigious awards in recognition of this. Specialising in local seafood, the 'Lochside Restaurant' serves an extensive menu comprising Loch Ewe langoustine, lobster and scallops, while the wine list offers a choice to suit every palate and pocket. Some of the more unusual whiskies can be sampled in the Rowallan bar, which is also the place to enjoy an informal meal. Hill walkers, keen ornithologists and wildlife enthusiasts will all be delighted by the excellent opportunities to indulge their favourite pastimes. **Directions:** Pool House is on A832 to Poolewe, 6 miles north-east of Gairloch. Price guide: Single £45–£60; double £90–£150.

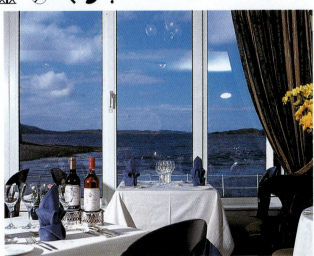

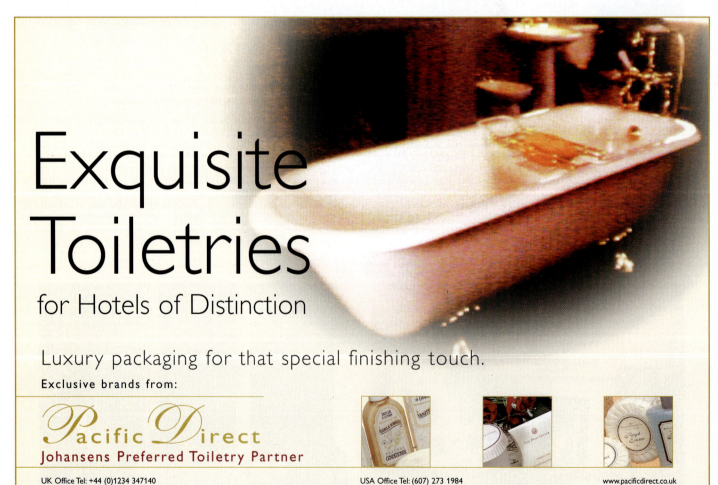

Johansens Recommended Traditional Inns, Hotels and Restaurants
Channel Islands

With a wealth of wonderful scenery, magnificent coastlines, historic buildings, natural and man-made attractions plus mouthwatering local produce, the Channel Islands provide a memorable destination that is distinctly different.

St. Aubins Harbour, Jersey

What's happening in Guernsey?

• Millennium Eve Carnival, 31st December 1999 – to start the evening there will be a true Guernsey 'budloe' style boat burning in St Peter Port Harbour, then a torchlit procession, a magical parade of light and music through the streets of St Peter Port. There will also be an Octopussy Big Top with an early evening cabaret, live bands, DJs, sideshows and various artists. The Big Top will be situated on North Beach.

• Gala Millennium Concert – a fantastic musical event featuring the Guernsey Symphony Orchestra, the Guernsey Choral Society, the Guernsey Sinfonia Chorus and the Guernsey Youth Choir all join together for a performance of Beethoven's Symphony No. 9. To be held on 1st July 2000 at Beau Sejour.

For further information, please contact:-

Guernsey Tourist Board
PO Box 23
St Peter Port
Guernsey GY1 3AN
Tel: 01481 723557

What's happening in Jersey?

• Jersey Jazz Festival – taking place at various venues around the Island. Held between 6th and 9th April 2000.

• The Jersey International Food Festival – this event gives visitors the chance to taste the finest local produce and experience the skills of top Jersey Chefs. Held between 13th and 21st May 2000.

• Jersey Battle of Flowers – this parade is held on 10th August 2000 and features floats covered in flowers, musicians, dancers and carnival queens.

For further information, please contact:-

Jersey Tourism
Liberation Square
St Helier
Jersey JE1 1BB
Tel: 01534 500700

LES ROCQUETTES HOTEL

LES GRAVEES, ST PETER PORT, GUERNSEY, CHANNEL ISLANDS GY1 1RN
TEL: 01481 722146 FAX: 01481 714543

Originally a country mansion, this much extended hotel provides guests with all the modern amenities in a relaxed and friendly atmosphere. Strolling around the tranquil gardens of Les Rocquettes, guests could easily forget that they are within walking distance of the financial heartland of Guernsey. All 51 en suite bedrooms are comfortably appointed, with several adapted to allow wheelchair access. There is also the choice of two well-equipped self catering apartments which can accommodate either four or six guests. The new Mulberry Health suite boasts state-of-the-art facilities which feature both cardiovascular and toning equipment, as well as a large indoor pool, Jacuzzi and sauna. The Beauty Box treatment room offers a number of treats. Light lunches and afternoon teas are enjoyed in the cosy Mulberry Bar or alfresco on the terrace. For those exploring the surrounding areas, a picnic can be provided upon request. In the evening, the Tartan Bar proves as popular with the guests and locals alike for fine fare and good company. There is plenty to do nearby, including walking and cycling along the exquisite Guernsey coastline. Places of interest include the maritime museum at Castle Cornet, Hauteville House, which was the home of Victor Hugo during his exile in Guernsey and the islands of Herm and Sark. **Directions:** The hotel is a 15 minutes drive from the airport and 5 minutes drive from the ferry port. Price guide: Single £33–£68; double/twin £56–£94 .

PREFERRED PARTNERS

Preferred partners are those organisations specifically chosen and exclusively recommended by Johansens for the quality and excellence of their products and services for the mutual benefit of Johansens members, readers and independent travellers.

 Barrels & Bottles

 Classic Malts of Scotland

 Conqueror

 Dorlux

 Ercol Furniture Ltd

 Hildon Ltd

 Marsh UK Ltd

 Knight Frank International

 Honda (UK)

 Moët Hennessy

 Pacific Direct

To Dublin/ Dun Laoghaire

Holyhead
ANGLESEY
BEAUMARIS
CONWY
LLANDUDNO

CAERNARFON
BETWS-Y-COED

CRICCIETH
PORTMEIRION VILLAGE
PWLLHELI
ABERSOCH
HARLECH
BALA
CORWEN

BARMOUTH
DOLGELLAU
LLANARMON DYFFRYN CEIRIOG
LAKE VYRNWY

ABERDOVEY
MACHYNLLETH

ABERYSTWYTH

To Rosslare

FISHGUARD
ST DAVID'S

To Rosslare

Carmarthen
LLANGAMMARCH WELLS

BRECON
LLANDEILO

CRICKHOWELL
MILFORD HAVEN
PEMBROKE
TENBY

To Cork

SWANSEA
ABERDARE
ABERGAVENNY

BRIDGEND
USK
TINTERN
CHEPSTOW

CARDIFF

● JOHANSENS RECOMMENDED HOTEL
▲ JOHANSENS RECOMMENDED INN OR RESTAURANT
■ JOHANSENS RECOMMENDED COUNTRY HOUSE

BOLTON SADDLEWORTH
MANCHESTER
ALTRINCHAM
GLOSSOP
HAYFIELD
MANCHESTER AIRPORT
MANCHESTER
ALDERLEY EDGE
KNUTSFORD
PRESTBURY
MACCLESFIELD
BUXTON
CHESTER
TARPORLEY
LEEK
LLANDEGLA
NANTWICH
WREXHAM
Stoke
OSWESTRY
ECCLESHALL
WEM
STAFFORD
SHREWSBURY
ACTON TRUSSELL
TELFORD
SHIFNAL
WOLVERHAMPTON
CHURCH STRETTON
BRIDGNORTH
BIRMINGHAM
KIDDERMINSTER
CHADDESLEY CORBETT
LUDLOW
CLEOBURY MORTIMER
BROMSGROVE
PRESTEIGNE
ABBERLEY
ALCESTER
LEOMINSTER
WEOBLEY
MALVERN WELLS
UPTON-ON-SEVERN
EVESHAM
HAY-ON-WYE
HEREFORD
LEDBURY
BROADWAY
TEWKESBURY
ROSS-ON-WYE
CHELTENHAM
MONMOUTH
PAINSWICK
STONEHOUSE
CLEARWELL
CIRENCESTER
STROUD
MINCHIN-HAMPTON
OWLPEN
TETBURY
MALMESBURY
CHIPPING SODBURY
CASTLE COMBE
FORD
CHIPPENHAM
BRISTOL
LACOCK
BATH
BRADFORD-ON-AVON
BECKINGTON
LONGLEAT
MELLS
WARMINSTER
WELLS
SHEPTON MALLET
HINDON
DITCHEAT
CASTLE CARY
WINCANTON
FIFEFIELD
ILCHESTER
SHERBORNE
STURMINSTER NEWTON
ILMINSTER
SEAVINGTON ST MARY
EVERSHOT
WIMBORNE MINSTER
BOURNEMOUTH

COMBE MARTIN
LYNTON
LYNMOUTH
PORLOCK WEIR
MIDDLECOMBE
WOOLACOMBE
SIMONSBATH
EXMOOR
EXFORD
SAUNTON
BARNSTAPLE
DULVERTON
CLOVELLY
BIDEFORD
SOUTH MOLTON
TAUNTON
BURRINGTON
MORCHARD BISHOP
BICKLEIGH
HONITON
BEAMINSTER
COLEFORD
CREDITON
AXMINSTER
TINTAGEL
LEWDOWN
CHAGFORD
EXETER
BRIDPORT
DORCHESTER
PORT GAVERNE
LIFTON
LYDFORD
BOVEY TRACEY
SIDMOUTH
LYME REGIS
WAREHAM
PADSTOW
DARTMOOR
ILSINGTON
WEYMOUTH
WADEBRIDGE
TAVISTOCK
ASHBURTON
ST KEYNE
PELYNT
STAVERTON
KINGSKERSWELL
TORQUAY
GOLANT BY FOWEY
LOOE
PLYMOUTH
TOTNES
ST AGNES
FOWEY
POLPERRO
DARTMOUTH
CAMBORNE
VERYAN
KINGSBRIDGE
ST IVES
THURLESTONE SANDS
SALCOMBE
PENZANCE
HELSTON
ST MAWES
PORTHLEVEN
FALMOUTH

ISLES OF SCILLY

0   20   40   60   80   100 Kilometres

0   10   20   30   40   50 Miles

To Santander
To Roscoff
To Guernsey

196

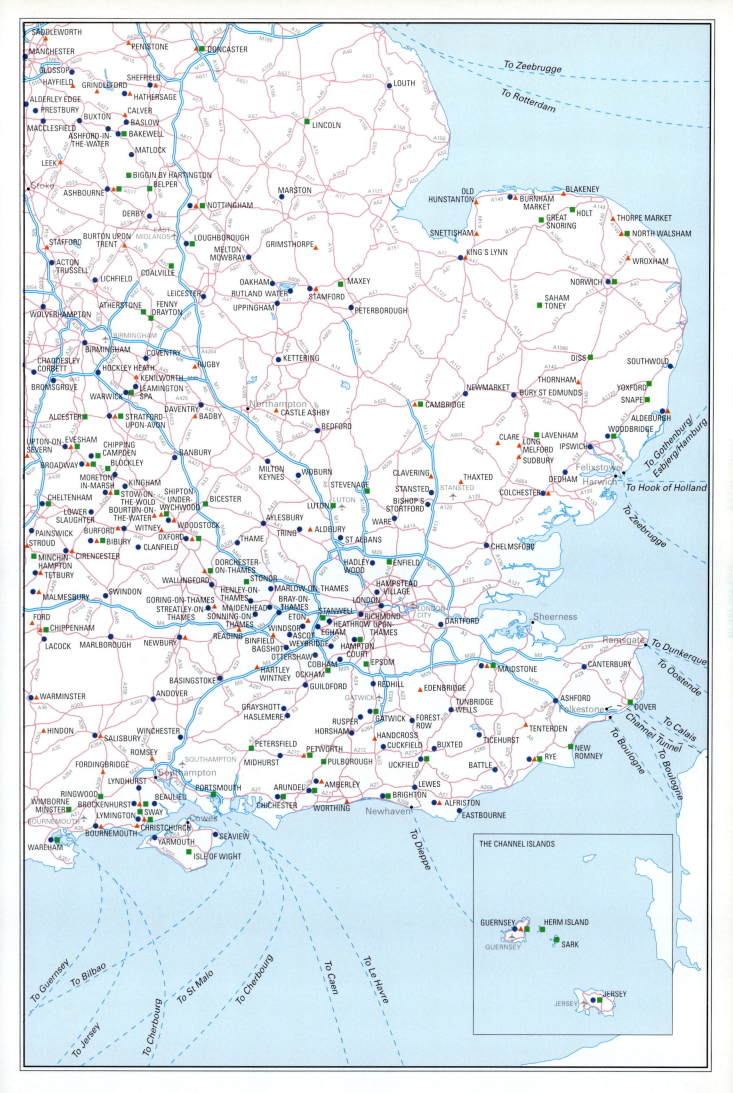

BERWICK-UPON-TWEED

BELFORD BAMBURGH

WOOLER

OTTERBURN

To Stavanger/Bergen
To Gothenburg
To Esbjerg

To Hamburg

NEWCASTLE
NEWCASTLE

STANHOPE DURHAM

HAMSTERLEY NEWTON AYCLIFFE

WEST AUCKLAND DARLINGTON Middlesbrough EASINGTON

TEESSIDE CRATHORNE EGTON

WEST WITTON APPLETON-LE-MOORS SCARBOROUGH

MIDDLEHAM HELMSLEY AMPLEFORTH
EAST WITTON THIRSK
HOVINGHAM MALTON

BURNSALL BOLTON ABBEY HARROGATE

ILKLEY YORK

OTLEY WETHERBY

BURNLEY LEEDS/BRADFORD HAZLEWOOD
LEEDS BEVERLEY

HALIFAX Wakefield HULL

HUDDERSFIELD

SADDLEWORTH PENISTONE

MANCHESTER DONCASTER

GLOSSOP

HAYFIELD SHEFFIELD

GRINDLEFORD HATHERSAGE LOUTH

ALDERLEY EDGE CALVER
PRESTBURY BUXTON BASLOW
MACCLESFIELD BAKEWELL LINCOLN
ASHFORD-IN-THE-WATER MATLOCK

LEEK

Stoke BIGGIN BY HARTINGTON
BELPER

ASHBOURNE

DERBY MARSTON

OLD HUNSTANTON BLAKENEY
BURNHAM MARKET
STAFFORD BURTON UPON TRENT NOTTINGHAM
EAST MIDLANDS LOUGHBOROUGH GREAT SNORING HOLT THORPE MARKET
ACTON TRUSSELL GRIMSTHORPE SNETTISHAM NORTH WALSHAM
MELTON MOWBRAY
LICHFIELD COALVILLE KING'S LYNN WROXHAM
OAKHAM MAXEY
WOLVERHAMPTON LEICESTER RUTLAND WATER NORWICH
ATHERSTONE FENNY DRAYTON UPPINGHAM STAMFORD SAHAM TONEY
BIRMINGHAM PETERBOROUGH
BIRMINGHAM DISS SOUTHWOLD
CHADDESLEY CORBETT COVENTRY KETTERING
HOCKLEY HEATH RUGBY

To Zeebrugge

To Rotterdam

● JOHANSENS RECOMMENDED HOTEL
▲ JOHANSENS RECOMMENDED INN OR RESTAURANT
■ JOHANSENS RECOMMENDED COUNTRY HOUSE

0   20   40   60   80   100 Kilometres

0   10   20   30   40   50 Miles

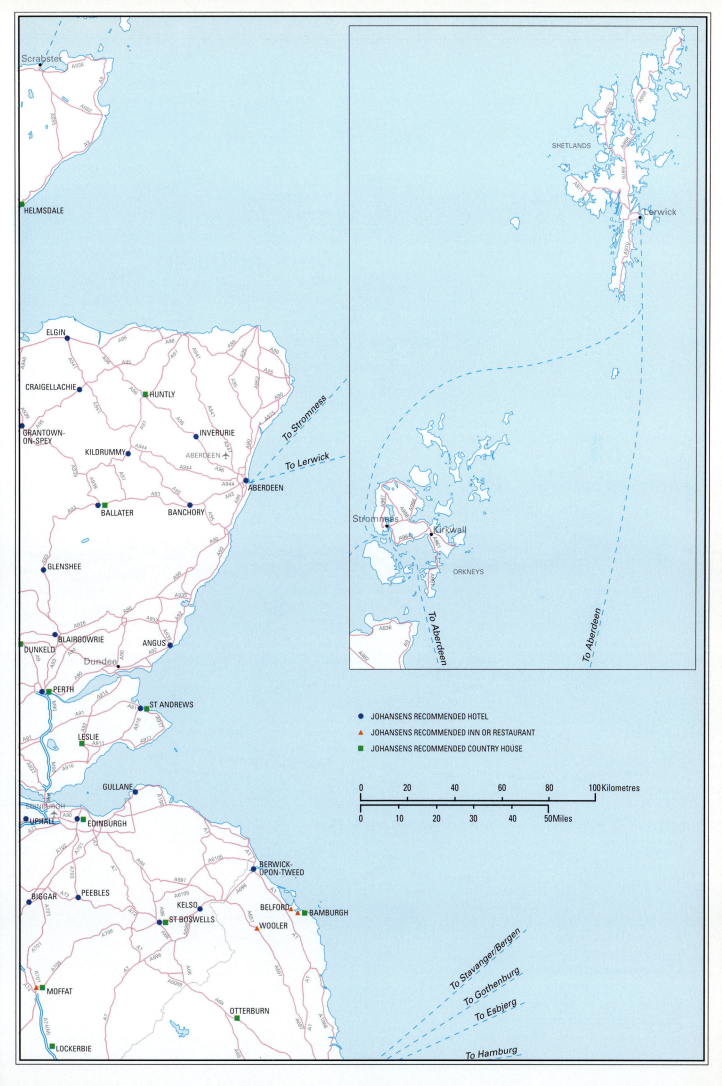

Scrabster

HELMSDALE

ELGIN
CRAIGELLACHIE
HUNTLY
INVERURIE
GRANTOWN-ON-SPEY
KILDRUMMY
ABERDEEN
BALLATER
BANCHORY
GLENSHEE
BLAIRGOWRIE
DUNKELD
ANGUS
Dundee
PERTH
ST ANDREWS
LESLIE
GULLANE
EDINBURGH
UPHALL
EDINBURGH
BERWICK-UPON-TWEED
BIGGAR
PEEBLES
KELSO
BELFORD
BAMBURGH
ST BOSWELLS
WOOLER
MOFFAT
OTTERBURN
LOCKERBIE

To Stromness
To Lerwick

SHETLANDS
Lerwick

Stromness
Kirkwall
ORKNEYS

To Aberdeen
To Aberdeen

To Stavanger/Bergen
To Gothenburg
To Esbjerg
To Hamburg

● JOHANSENS RECOMMENDED HOTEL
▲ JOHANSENS RECOMMENDED INN OR RESTAURANT
■ JOHANSENS RECOMMENDED COUNTRY HOUSE

| 0 | 20 | 40 | 60 | 80 | 100 Kilometres |

| 0 | 10 | 20 | 30 | 40 | 50 Miles |

JOHANSENS RECOMMENDED HOTEL

▲ **JOHANSENS RECOMMENDED INN OR RESTAURANT**

■ **JOHANSENS RECOMMENDED COUNTRY HOUSE**

0   20   40   60   80   100 Kilometres

0   10   20   30   40   50 Miles

Johansens Recommended Country Houses in Great Britain & Ireland

ENGLAND

Alcester (Arrow) – Arrow Mill Hotel And Restaurant, Arrow Mill Hotel And Restaurant, Arrow, Nr Alcester, Warwickshire B49 5NL. Tel: 01789 762419

Ambleside (Clappersgate) – Nanny Brow Country House Hotel & Restaurant, Nanny Brow Country House Hotel & Restaurant, Clappersgate, Ambleside, Cumbria LA22 9NF. Tel: 015394 32036

Ampleforth – Shallowdale House, Shallowdale House, Ampleforth, York, North Yorkshire YO62 4DY. Tel: 01439 788325

Appleton-Le-Moors – Appleton Hall, Appleton Hall, Appleton-Le-Moors, North Yorkshire YO6 6TF. Tel: 01751 417227

Arundel (Burpham) – Burpham Country House Hotel, Burpham Country House Hotel, Old Down, Burpham, Nr Arundel, West Sussex BN18 9RJ. Tel: 01903 882160

Atherstone – Chapel House, Chapel House, Friars' Gate, Atherstone, Warwickshire CV9 1EY. Tel: 01827 718949

Bakewell (Rowsley) – East Lodge Country House Hotel, East Lodge Country House Hotel, Rowsley, Matlock, Derbyshire DE4 2EF. Tel: 01629 734474

Bakewell (Rowsley) – The Peacock Hotel at Rowsley, The Peacock Hotel at Rowsley, Rowsley, Near Matlock, Derbyshire DE4 2EB. Tel: 01629 733518

Bamburgh – Waren House Hotel, Waren House Hotel, Waren Mill, Bamburgh, Northumberland NE70 7EE. Tel: 01668 214581

Barnstaple (Bishops Tawton) – Downrew House Hotel, Downrew House Hotel, Bishops Tawton, Barnstaple, Devon EX32 0DY. Tel: 01271 342497

Bath – Apsley House, Apsley House, 141 Newbridge Hill, Bath, Somerset BA1 3PT. Tel: 01225 336966

Bath – Bloomfield House, Bloomfield House, 146 Bloomfield Road, Bath, Somerset BA2 2AS. Tel: 01225 420105

Bath – Duke's Hotel, Duke's Hotel, Great Pulteney Street, Bath, Somerset BA2 4DN. Tel: 01225 463512

Bath – Eagle House, Eagle House, Church Street, Bathford, Somerset BA1 7RS. Tel: 01225 859946

Bath – Oldfields, Oldfields, 102 Wells Road, Bath, Somerset BA2 3AL. Tel: 01225 317984

Bath – Paradise House, Paradise House, Holloway, Bath, Somerset BA2 4PX. Tel: 01225 317723

Bath – Villa Magdala, Villa Magdala, Henrietta Road, Bath, Somerset BA2 6LX. Tel: 01225 466329

Bath (Bradford-On-Avon) – Widbrook Grange, Widbrook Grange, Trowbridge Road, Bradford-On-Avon, Wiltshire BA15 1UH. Tel: 01225 864750 / 863173

Bath (Midsomer Norton) – The Old Priory Hotel, The Old Priory Hotel, Church Square, Midsomer Norton, Somerset BA3 2HX. Tel: 01761 416784

Bath (Norton St Philip) – Bath Lodge Hotel, Bath Lodge Hotel, Norton St Philip, Bath, Somerset BA3 6NH. Tel: 01225 723040

Bath (Woolverton) – Woolverton House, Woolverton House, Woolverton, Nr Bath, Somerset BA3 6QS. Tel: 01373 830415

Belper (Shottle) – Dannah Farm Country Guest House, Dannah Farm Country Guest House, Bowman's Lane, Shottle, Nr Belper, Derbyshire DE56 2DR. Tel: 01773 550273 / 630

Beverley (Walkington) – The Manor House, The Manor House, Northlands, Walkington, East Yorkshire HU17 8RT. Tel: 01482 881645

Bibury – Bibury Court, Bibury Court, Bibury , Gloucestershire GL7 5NT. Tel: 01285 740337

Bicester (Chesterton) – Bignell Park Hotel, Bignell Park Hotel, Chesterton, Nr Bicester, OX6 8UE. Tel: 01869 241444

Bideford (Northam) – Yeoldon House Hotel, Yeoldon House Hotel, Durrant Lane, Northam, Nr Bideford, Devon EX39 2RL. Tel: 01237 474400

Biggin-By-Hartington – Biggin Hall, Biggin Hall, Biggin-By-Hartington, Buxton, Derbyshire SK17 0DH. Tel: 01298 84451

Blockley (Chipping Campden) – Lower Brook House, Lower Brook House, Blockley, Nr Moreton-In-Marsh, Gloucestershire GL56 9DS. Tel: 01386 700286

Bolton (Edgworth) – Pelton Fold Farm, Pelton Fold Farm, Bury Road, Edgworth, Bolton, Lancashire BL7 0BS. Tel: 01204 852207

Bolton (Edgworth) – Quarlton Manor Farm, Quarlton Manor Farm, Plantation Road , Edgeworth, Turton, Bolton , Lancashire BL7 0DD. Tel: 01204 852277

Bridgnorth – Cross Lane House Hotel, Cross Lane House Hotel, Cross Lane Head, Bridgnorth, Shropshire WV16 4SJ. Tel: 01746 764887

Brighton – The Granville, The Granville, 124 Kings Road, Brighton, East Sussex BN1 2FA. Tel: 01273 326302

Broadway – The Broadway Hotel, The Broadway Hotel, The Green, Broadway, Worcestershire WR12 7AA. Tel: 01386 852401

Broadway – Collin House Hotel, Collin House Hotel, Collin Lane, Broadway, Worcestershire WR12 7PB. Tel: 01386 858354

Broadway (Willersey) – The Old Rectory, The Old Rectory, Church Street, Willersey, Broadway, Gloucestershire WR12 7PN. Tel: 01386 853729

Brockenhurst – Thatched Cottage Hotel & Restaurant, Thatched Cottage Hotel & Restaurant, 16 Brookley Road, Brockenhurst, New Forest, Hampshire SO42 7RR. Tel: 01590 623090

Brockenhurst – Whitley Ridge & Country House Hotel, Whitley Ridge & Country House Hotel, Beaulieu Road, Brockenhurst, New Forest, Hampshire SO42 7QL. Tel: 01590 622354

Buttermere (Lorton Vale) – New House Farm, New House Farm, Lorton, Cockermouth, Cumbria CA13 9UU. Tel: 01900 85404

Cambridge (Melbourn) – Melbourn Bury, Melbourn Bury, Melbourn, Cambridgeshire, Nr Royston, Cambridgeshire SG8 6DE. Tel: 01763 261151

Carlisle (Crosby-On-Eden) – Crosby Lodge Country House Hotel, Crosby Lodge Country House Hotel, High Crosby, Crosby-On-Eden, Carlisle, Cumbria CA6 4QZ. Tel: 01228 573618

Cartmel – Aynsome Manor Hotel, Aynsome Manor Hotel, Cartmel, Grange-Over-Sands, Cumbria LA11 6HH. Tel: 015395 36653

Castle Cary – Bond's - Bistro with Rooms, Bond's - Bistro with Rooms, Ansford Hill, Castle Cary, Somerset BA7 7JP. Tel: 01963 350464

Chagford – Easton Court Hotel, Easton Court Hotel, Easton Cross, Chagford, Devon TQ13 8JL. Tel: 01647 433469

Chagford – Mill End Hotel, Mill End Hotel, Dartmoor National Park, Chagford, Devon TQ13 8JN. Tel: 01647 432282

Cheltenham (Charlton Kings) – Charlton Kings Hotel, Charlton Kings Hotel, Charlton Kings, Cheltenham, Gloucestershire GL52 6UU. Tel: 01242 231061

Cheltenham (Withington) – Halewell, Halewell, Halewell Close, Withington, Nr Cheltenham, Gloucestershire GL54 4BN. Tel: 01242 890238

Chester – Green Bough Hotel, Green Bough Hotel, 60 Hoole Road, Chester, Cheshire CH2 3NL. Tel: 01244 326241

Chichester (Apuldram) – Crouchers Bottom Country Hotel, Crouchers Bottom Country Hotel, Birdham Road, Apuldram, Nr Chichester, West Sussex PO20 7EH. Tel: 01243 784995

Chichester (Charlton) – Woodstock House Hotel, Woodstock House Hotel, Charlton, Nr Chichester, West Sussex PO18 0HU. Tel: 01243 811666

Chippenham – Stanton Manor, Stanton Manor, Stanton Saint Quinton, Nr Chippenham, Wiltshire SN14 6DQ. Tel: 01666 837552

Chipping Campden (Broad Campden) – The Malt House, The Malt House, Broad Campden, Gloucestershire GL55 6UU. Tel: 01386 840295

Church Stretton (Little Stretton) – Mynd House Hotel & Restaurant, Mynd House Hotel & Restaurant, Little Stretton, Church Stretton, Nr Shrewsbury, Shropshire SY6 6RB. Tel: 01694 722212

Clearwell – Tudor Farmhouse Hotel & Restaurant, Tudor Farmhouse Hotel & Restaurant, High Street, Clearwell, Nr Coleford, Gloucestershire GL16 8JS. Tel: 01594 833046

Clovelly (Horns Cross) – Foxdown Manor, Foxdown Manor, Horns Cross, Clovelly, Devon EX39 5PJ. Tel: 01237 451325

Coalville (Greenhill) – Abbots Oak, Abbots Oak, Greenhill, Coalville, Leicestershire LE67 4UY. Tel: 01530 832 328

Combe Martin (East Down) – Ashelford, Ashelford, Ashelford, East Down, Nr Barnstaple, Devon EX31 4LU. Tel: 01271 850469

Crediton (Coleford) – Coombe House Country Hotel, Coombe House Country Hotel, Coleford, Crediton, Devon EX17 5BY. Tel: 01363 84487

Dartmoor (Haytor Vale) – Bel Alp House, Bel Alp House, Haytor , Nr Bovey Tracey, Devon TQ13 9XX. Tel: 01364 661217

Diss (Fressingfield) – Chippenhall Hall, Chippenhall Hall, Fressingfield, Eye, Suffolk IP21 5TD. Tel: 01379 588180 / 586733

Diss (Starston) – Starston Hall, Starston Hall, Starston, Harleston, Norfolk IP20 9PU. Tel: 01379 854252

Doncaster – Hamilton's Restaurant & Hotel, Hamilton's Restaurant & Hotel, Carr House Road, Doncaster, South Yorkshire DN4 5HP. Tel: 01302 760770

Dorchester (Lower Bockhampton) – Yalbury Cottage Hotel, Yalbury Cottage Hotel, Lower Bockhampton, Dorchester, Dorset DT2 8PZ. Tel: 01305 262382

Dorchester-On-Thames – The George Hotel, The George Hotel, High Street, Dorchester-On-Thames, Oxford OX10 7HH. Tel: 01865 340404

Dover (Temple Ewell) – The Woodville Hall, The Woodville Hall, Temple Ewell, Dover , Kent CT16 3DJ. Tel: 01304 825256

Dover (West Cliffe) – Wallett's Court, Wallett's Court, West Cliffe, St. Margaret's-at-Cliffe, Nr Dover, Kent CT15 6EW. Tel: 01304 852424

Dulverton – Ashwick Country House Hotel, Ashwick Country House Hotel, Dulverton, Somerset TA22 9QD. Tel: 01398 323868

Enfield (London) – Oak Lodge Hotel, Oak Lodge Hotel, 80 Village Road, Bush Hill Park, Enfield, Middlesex EN1 2EU. Tel: 020 8360 7082

Epsom – Chalk Lane Hotel, Chalk Lane Hotel, Chalk Lane, Epsom, Surrey KT18 7BB. Tel: 01372 721179

Evershot – Rectory House, Rectory House, Fore Street, Evershot, Dorset DT2 0JW. Tel: 0193583 273

Evesham (Harvington) – The Mill At Harvington, The Mill At Harvington, Anchor Lane, Harvington, Evesham, Worcestershire WR11 5NR. Tel: 01386 870688

Exford (Exmoor) – The Crown Hotel, The Crown Hotel, Exford , Exmoor National Park, Somerset TA24 7PP. Tel: 01643 831554/5

Exmoor (Minehead) – The Beacon Country House Hotel, The Beacon Country House Hotel, Beacon Road, Minehead, Somerset TA24 5SD. Tel: 01643 703476

Falmouth (Mawnan Smith) – Trelawne Hotel-The Hutches Restaurant, Trelawne Hotel-The Hutches Restaurant, Mawnan Smith, Nr Falmouth, Cornwall TR11 5HS. Tel: 01326 250226

Fenny Drayton (Leicestershire) – White Wings, White Wings, Quaker Close, Fenny Drayton, Nr Nuneaton, Leicestershire CV13 6BS. Tel: 01827 716100

Gatwick (Charlwood) – Stanhill Court Hotel, Stanhill Court Hotel, Stan Hill , Charlwood, Nr Horley, Surrey RH6 0EP. Tel: 01293 862166

Golant by Fowey – The Cormorant Hotel, The Cormorant Hotel, Golant, Fowey, Cornwall PL23 1LL. Tel: 01726 833426

Grasmere (Rydal Water) – White Moss House, White Moss House, Rydal Water, Grasmere, Cumbria LA22 9SE. Tel: 015394 35295

Great Snoring – The Old Rectory, The Old Rectory, Barsham Road, Great Snoring, Norfolk NR21 0HP. Tel: 01328 820597

Hampton Court (Hampton Wick) – Chase Lodge, Chase Lodge, 10 Park Road, Hampton Wick, Kingston Upon Thames, Surrey KT1 4AS. Tel: 020 8943 1862

Hamsterley Forest (Near Durham) – Grove House, Grove House, Hamsterley Forest, Nr Bishop Auckland, Co.Durham DL13 3NL. Tel: 01388 488203

Harrogate – The White House, The White House, 10 Park Parade, Harrogate, North Yorkshire HG1 5AH. Tel: 01423 501388

Hawes (Wensleydale) – Rookhurst Country House Hotel, Rookhurst Country House Hotel, West End, Gayle, Hawes, North Yorkshire DL8 3RT. Tel: 01969 667454

Hawkshead (Near Sawrey) – Sawrey House Country Hotel, Sawrey House Country Hotel, Near Sawrey, Hawkshead, Ambleside, Cumbria LA22 OLF. Tel: 015394 36387

Helston – Nansloe Manor, Nansloe Manor, Meneage Road, Helston, Cornwall TR13 0SB. Tel: 01326 574691

Hereford (Fownhope) – The Bowens Country House, The Bowens Country House, Fownhope, Herefordshire HR1 4PS. Tel: 01432 860430

Hereford (Ullingswick) – The Steppes, The Steppes, Ullingswick, Nr Hereford, Herefordshire HR1 3JG. Tel: 01432 820424

Holt (Felbrigg) – Felbrigg Lodge, Felbrigg Lodge, Aylmerton, Norfolk NR11 8RA. Tel: 01263 837588

Ilminster (Cricket Malherbie) – The Old Rectory, The Old Rectory, Cricket Malherbie, Ilminster, Somerset TA19 0PW. Tel: 01460 54364

Ilsington (Dartmoor) – Ilsington Country Hotel, Ilsington Country Hotel, Ilsington, Newton Abbot, Devon TQ13 9RR. Tel: 01364 661452

Isle of Wight (Shanklin) – Rylstone Manor, Rylstone Manor, Rylstone Gardens, Shanklin, Isle of Wight PO37 6RG. Tel: 01983 862806

Keswick (LakeThirlmere) – Dale Head Hall Lakeside Hotel, Dale Head Hall Lakeside Hotel, Thirlmere, Keswick, Cumbria CA12 4TN. Tel: 017687 72478

Keswick (Newlands) – Swinside Lodge Hotel, Swinside Lodge Hotel, Grange Road, Newlands, Keswick, Cumbria CA12 5UE. Tel: 017687 72948

Kirkby Lonsdale – Hipping Hall, Hipping Hall, Cowan Bridge, Kirkby Lonsdale, Cumbria LA6 2JJ. Tel: 015242 71187

Lavenham – Lavenham Priory, Lavenham Priory, Water Street, Lavenham, Sudbury, Suffolk CO10 9RW. Tel: 01787 247404

Leominster – Lower Bache House, Lower Bache House, Kimbolton, Nr Leominster, Herefordshire HR6 0ER. Tel: 01568 750304

Lifton (Sprytown) – The Thatched Cottage Country Hotel And Restaurant, The Thatched Cottage Country Hotel And Restaurant, Sprytown, Lifton, Devon PL16 0AY. Tel: 01566 784224

Lincoln (Washingborough) – Washingborough Hall, Washingborough Hall, Church Hill, Washingborough, Lincoln, Lincolnshire LN4 1BE. Tel: 01522 790340

Looe (Widegates) – Coombe Farm, Coombe Farm, Widegates, Looe, Cornwall PL13 1QN. Tel: 01503 240223

Lorton – Winder Hall, Winder Hall, Low Lorton, Nr Cockermouth, Cumbria CA13 9UP. Tel: 01900 85107

Loughborough – The Old Manor Hotel, The Old Manor Hotel, 11-14 Sparrow Hill, Loughborough, Leicestershire LE11 1BT. Tel: 01509 211228

Ludlow (Diddlebury) – Delbury Hall, Delbury Hall, Diddlebury, Craven Arms, Shropshire SY7 9DH. Tel: 01584 841267

Ludlow (Overton) – Overton Grange Hotel, Overton Grange Hotel, Overton, Ludlow, Shropshire SY8 4AD. Tel: 01584 873500

Luton (Little Offley) – Little Offley, Little Offley, Hitchin, Hertfordshire SG5 3BU. Tel: 01462 768243

Lydford (Vale Down) – Moor View House, Moor View House, Vale Down, Lydford, Devon EX20 4BB. Tel: 01822 820220

Lyme Regis (Charmouth) – Thatch Lodge Hotel, Thatch Lodge Hotel, The Street, Charmouth, Nr Lyme Regis, Dorset DT6 6PQ. Tel: 01297 560407

Lymington – Rosefield House, Rosefield House, Sway Road, Lymington, New Forest, Hampshire SO41 8LR. Tel: 01590 671526

Lymington (Hordle) – Hotel Gordleton Mill, Hotel Gordleton Mill, Silver Street, Hordle, Nr Lymington, Hampshire SO41 6DJ. Tel: 01590 682219

Lynton – Hewitt's Hotel, Hewitt's Hotel, North Walk, Lynton, Devon EX35 6HJ. Tel: 01598 752293

Maidstone (Boughton Monchelsea) – Tanyard, Tanyard, Wierton Hill, Boughton Monchelsea, Nr Maidstone, Kent ME17 4JT. Tel: 01622 744705

Malton – Newstead Grange, Newstead Grange, Norton-On-Derwent, Malton, North Yorkshire YO17 9PJ. Tel: 01653 692502

Maxey (Nr Stamford) – Abbey House & Coach House, Abbey House & Coach House, West End Road, Maxey, Cambridge PE6 9EJ. Tel: 01778 344642

Middlecombe (Minehead) – Periton Park Hotel, Periton Park Hotel, Middlecombe, Nr Minehead, Somerset TA24 8SN. Tel: 01643 706885

Middleham (Wensleydale) – Millers House Hotel, Millers House Hotel, Middleham, Wensleydale, North Yorkshire DL8 4NR. Tel: 01969 622630

Middleham (Wensleydale) – Waterford House, Waterford House, 19 Kirkgate, Middleham, North Yorkshire DL8 4PG. Tel: 01969 622090

Minchinhampton – Burleigh Court, Burleigh Court, Minchinhampton, Gloucestershire GL5 2PF. Tel: 01453 883804

Morchard Bishop – Wigham, Wigham, Morchard Bishop, Crediton, Devon EX17 6RJ. Tel: 01363 877350

New Romney (Littlestone) – Romney Bay House, Romney Bay House, Coast Road, Littlestone, New Romney, Kent TN28 8QY. Tel: 01797 364747

North Walsham – Beechwood Hotel, Beechwood Hotel, Cromer Road, North Walsham, Norfolk NR28 0HD. Tel: 01692 403231

Norwich – The Beeches Hotel & Victorian Gardens, The Beeches Hotel & Victorian Gardens, 2-6 Earlham Road, Norwich, Norfolk NR2 3DB. Tel: 01603 621167

Norwich (Coltishall) – Norfolk Mead Hotel, Norfolk Mead Hotel, Coltishall, Norwich, Norfolk NR12 7DN. Tel: 01603 737531

Norwich (Drayton) – The Stower Grange, The Stower Grange, School Road, Drayton, Norfolk NR8 6EF. Tel: 01603 860210

Norwich (Old Catton) – Catton Old Hall, Catton Old Hall, Lodge Lane, Catton, Norwich, Norfolk NR6 7HG. Tel: 01603 419379

Norwich (Thorpe St Andrew) – The Old Rectory, The Old Rectory, 103 Yarmouth Road, Thorpe St Andrew, Norwich, Norfolk NR7 0HF. Tel: 01603 700772

Nottingham – Cockliffe Country House Hotel, Cockliffe Country House Hotel, Nottingham, Nottinghamshire NG5 8PQ. Tel: 01159 680179

Nottingham (Langar) – Langar Hall, Langar Hall, Langar, Nottinghamshire NG13 9HG. Tel: 01949 860559

Nottingham (Redmile) – L'Auberge, L'Auberge, 29 Main Street, Redmile, Nottinghamshire NG13 0GA. Tel: 01949 843086

Nottingham (Ruddington) – The Cottage Country House Hotel, The Cottage Country House Hotel, Easthorpe Street, Ruddington, Nottingham, Nottinghamshire NG11 6LA. Tel: 01159 846882

Ockham – The Hautboy, The Hautboy, Ockham Lane, Ockham, Surrey GU23 6. Tel: 01483 225355

Oswestry – Pen-y-Dyffryn Country Hotel, Pen-y-Dyffryn Country Hotel, Rhydycroesau, Nr Oswestry, Shropshire SY10 7JD. Tel: 01691 653700

Otterburn – The Tower, The Tower, Otterburn, Northumberland NE19 1NS. Tel: 01830 520620

Owlpen – Owlpen Manor, Owlpen Manor, Near Uley, Gloucestershire GL11 5BZ. Tel: 01453 860261

Oxford (Kingston Bagpuize) – Fallowfields, Fallowfields, Kingston Bagpuize With Southmoor, Oxfordshire OX13 5BH. Tel: 01865 820416

Padstow – Cross House Hotel, Cross House Hotel, Church Street, Padstow, Cornwall PL28 8BG. Tel: 01841 532391

Penrith (Temple Sowerby) – Temple Sowerby House Hotel, Temple Sowerby House Hotel, Temple Sowerby, Penrith, Cumbria CA10 1RZ. Tel: 017683 61578

Penzance – The Summer House, The Summer House, Cornwall Terrace, Penzance, Cornwall TR18 4HL. Tel: 01736 363744

Petersfield (Langrish) – Langrish House, Langrish House, Langrish, Nr Petersfield, Hampshire GU32 1RN. Tel: 01730 266941

Petworth – The Old Railway Station, The Old Railway Station, Coultershaw Bridge, Petworth, West Sussex GU28 0JF. Tel: 01798 342346

Porlock Weir – The Cottage Hotel, The Cottage Hotel, Porlock Weir, Porlock, Somerset TA24 8PB. Tel: 01643 863300

Porlock Weir – Porlock Vale House, Porlock Vale House, Porlock Weir, Somerset TA24 8NY. Tel: 01643 862338

Porthleven (Nr Helston) – Tye Rock Country House Hotel, Tye Rock Country House Hotel, Loe Bar Road, Porthleven, Nr Helston, Cornwall TR13 9EW. Tel: 01326 572695

Portsmouth – The Beaufort Hotel, The Beaufort Hotel, 71 Festing Road, Portsmouth, Hampshire PO4 0NQ. Tel: 023 92823707

Preston (Gardstang) – Pickering Park Country House, Pickering Park Country House, Gardstang Road, Catterall, Gardstang, Lancashire PR3 0HD. Tel: 01995 600999

Pulborough – Chequers Hotel, Chequers Hotel, Church Place, Pulborough, West Sussex RH20 1AD. Tel: 01798 872486

Ringwood – Moortown Lodge, Moortown Lodge, 244 Christchurch Road, Ringwood, Hampshire BH24 3AS. Tel: 01425 471404

Ross-On-Wye (Glewstone) – Glewstone Court, Glewstone Court, Nr Ross-On-Wye, Herefordshire HR9 6AW. Tel: 01989 770367

Rye – White Vine House, White Vine House, High Street, Rye, East Sussex TN31 7JF. Tel: 01797 224748

Saham Toney (Thetford) – Broom Hall, Broom Hall, Richmond Road, Saham Toney, Thetford, Norfolk IP25 7EX. Tel: 01953 882125

Saunton – Preston House Hotel, Preston House Hotel, Saunton, Braunton, Devon EX33 1LG. Tel: 01271 890472

Seavington St Mary, Nr Ilminster – The Pheasant Hotel, The Pheasant Hotel, Seavington St Mary, Nr Ilminster, Somerset TA19 0HQ. Tel: 01460 240502

Sherborne – The Eastbury Hotel, The Eastbury Hotel, Long Street, Sherborne, Dorset DT9 3BY. Tel: 01935 813131

Shipton-Under-Wychwood – The Shaven Crown Hotel, The Shaven Crown Hotel, High Street, Shipton-Under-Wychwood, Oxfordshire OX7 6BA. Tel: 01993 830330

Shrewsbury – Upper Brompton Farm, Upper Brompton Farm, Cross houses, Shrewsbury, Shropshire SY5 6LE. Tel: 01743 761629

Simonsbath (Exmoor) – Simonsbath House Hotel, Simonsbath House Hotel, Simonsbath, Exmoor, Somerset TA24 7SH. Tel: 01643 831259

Snape (Butley) – Butley Priory, Butley Priory, Nr Woodbridge, Suffolk IP12 3NR. Tel: 01394 450046

St Ives (Trink) – The Countryman At Trink Hotel, The Countryman At Trink Hotel, Old Coach Road, St Ives, Cornwall TR26 3JQ. Tel: 01736 797571

St Mawes (Ruan Highlanes) – The Hundred House Hotel, The Hundred House Hotel, Ruan Highlanes, Truro, Cornwall TR2 5JR. Tel: 01872 501336

Stanhope (Weardale) – Horsley Hall, Horsley Hall, East Gate, Nr Stanhope, Bishop Auckland, Co.Durham DL13 2LJ. Tel: 01388 517239

Stanwell (Nr Heathrow) – Stanwell Hall, Stanwell Hall, Town Lane, Stanwell, Nr Staines, Middlesex TW19 7PW. Tel: 01784 252292

Staverton (Nr Totnes) – Kingston House, Kingston House, Staverton, Totnes, Devon TQ9 6AR. Tel: 01803 762 235

Stevenage (Hitchin) – Redcoats Farmhouse Hotel & Restaurant, Redcoats Farmhouse Hotel & Restaurant, Redcoats Green, Nr Hitchin, Hertfordshire SG4 7JR. Tel: 01438 729500

Stonor (Henley-on-Thames) – The Stonor Arms Hotel, The Stonor Arms Hotel, Stonor, Nr Henley-on-Thames, Oxfordshire RG9 6HE. Tel: 01491 638866

Stow-on-the-Wold – The Unicorn Hotel, The Unicorn Hotel, Sheep Street, Stow-on-the-Wold, Gloucestershire GL54 1HQ. Tel: 01451 830257

Stow-On-The-Wold (Kingham) – The Tollgate Inn, The Tollgate Inn, Church Street, Kingham, Oxfordshire OX7 6YA . Tel: 01608 658389

Stratford-upon-Avon (Loxley) – Glebe Farm House, Glebe Farm House, Loxley, Warwickshire CV35 9JW. Tel: 01789 842501

Sway – The Nurse's Cottage, The Nurse's Cottage, Station Road, Sway, Lymington, Hampshire SO41 6BA. Tel: 01590 683402

Tarporley (Willington) – Willington Hall Hotel, Willington Hall Hotel, Willington, Near Tarporley, Cheshire CW6 0NB. Tel: 01829 752321

Tewkesbury (Kemerton) – Upper Court, Upper Court, Kemerton, Tewkesbury, Gloucestershire GL20 7HY. Tel: 01386 725351

Thurlestone Sands (Nr Salcombe) – Heron House Hotel, Heron House Hotel, Thurlestone Sands, Nr Salcombe, South Devon TQ7 3JY. Tel: 01548 561308

Tintagel (Trenale) – Trebrea Lodge, Trebrea Lodge, Trenale, Tintagel , Cornwall PL34 0HR. Tel: 01840 770410

Uckfield – Hooke Hall, Hooke Hall, High Street, Uckfield, East Sussex TN22 1EN. Tel: 01825 761578

Wadebridge (Washaway) – Trehellas House & Memories of Malaya Restaurant, Trehellas House & Memories of Malaya Restaurant, Washaway, Bodmin, Cornwall PL30 3AD. Tel: 01208 72700

Wareham (East Stoke) – Kemps Country House Hotel & Restaurant, Kemps Country House Hotel & Restaurant, East Stoke, Wareham, Dorset BH20 6AL. Tel: 01929 462563

Warwick (Claverdon) – The Ardencote Manor Hotel & Country Club, The Ardencote Manor Hotel & Country Club, Lye Green Road, Claverdon, Warwickshire CV35 8LS. Tel: 01926 843111

Wells – Beryl, Beryl, Wells, Somerset BA5 3JP. Tel: 01749 678738

Wells – Glencot House, Glencot House, Glencot Lane, Wookey Hole, Nr Wells, Somerset BA5 1BH. Tel: 01749 677160

Wells (Coxley) – Coxley Vineyard, Coxley Vineyard, Coxley, Wells, Somerset BA5 1RQ. Tel: 01749 670285

Wem – Soulton Hall, Soulton Hall, Near Wem, Shropshire SY4 5RS. Tel: 01939 232786

Wimborne Minster – Beechleas, Beechleas, 17 Poole Road, Wimborne Minster, Dorset BH21 1QA. Tel: 01202 841684

Wincanton (Holbrook) – Holbrook House Hotel, Holbrook House Hotel, Wincanton, Somerset BA9 8BS. Tel: 01963 32377

Windermere – Quarry Garth Country House Hotel, Quarry Garth Country House Hotel, Windermere, Lake District, Cumbria LA23 1LF. Tel: 015394 88282

Windermere (Bowness) – Fayrer Garden House Hotel, Fayrer Garden House Hotel, Lyth Valley Road, Bowness-On - Windermere, Cumbria LA23 3JP. Tel: 015394 88195

Witherslack – The Old Vicarage Country House Hotel, The Old Vicarage Country House Hotel, Church Road, Witherslack, Grange-Over-Sands, Cumbria LA11 6RS. Tel: 015395 52381

Woodbridge – Wood Hall Country House Hotel, Wood Hall Country House Hotel, Shottisham, Woodbridge, Suffolk IP12 3EG. Tel: 01394 411283

York (Escrick) – The Parsonage Country House Hotel, The Parsonage Country House Hotel, Escrick, York, North Yorkshire YO19 6LF. Tel: 01904 728111

Yoxford – Hope House, Hope House, High Street, Yoxford, Saxmundham, Suffolk IP17 3HP. Tel: 01728 668281

WALES

Aberdovey – Plas Penhelig Country House Hotel, Plas Penhelig Country House Hotel, Aberdovey, Gwynedd LL35 0NA. Tel: 01654 767676

Abergavenny (Glangrwyney) – Glangrwyney Court, Glangrwyney Court, Glangrwyney, Nr Crickhowell, Powys NP8 1ES. Tel: 01873 811288

Abergavenny (Govilon) – Llanwenarth House, Llanwenarth House, Govilon, Abergavenny, Monmouthshire NP7 9SF. Tel: 01873 830289

Anglesey (Llangefni) – Tre-Ysgawen Hall, Tre-Ysgawen Hall, Capel Coch, Llangefni, Ynys Yuon LL77 7UR. Tel: 01248 750750

Betws-y-Coed – Tan-y-Foel, Tan-y-Foel, Capel Garmon, Nr Betws-y-Coed, Conwy LL26 0RE. Tel: 01690 710507

Brecon (Three Cocks) – Old Gwernyfed Country Manor, Old Gwernyfed Country Manor, Felindre, Three Cocks, Brecon, Powys LD3 0SU. Tel: 01497 847376

Caernarfon – Ty'n Rhos Country Hotel, Ty'n Rhos Country Hotel, Seion Llanddeiniolen, Caernarfon, Gwynedd LL55 3AE. Tel: 01248 670489

Conwy – The Old Rectory, The Old Rectory, Llanrwst Road, Llansanffried Glan Conwy, Colwyn Bay, Conwy LL28 5LF. Tel: 01492 580611

Dolgellau (Ganllwyd) – Plas Dolmelynllyn, Plas Dolmelynllyn, Ganllwyd, Dolgellau, Gwynedd LL40 2HP. Tel: 01341 440273

Fishguard (Welsh Hook) – Stone Hall, Stone Hall, Welsh Hook, Haverfordwest, Pembrokeshire, Dyfed SA62 5NS. Tel: 01348 840212

Monmouth (Whitebrook) – The Crown At Whitebrook, The Crown At Whitebrook, Restaurant With Rooms, Whitebrook, Monmouth, Monmouthshire NP5 4TX. Tel: 01600 860254

Pwllheli – Plas Bodegroes, Plas Bodegroes, Nefyn Road, Pwllheli, Gwynedd LL53 5TH. Tel: 01758 612363

Swansea (Mumbles) – Norton House Hotel & Restaurant, Norton House Hotel & Restaurant, Norton Road, Mumbles, Swansea, West Glamorgan SA3 5TQ. Tel: 01792 404891

Tenby (Waterwynch Bay) – Waterwynch House Hotel, Waterwynch House Hotel, Waterwynch Bay, Tenby, Pembrokeshire SA70 8JT. Tel: 01834 842464

Tintern – Parva Farmhouse and Restaurant, Parva Farmhouse and Restaurant, Tintern, Chepstow, Monmouthshire NP16 6SQ. Tel: 01291 689411

SCOTLAND

Ballater, Royal Deeside – Balgonie Country House, Balgonie Country House, Braemar Place, Royal Deeside, Ballater, Aberdeenshire AB35 5NQ. Tel: 013397 55482

By Huntly (Bridge of Marnoch) – The Old Manse of Marnoch, The Old Manse of Marnoch, Bridge of Marnoch, By Huntly, Aberdeenshire AB54 7RS. Tel: 01466 780873

Castle Douglas – Longacre Manor, Longacre Manor, Ernespie Road, Castle Douglas, Dumfries & Galloway DG7 1LE. Tel: 01556 503576

Comrie (Perthshire) – The Royal Hotel, The Royal Hotel, Melville Square, Comrie, Perthshire PH6 2DN. Tel: 01764 679200

Dunfries (Thornhill) – Trigony House Hotel, Trigony House Hotel, Closeburn, Thornhill, Dunfriesshire DG3 5EZ. Tel: 01848 331211

Dunkeld – The Pend, The Pend, 5 Brae Street, Dunkeld, Perthshire PH8 0BA. Tel: 01350 727586

Edinburgh (Dunfermline) – Garvock House Hotel, Garvock House Hotel, St. Johns Drive, Transy, Dunfermline, Fife KY12 7TU. Tel: 01383 621067

Fintry (Stirlingshire) – Culcreuch Castle Hotel & Country Park, Culcreuch Castle Hotel & Country Park, Fintry, Loch Lomond, Stirling & Trossachs G63 0LW. Tel: 01360 860555

Glasgow – Nairns, Nairns, 13 Woodside Crescent, Glasgow, G3 7UP. Tel: 0141 353 0707

Glen Cannich (By Beauly) – Mullardoch House Hotel, Mullardoch House Hotel, Glen Cannich, By Beauly, Inverness-shire IV4 7LX. Tel: 01456 415460

Helmsdale (Sutherland) – Navidale House Hotel, Navidale House Hotel, Helmsdale, Sutherland KW8 6JS. Tel: 01431 821 258

Inverness – Culduthel Lodge, Culduthel Lodge, 14 Culduthel Road, Inverness, Inverness-shire IV2 4AG. Tel: 01463 240089

Inverness – Maple Court & Chandlery Restaurant, Maple Court & Chandlery Restaurant, No12 Ness Walk, Inverness, Inverness-shire IV3 5SQ. Tel: 01463 230330

Isle Of Harris – Ardvourlie Castle, Ardvourlie Castle, Aird A Mhulaidh, Isle Of Harris, Western Isles HS3 3AB. Tel: 01859 502307

Isle Of Mull – Killiechronan, Killiechronan, Killiechronan, Isle Of Mull, Argyllshire PA72 6JU. Tel: 01680 300403

Isle of Mull (Tobermory) – Highland Cottage, Highland Cottage, Breadalbane Street, Tobermory, Isle of Mull, Argyll PA75 6PD. Tel: 01688 302030

Isle of Skye (Portree) – Bosville Hotel & Chandlery Seafood Restaurant, Bosville Hotel & Chandlery Seafood Restaurant, Bosville Terrace, Portree, Isle of Skye IV51 9DG. Tel: 01478 612846

Kentallen Of Appin – Ardsheal House, Ardsheal House, Kentallen Of Appin, Argyll PA38 4BX. Tel: 01631 740227

Killiecrankie, By Pitlochry – The Killiecrankie Hotel, The Killiecrankie Hotel, Killiecrankie, By Pitlochry, Perthshire PH16 5LG. Tel: 01796 473220

Kinlochbervie – The Kinlochbervie Hotel, The Kinlochbervie Hotel, Kinlochbervie, By Lairg, Sutherland IV27 4RP. Tel: 01971 521275

Leslie (Fife) – Balgeddie House Hotel, Balgeddie House Hotel, Balgeddie Way, Glenrothes, Fife KY6 3ET. Tel: 01592 742511

Loch Ness (Drumnadrochit) – Polmaily House Hotel, Polmaily House Hotel, Drumnadrochit, Loch Ness, Inverness-shire IV3 6XT. Tel: 01456 450343

Lockerbie – The Dryfesdale Hotel, The Dryfesdale Hotel, Lockerbie, Dumfriesshire DG11 2SF. Tel: 01576 202427

Maybole (Ayrshire) – Culzean Castle, Culzean Castle, Maybole, Ayrshire KA19 8LE. Tel: 01655 760274

Moffat – Well View Hotel, Well View Hotel, Ballplay Road, Moffat, Dumfriesshire DG10 9JU. Tel: 01683 220184

Nairn (Auldearn) – Boath House, Boath House, Auldearn, Nairn, Inverness IV12 5TE. Tel: 01667 454896

Oban – Dungallan House Hotel, Dungallan House Hotel, Gallanach Road, Oban, Argyllshire PA34 4PD. Tel: 01631 563799

Oban – The Manor House Hotel, The Manor House Hotel, Gallanch Road, Oban, Argyllshire PA34 4LS. Tel: 01631 562087

Pitlochry – Knockendarroch House, Knockendarroch House, Higher Oakfield, Pitlochry, Perthshire PH16 5HT. Tel: 01796 473473

Port Of Menteith – The Lake Hotel, The Lake Hotel, Port Of Menteith, Perthshire FK8 3RA. Tel: 01877 385258

Rothiemurchus (Highland) – Corrour House Hotel, Corrour House Hotel, Inverdruie, Aviemore, Inverness-shire PH22 1QH. Tel: 01479 810220

St. Andrews – The Argyle House Hotel, The Argyle House Hotel, 127 Norton Street, St. Andrews, KY16 9AG. Tel: 01334 473387

St. Boswell By Melrose – Clint Lodge, Clint Lodge, St. Boswells, Melrose, Roxburgshire TD6 0DZ. Tel: 01835 822027

St Fillans (Perthshire) – The Four Seasons Hotel, The Four Seasons Hotel, St Fillans , Perthshire PH6 2NF. Tel: 01764 685333

Strathtummel (By Pitlochry) – Queen's View Hotel, Queen's View Hotel, Strathtummel, By Pitlochry, Perthshire PH16 5NR. Tel: 01796 473291

Tain (Ross-shire) – Glenmorangie House at Cadbol, Glenmorangie House at Cadbol, Cadbol, Fearn, By Tain, IV20 1XP. Tel: 01862 871671

The Great Glen (Fort William) – Corriegour Lodge Hotel, Corriegour Lodge Hotel, Loch Lochy, By Spean Bridge, Inverness-shire PH34 4EB. Tel: 01397 712685

IRELAND

Caragh Lake Co Kerry – Caragh Lodge, Caragh Lodge, Caragh Lake, Co Kerry. Tel: 00 353 66 9769115

Cashel Co Tipperary – Cashel Palace Hotel, Cashel Palace Hotel, Cashel, Co Tipperary. Tel: 00 353 62 62707

Connemara (Co Galway) – Ross Lake House Hotel, Ross Lake House Hotel, Rosscahill, Oughterard, Co Galway. Tel: 00 353 91 550109

Craughwell (Co.Galway) – St. Clerans, St. Clerans, Craughwell, Co.Galway. Tel: 00 353 91 846 555

Dublin – Aberdeen Lodge, Aberdeen Lodge, 53-55 Park Avenue, Ailesbury Road, Dublin 4. Tel: 00 353 1 2838155

Dublin – Fitzwilliam Park, Fitzwilliam Park, No5 Fitzwilliam Square, Dublin 2. Tel: 00 353 1 6628 280

Kilkee Co Clare – Halpins Hotel & Vittles Restaurant, Halpins Hotel & Vittles Restaurant, Erin Street, Kilkee, Co Clare. Tel: 00 353 65 9056032

Killarney Co Kerry – Earls Court House, Earls Court House, Woodlawn Junction, Muckross Road, Co Kerry. Tel: 00 353 64 34009

Kilmeaden (Co. Waterford) – The Old Rectory - Kilmeaden House, The Old Rectory - Kilmeaden House, Kilmeaden, Co Waterford. Tel: 00 353 51 384254

Letterkenny (Co Donegal) – Castle Grove Country House, Castle Grove Country House, Ramelton Road, Letterkenny, Co Donegal. Tel: 00 353 745 1118

Riverstown, Co Sligo – Coopershill House, Coopershill House, Riverstown, Co Sligo. Tel: 00 353 71 65108

Sligo, Co Sligo – Markree Castle, Markree Castle, Colooney, Co Sligo. Tel: 00 353 71 67800

Wicklow, Co Wicklow – The Old Rectory, The Old Rectory, Wicklow Town, Co Wicklow. Tel: 00 353 404 67048

CHANNEL ISLANDS

Guernsey (Fermain Bay) – La Favorita Hotel, La Favorita Hotel, Fermain Bay, Guernsey GY4 6SD. Tel: 01481 35666

Guernsey (St Martin) – Bella Luce Hotel & Restaurant, Bella Luce Hotel & Restaurant, La Fosse, St Martin, Guernsey, GY4 6EB. Tel: 01481 38764

Herm Island (Guernsey) – The White House, The White House, Herm Island, Guernsey, GY1 3HR. Tel: 01481 722159

Jersey (St Aubin) – Hotel La Tour, Hotel La Tour, Rue de Croquet, St Aubin, Jersey, JE3 8BR. Tel: 01534 743770

Sark Island (Guernsey) – La Sablonnerie, La Sablonnerie, Little Sark, Sark Island, Guernsey. Tel: 01481 832061

MARSH
An *MMC* Company

Marsh, the world's leading insurance broker,
is proud to be the appointed Preferred Insurance Provider
to Johansens Members Worldwide

ARE YOU A HOTELIER?

There is never a spare moment when you're running a Hotel, Inn, Restaurant or Country House. If you're not with a customer, your mind is on stocktaking. Sound familiar?

At Marsh, we realise you have little time to worry about your insurance policy, instead, you require peace of mind that you are covered.

That is why for over 20 years Marsh have been providing better cover for businesses like yours.

Our unique services are developed specifically for establishments meeting the high standards required for entry in a Johansens guide.

CONTACT US NOW FOR DETAILS OF THE INSURANCE POLICY FOR JOHANSENS
01892 553160 (UK)

ARE YOU AN INDEPENDENT TRAVELLER?

Insurance is probably the last thing on your mind. Especially when you are going on holiday or on a business trip. But are you protected when travelling? Is your home protected while you are away?

Marsh offer a wide range of insurances that gives you peace of mind when travelling.

FOR DETAILS ON THESE SERVICES RING (UK):

TRAVEL	**01462 428041**
PENSIONS & FINANCIAL SERVICES	**0171 357 3307**
HOUSEHOLD	**01462 428200**
MOTOR	**01462 428100**
HEALTHCARE	**01462 428000**

Insurance Policy for Johansens members arranged by:
Marsh UK Ltd.
Mount Pleasant House,
Lonsdale Gardens,
Tunbridge Wells, Kent TN1 1NY

To enable you to use your 2000 Johansens Recommended Traditional Inns, Hotels & Restaurants Guide more effectively, the following four pages of indexes contain a wealth of useful information about the establishments featured in the Guide. As well as listing them alphabetically, by region and by county, the indexes also show at a glance which properties offer certain specialised facilities. The indexes are listed as follows:

- Alphabetically by region
- By county
- With a swimming pool
- With fishing nearby
- With shooting nearby
- With golf nearby
- With conference facilities for 100 delegates or more
- Double rooms for £55 or under
- Johansens Preferred Partners

Johansens Recommended Traditional Inns, Hotels & Restaurants listed alphabetically by region

What does your paper say about you?

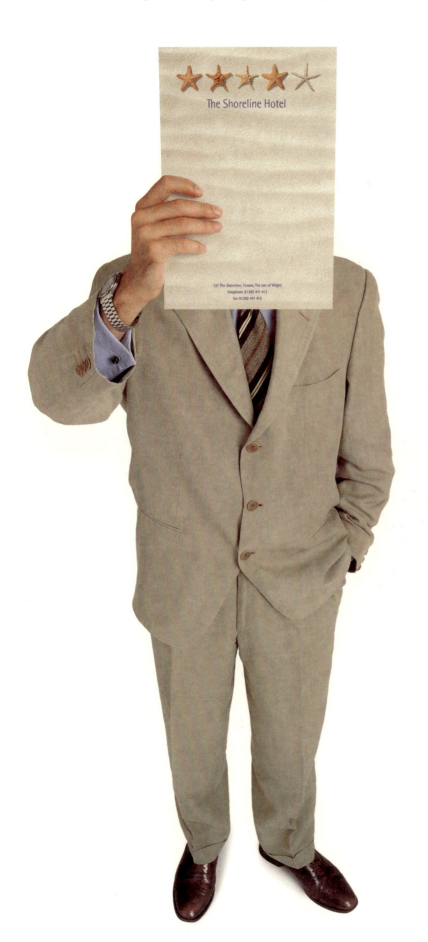

Jeremy Hoskins, hotelier, chooses Conqueror* Contour in Oyster, printed in colour.

Starring role. Jeremy Hoskins combed the Conqueror* range to discover the perfect texture for his hotel's letterhead. Ideal for brochures, menus, wine-lists and letterheads, as well as for all corporate and conference stationery, the colours, textures and weights of the Conqueror* range are the best in the business. For a free sample pack or advice on the Conqueror* range and where to find it, call + 44 (0) 1256 728665 or visit www.conqueror.com now. You'll get five stars for presentation.

 Star quality. For a free sample pack or advice on the Conqueror* range and where to find it, call + 44 (0) 1256 728665 or visit www.conqueror.com now.

With a swimming pool

With fishing nearby

With shooting nearby

With golf nearby

With conference facilities for 100 delegates or more

With double rooms for £55 per night or under

Johansens Preferred Partners

ORDER FORM

Call our 24hr credit card hotline FREEPHONE 0800 269 397.

Simply indicate which title(s) you require by putting the quantity in the boxes provided. Choose your preferred method of payment and mail to Johansens, FREEPOST (CB 264), 43 Millharbour, London E14 9BR, England (no stamp needed). Your FREE gifts will automatically be dispatched with your order. Fax orders welcome on 0171 537 3594

CHOOSE FROM 7 SPECIAL GUIDE COLLECTIONS – SAVE UP TO £56

TITLE	Normal Price	PRICE	SAVE	QTY	TOTAL
OFFER ONE					
3 Johansens Guides A+B+C	£42.85	£36.00	£6.85		
OFFER TWO					
4 Johansens Guides A+B+C+G	£58.80	£46.00	£12.80		
OFFER THREE					
5 Johansens Guides A+B+C+G+K **PLUS** Southern Africa Guide **FREE**	£71.75	£56.00	£15.75		
OFFER FOUR - The Executive Collection					
Business Meeting Venues Guide & CD-ROM M+R	£40.00	£30.00	£10.00		
OFFER FIVE - The Holiday Pack					
3 Johansens Guides D+E+F	£18.93	£9.99	£8.94		
OFFER SIX - The Digital Collection					
3 Johansens CD-ROMs N+O+P **PLUS** Southern Africa CD-ROM Q **FREE**	£69.85	£59.85	£10.00		
OFFER SEVEN - The Chairman's Collection					
Business Meeting Venues Guide & CD-ROMs M+R **PLUS** 5 Johansens Boxed Guides A+B+C+G+K, **PLUS** 3 CD-ROMs N+O+P **PLUS** Southern Africa Guide/CD ROM Q **FREE**, **PLUS** Mystery Gift **FREE**	£200.53	£149.00	£56.53		
Privilege Card PLUS The Millennium Guide		**FREE**			
1 Presentation box for offers 1, 2 and 3		£5.00	£20.00		
			TOTAL 1		

JOHANSENS PRINTED GUIDES 2000

CODE	TITLE	PRICE	QTY	TOTAL
A	Recommended Hotels – Great Britain & Ireland 2000	£19.95		
B	Recommended Country Houses & Small Hotels – Great Britain & Ireland 2000	£11.95		
C	Recommended Traditional Inns, Hotels & Restaurants – Great Britain 2000	£10.95		
NEW D	Recommended Holiday Cottages – Great Britain & Ireland 2000	£4.99		
E	Historic Houses, Castles & Gardens 2000	£4.99		
F	Museums & Galleries 2000	£8.95		
G	Recommended Hotels – Europe & The Mediterranean 2000	£15.95		
NEW H	Recommended Hotels – Europe & The Mediterranean 2000 (French Language)	£15.95		
NEW J	Recommended Hotels – Europe & The Mediterranean 2000 (German Language)	£15.95		
K	Recommended Hotels & Inns – North America, Bermuda & The Caribbean 2000	£12.95		
NEW L	Recommended Hotels & Game Lodges – Southern Africa, Mauritius & The Seychelles 2000	£9.95		
M	Recommended Business Meeting Venues 2000	£20.00		

JOHANSENS CD ROMs DIGITAL COLLECTION 2000

CODE	TITLE	PRICE	QTY	TOTAL
N	The Guide 2000 – Great Britain & Ireland	£29.95		
O	The Guide 2000 – Europe & The Mediterranean (English, French, German Language)	£22.95		
P	The Guide 2000 – North America, Bermuda & The Caribbean	£16.95		
NEW Q	The Guide 2000 – Southern Africa, Mauritius & The Seychelles	£16.95		
R	Business Meeting Venues 2000	£20.00		
S	Privilege Card 2000 (Free with your order. Additional Cards £20 each)	£20.00		

Postage & Packing (UK) £4.50 or £2.50 for single order and CD-ROMs

Outside UK add £5 or £3 for single orders and CD-ROMs

TOTAL 2

GRAND TOTAL 1+2+P&P

Name (Mr/Mrs/Miss)

Address

Postcode

Card No.

Exp Date

Signature

I have chosen my Johansens Guides/CD-ROMs and

☐ I enclose a cheque for £ _____ payable to Johansens

☐ I enclose my order on company letterheading, please invoice (UK only)

☐ Please debit my credit/charge card account (please tick).

☐ MasterCard ☐ Diners ☐ Amex

☐ Visa ☐ Switch (Issue Number)

A15

GUEST SURVEY REPORT

Your own Johansens 'inspection' gives reliability to our guides and assists in the selection of Award Nominations

Name of Hotel: _____

Location of Hotel: _____

Page No: _____

Date of visit: _____

Name of guest _____

Address of guest: _____

_____ **Postcode** _____

Please tick one box in each category below:	Excellent	Good	Disappointing	Poor
Bedrooms				
Public Rooms				
Restaurant/Cuisine				
Service				
Welcome/Friendliness				
Value For Money				

Occasionally we may allow other reputable organisations to write with offers which may be of interest.
If you prefer not to hear from them, tick this box ☐

To: Johansens, FREEPOST (CB264), 43 Millharbour, London E14 9BR

ORDER FORM

Call our 24hr credit card hotline FREEPHONE 0800 269 397.

Simply indicate which title(s) you require by putting the quantity in the boxes provided. Choose your preferred method of payment and mail to Johansens, FREEPOST (CB 264), 43 Millharbour, London E14 9BR, England (no stamp needed). Your FREE gifts will automatically be dispatched with your order. Fax orders welcome on 0171 537 3594

CHOOSE FROM 7 SPECIAL GUIDE COLLECTIONS – SAVE UP TO £56

TITLE	Normal Price	PRICE	SAVE	QTY	TOTAL
OFFER ONE					
3 Johansens Guides A+B+C	£42.85	£36.00	£6.85		
OFFER TWO					
4 Johansens Guides A+B+C+G	£58.80	£46.00	£12.80		
OFFER THREE					
5 Johansens Guides A+B+C+G+K **PLUS** Southern Africa Guide **FREE**	£71.75	£56.00	£15.75		
OFFER FOUR - The Executive Collection					
Business Meeting Venues Guide & CD-ROM M+R	£40.00	£30.00	£10.00		
OFFER FIVE - The Holiday Pack					
3 Johansens Guides D+E+F	£18.93	£9.99	£8.94		
OFFER SIX - The Digital Collection					
3 Johansens CD-ROMs N+O+P **PLUS** Southern Africa CD-ROM Q **FREE**	£69.85	£59.85	£10.00		
OFFER SEVEN - The Chairman's Collection					
Business Meeting Venues Guide & CD-ROMs M+R **PLUS** 5 Johansens Boxed Guides A+B+C+G+K, **PLUS** 3 CD-ROMs N+O+P **PLUS** Southern Africa Guide/CD ROM Q **FREE**, **PLUS** Mystery Gift **FREE**	£200.53	£149.00	£56.53		
Privilege Card PLUS The Millennium Guide		**FREE**			
1 Presentation box for offers 1, 2 and 3		£5.00	£20.00		
			TOTAL 1		

JOHANSENS PRINTED GUIDES 2000

CODE	TITLE	PRICE	QTY	TOTAL
A	Recommended Hotels – Great Britain & Ireland 2000	£19.95		
B	Recommended Country Houses & Small Hotels – Great Britain & Ireland 2000	£11.95		
C	Recommended Traditional Inns, Hotels & Restaurants – Great Britain 2000	£10.95		
NEW D	Recommended Holiday Cottages – Great Britain & Ireland 2000	£4.99		
E	Historic Houses, Castles & Gardens 2000	£4.99		
F	Museums & Galleries 2000	£8.95		
G	Recommended Hotels – Europe & The Mediterranean 2000	£15.95		
NEW H	Recommended Hotels – Europe & The Mediterranean 2000 (French Language)	£15.95		
NEW J	Recommended Hotels – Europe & The Mediterranean 2000 (German Language)	£15.95		
K	Recommended Hotels & Inns – North America, Bermuda & The Caribbean 2000	£12.95		
NEW L	Recommended Hotels & Game Lodges – Southern Africa, Mauritius & The Seychelles 2000	£9.95		
M	Recommended Business Meeting Venues 2000	£20.00		

JOHANSENS CD ROMs DIGITAL COLLECTION 2000

CODE	TITLE	PRICE	QTY	TOTAL
N	The Guide 2000 – Great Britain & Ireland	£29.95		
O	The Guide 2000 – Europe & The Mediterranean (English, French, German Language)	£22.95		
P	The Guide 2000 – North America, Bermuda & The Caribbean	£16.95		
NEW Q	The Guide 2000 – Southern Africa, Mauritius & The Seychelles	£16.95		
R	Business Meeting Venues 2000	£20.00		
S	Privilege Card 2000 (Free with your order. Additional Cards £20 each)	£20.00		

Postage & Packing (UK) £4.50 or £2.50 for single order and CD-ROMs

Outside UK add £5 or £3 for single orders and CD-ROMs

TOTAL 2

GRAND TOTAL 1+2+P&P

Name (Mr/Mrs/Miss)

Address

Postcode

Card No.

Exp Date

Signature

I have chosen my Johansens Guides/CD-ROMs and

☐ I enclose a cheque for £ _____ payable to Johansens

☐ I enclose my order on company letterheading, please invoice (UK only)

☐ Please debit my credit/charge card account (please tick).

☐ MasterCard ☐ Diners ☐ Amex

☐ Visa ☐ Switch (Issue Number)

A15

GUEST SURVEY REPORT

Your own Johansens 'inspection' gives reliability to our guides and assists in the selection of Award Nominations

Name of Hotel: _____

Location of Hotel: _____

Page No: _____

Date of visit: _____

Name of guest _____

Address of guest: _____

_____Postcode _____

Please tick one box in each category below:	Excellent	Good	Disappointing	Poor
Bedrooms				
Public Rooms				
Restaurant/Cuisine				
Service				
Welcome/Friendliness				
Value For Money				

Occasionally we may allow other reputable organisations to write with offers which may be of interest.
If you prefer not to hear from them, tick this box ☐

To: Johansens, FREEPOST (CB264), 43 Millharbour, London E14 9BR

ORDER FORM

Call our 24hr credit card hotline FREEPHONE 0800 269 397.

Simply indicate which title(s) you require by putting the quantity in the boxes provided. Choose your preferred method of payment and mail to Johansens, FREEPOST (CB 264), 43 Millharbour, London E14 9BR, England (no stamp needed). Your FREE gifts will automatically be dispatched with your order. Fax orders welcome on 0171 537 3594

CHOOSE FROM 7 SPECIAL GUIDE COLLECTIONS – SAVE UP TO £56

TITLE	*Normal Price*	PRICE	SAVE	QTY	TOTAL
OFFER ONE					
3 Johansens Guides A+B+C	£42.85	£36.00	£6.85		
OFFER TWO					
4 Johansens Guides A+B+C+G	£58.80	£46.00	£12.80		
OFFER THREE					
5 Johansens Guides A+B+C+G+K **PLUS** Southern Africa Guide **FREE**	£71.75	£56.00	£15.75		
OFFER FOUR - The Executive Collection					
Business Meeting Venues Guide & CD-ROM M+R	£40.00	£30.00	£10.00		
OFFER FIVE - The Holiday Pack					
3 Johansens Guides D+E+F	£18.93	£9.99	£8.94		
OFFER SIX - The Digital Collection					
3 Johansens CD-ROMs N+O+P **PLUS** Southern Africa CD-ROM Q **FREE**	£69.85	£59.85	£10.00		
OFFER SEVEN - The Chairman's Collection					
Business Meeting Venues Guide & CD-ROMs M+R **PLUS** 5 Johansens Boxed Guides A+B+C+G+K, **PLUS** 3 CD-ROMs N+O+P **PLUS** Southern Africa Guide/CD ROM Q **FREE**, **PLUS** Mystery Gift **FREE**	£200.53	£149.00	£56.53		
Privilege Card PLUS The Millennium Guide		**FREE**			
1 Presentation box for offers 1, 2 and 3		£5.00	£20.00		
			TOTAL 1		

JOHANSENS PRINTED GUIDES 2000

CODE	TITLE	PRICE	QTY	TOTAL
A	Recommended Hotels – Great Britain & Ireland 2000	£19.95		
B	Recommended Country Houses & Small Hotels – Great Britain & Ireland 2000	£11.95		
C	Recommended Traditional Inns, Hotels & Restaurants – Great Britain 2000	£10.95		
NEW D	Recommended Holiday Cottages – Great Britain & Ireland 2000	£4.99		
E	Historic Houses, Castles & Gardens 2000	£4.99		
F	Museums & Galleries 2000	£8.95		
G	Recommended Hotels – Europe & The Mediterranean 2000	£15.95		
NEW H	Recommended Hotels – Europe & The Mediterranean 2000 *(French Language)*	£15.95		
NEW J	Recommended Hotels – Europe & The Mediterranean 2000 *(German Language)*	£15.95		
K	Recommended Hotels & Inns – North America, Bermuda & The Caribbean 2000	£12.95		
NEW L	Recommended Hotels & Game Lodges – Southern Africa, Mauritius & The Seychelles 2000	£9.95		
M	Recommended Business Meeting Venues 2000	£20.00		

JOHANSENS CD ROMs DIGITAL COLLECTION 2000

CODE	TITLE	PRICE	QTY	TOTAL
N	The Guide 2000 – Great Britain & Ireland	£29.95		
. O	The Guide 2000 – Europe & The Mediterranean *(English, French, German Language)*	£22.95		
P	The Guide 2000 – North America, Bermuda & The Caribbean	£16.95		
NEW Q	The Guide 2000 – Southern Africa, Mauritius & The Seychelles	£16.95		
R	Business Meeting Venues 2000	£20.00		
S	Privilege Card 2000 *(Free with your order. Additional Cards £20 each)*	£20.00		

Postage & Packing (UK) £4.50 or £2.50 for single order and CD-ROMs

Outside UK add £5 or £3 for single orders and CD-ROMs

TOTAL 2

GRAND TOTAL 1+2+P&P

Name (Mr/Mrs/Miss)

Address

Postcode

Card No.

Exp Date

Signature

I have chosen my Johansens Guides/CD-ROMs and

☐ I enclose a cheque for £ _____ payable to Johansens

☐ I enclose my order on company letterheading, please invoice (UK only)

☐ Please debit my credit/charge card account (please tick).

☐ MasterCard ☐ Diners ☐ Amex

☐ Visa ☐ Switch (Issue Number) _____

A15

GUEST SURVEY REPORT

Your own Johansens 'inspection' gives reliability to our guides

and assists in the selection of Award Nominations

Name of Hotel: _____

Location of Hotel: _____

Page No: _____

Date of visit: _____

Name of guest _____

Address of guest: _____

_____Postcode _____

Please tick one box in each category below:	Excellent	Good	Disappointing	Poor
Bedrooms				
Public Rooms				
Restaurant/Cuisine				
Service				
Welcome/Friendliness				
Value For Money				

To: Johansens, FREEPOST (CB264), 43 Millharbour, London E14 9BR

ORDER FORM

Call our 24hr credit card hotline FREEPHONE 0800 269 397.

Simply indicate which title(s) you require by putting the quantity in the boxes provided. Choose your preferred method of payment and mail to Johansens, FREEPOST (CB 264), 43 Millharbour, London E14 9BR, England (no stamp needed). Your FREE gifts will automatically be dispatched with your order. Fax orders welcome on 0171 537 3594

CHOOSE FROM 7 SPECIAL GUIDE COLLECTIONS – SAVE UP TO £56

TITLE	Normal Price	PRICE	SAVE	QTY	TOTAL
OFFER ONE					
3 Johansens Guides A+B+C	£42.85	£36.00	£6.85		
OFFER TWO					
4 Johansens Guides A+B+C+G	£58.80	£46.00	£12.80		
OFFER THREE					
5 Johansens Guides A+B+C+G+K **PLUS** Southern Africa Guide **FREE**	£71.75	£56.00	£15.75		
OFFER FOUR - The Executive Collection					
Business Meeting Venues Guide & CD-ROM M+R	£40.00	£30.00	£10.00		
OFFER FIVE - The Holiday Pack					
3 Johansens Guides D+E+F	£18.93	£9.99	£8.94		
OFFER SIX - The Digital Collection					
3 Johansens CD-ROMs N+O+P **PLUS** Southern Africa CD-ROM Q **FREE**	£69.85	£59.85	£10.00		
OFFER SEVEN - The Chairman's Collection					
Business Meeting Venues Guide & CD-ROMs M+R **PLUS** 5 Johansens Boxed Guides A+B+C+G+K, **PLUS** 3 CD-ROMs N+O+P **PLUS** Southern Africa Guide/CD ROM Q **FREE**, **PLUS** Mystery Gift **FREE**	£200.53	£149.00	£56.53		
Privilege Card PLUS The Millennium Guide		**FREE**			
1 Presentation box for offers 1, 2 and 3		£5.00	£20.00		

TOTAL 1

JOHANSENS PRINTED GUIDES 2000

CODE	TITLE	PRICE	QTY	TOTAL
A	Recommended Hotels – Great Britain & Ireland 2000	£19.95		
B	Recommended Country Houses & Small Hotels – Great Britain & Ireland 2000	£11.95		
C	Recommended Traditional Inns, Hotels & Restaurants – Great Britain 2000	£10.95		
NEW D	Recommended Holiday Cottages – Great Britain & Ireland 2000	£4.99		
E	Historic Houses, Castles & Gardens 2000	£4.99		
F	Museums & Galleries 2000	£8.95		
G	Recommended Hotels – Europe & The Mediterranean 2000	£15.95		
NEW H	Recommended Hotels – Europe & The Mediterranean 2000 (French Language)	£15.95		
NEW J	Recommended Hotels – Europe & The Mediterranean 2000 (German Language)	£15.95		
K	Recommended Hotels & Inns – North America, Bermuda & The Caribbean 2000	£12.95		
NEW L	Recommended Hotels & Game Lodges – Southern Africa, Mauritius & The Seychelles 2000	£9.95		
M	Recommended Business Meeting Venues 2000	£20.00		

JOHANSENS CD ROMs DIGITAL COLLECTION 2000

CODE	TITLE	PRICE	QTY	TOTAL
N	The Guide 2000 – Great Britain & Ireland	£29.95		
O	The Guide 2000 – Europe & The Mediterranean (English, French, German Language)	£22.95		
P	The Guide 2000 – North America, Bermuda & The Caribbean	£16.95		
NEW Q	The Guide 2000 – Southern Africa, Mauritius & The Seychelles	£16.95		
R	Business Meeting Venues 2000	£20.00		
S	Privilege Card 2000 (Free with your order. Additional Cards £20 each)	£20.00		

Postage & Packing (UK) £4.50 or £2.50 for single order and CD-ROMs

Outside UK add £5 or £3 for single orders and CD-ROMs

TOTAL 2

GRAND TOTAL 1+2+P&P

Name (Mr/Mrs/Miss)

Address

Postcode

Card No.

Exp Date

Signature

I have chosen my Johansens Guides/CD-ROMs and

☐ I enclose a cheque for £ _____ payable to Johansens

☐ I enclose my order on company letterheading, please invoice (UK only)

☐ Please debit my credit/charge card account (please tick).

☐ MasterCard ☐ Diners ☐ Amex

☐ Visa ☐ Switch (Issue Number) _____

A15

GUEST SURVEY REPORT

Your own Johansens 'inspection' gives reliability to our guides and assists in the selection of Award Nominations

Name of Hotel: _____

Location of Hotel: _____

Page No: _____

Date of visit: _____

Name of guest _____

Address of guest: _____

_____Postcode _____

Please tick one box in each category below:	Excellent	Good	Disappointing	Poor
Bedrooms				
Public Rooms				
Restaurant/Cuisine				
Service				
Welcome/Friendliness				
Value For Money				

Occasionally we may allow other reputable organisations to write with offers which may be of interest. If you prefer not to hear from them, tick this box ☐

To: Johansens, FREEPOST (CB264), 43 Millharbour, London E14 9BR

ORDER FORM

Call our 24hr credit card hotline FREEPHONE 0800 269 397.

Simply indicate which title(s) you require by putting the quantity in the boxes provided. Choose your preferred method of payment and mail to Johansens, FREEPOST (CB 264), 43 Millharbour, London E14 9BR, England (no stamp needed). Your FREE gifts will automatically be dispatched with your order. Fax orders welcome on 0171 537 3594

CHOOSE FROM 7 SPECIAL GUIDE COLLECTIONS – SAVE UP TO £56

TITLE	Normal Price	PRICE	SAVE	QTY	TOTAL
OFFER ONE					
3 Johansens Guides A+B+C	£42.85	£36.00	£6.85		
OFFER TWO					
4 Johansens Guides A+B+C+G	£58.80	£46.00	£12.80		
OFFER THREE					
5 Johansens Guides A+B+C+G+K PLUS Southern Africa Guide FREE	£71.75	£56.00	£15.75		
OFFER FOUR - The Executive Collection					
Business Meeting Venues Guide & CD-ROM M+R	£40.00	£30.00	£10.00		
OFFER FIVE - The Holiday Pack					
3 Johansens Guides D+E+F	£18.93	£9.99	£8.94		
OFFER SIX - The Digital Collection					
3 Johansens CD-ROMs N+O+P PLUS Southern Africa CD-ROM Q FREE	£69.85	£59.85	£10.00		
OFFER SEVEN - The Chairman's Collection					
Business Meeting Venues Guide & CD-ROMs M+R PLUS 5 Johansens Boxed Guides A+B+C+G+K, PLUS 3 CD-ROMs N+O+P PLUS Southern Africa Guide/CD ROM Q FREE, PLUS Mystery Gift FREE	£200.53	£149.00	£56.53		
Privilege Card PLUS The Millennium Guide		FREE			
1 Presentation box for offers 1, 2 and 3		£5.00	£20.00		

TOTAL 1

JOHANSENS PRINTED GUIDES 2000

CODE	TITLE	PRICE	QTY	TOTAL
A	Recommended Hotels – Great Britain & Ireland 2000	£19.95		
B	Recommended Country Houses & Small Hotels – Great Britain & Ireland 2000	£11.95		
C	Recommended Traditional Inns, Hotels & Restaurants – Great Britain 2000	£10.95		
NEW D	Recommended Holiday Cottages – Great Britain & Ireland 2000	£4.99		
E	Historic Houses, Castles & Gardens 2000	£4.99		
F	Museums & Galleries 2000	£8.95		
G	Recommended Hotels – Europe & The Mediterranean 2000	£15.95		
NEW H	Recommended Hotels – Europe & The Mediterranean 2000 (French Language)	£15.95		
NEW J	Recommended Hotels – Europe & The Mediterranean 2000 (German Language)	£15.95		
K	Recommended Hotels & Inns – North America, Bermuda & The Caribbean 2000	£12.95		
NEW L	Recommended Hotels & Game Lodges – Southern Africa, Mauritius & The Seychelles 2000	£9.95		
M	Recommended Business Meeting Venues 2000	£20.00		

JOHANSENS CD ROMs DIGITAL COLLECTION 2000

CODE	TITLE	PRICE	QTY	TOTAL
N	The Guide 2000 – Great Britain & Ireland	£29.95		
O	The Guide 2000 – Europe & The Mediterranean (English, French, German Language)	£22.95		
P	The Guide 2000 – North America, Bermuda & The Caribbean	£16.95		
NEW Q	The Guide 2000 – Southern Africa, Mauritius & The Seychelles	£16.95		
R	Business Meeting Venues 2000	£20.00		
S	Privilege Card 2000 (Free with your order. Additional Cards £20 each)	£20.00		

Postage & Packing (UK) £4.50 or £2.50 for single order and CD-ROMs
Outside UK add £5 or £3 for single orders and CD-ROMs

TOTAL 2

GRAND TOTAL 1+2+P&P

Name (Mr/Mrs/Miss)

Address

Postcode

Card No.

Exp Date

Signature

I have chosen my Johansens Guides/CD-ROMs and

☐ I enclose a cheque for £ _____ payable to Johansens

☐ I enclose my order on company letterheading, please invoice (UK only)

☐ Please debit my credit/charge card account (please tick).

☐ MasterCard ☐ Diners ☐ Amex

☐ Visa ☐ Switch (Issue Number)

A15

GUEST SURVEY REPORT

Your own Johansens 'inspection' gives reliability to our guides

and assists in the selection of Award Nominations

Name of Hotel: _____

Location of Hotel: _____

Page No: _____

Date of visit: _____

Name of guest _____

Address of guest: _____

_____ Postcode _____

Please tick one box in each category below:	Excellent	Good	Disappointing	Poor
Bedrooms				
Public Rooms				
Restaurant/Cuisine				
Service				
Welcome/Friendliness				
Value For Money				

Occasionally we may allow other reputable organisations to write with offers which may be of interest.
If you prefer not to hear from them, tick this box ☐

To: Johansens, FREEPOST (CB264), 43 Millharbour, London E14 9BR

ORDER FORM

Call our 24hr credit card hotline FREEPHONE 0800 269 397.

Simply indicate which title(s) you require by putting the quantity in the boxes provided. Choose your preferred method of payment and mail to Johansens, FREEPOST (CB 264), 43 Millharbour, London E14 9BR, England (no stamp needed). Your FREE gifts will automatically be dispatched with your order. Fax orders welcome on 0171 537 3594

CHOOSE FROM 7 SPECIAL GUIDE COLLECTIONS – SAVE UP TO £56

TITLE	Normal Price	PRICE	SAVE	QTY	TOTAL
OFFER ONE					
3 Johansens Guides A+B+C	£42.85	£36.00	£6.85		
OFFER TWO					
4 Johansens Guides A+B+C+G	£58.80	£46.00	£12.80		
OFFER THREE					
5 Johansens Guides A+B+C+G+K PLUS Southern Africa Guide FREE	£71.75	£56.00	£15.75		
OFFER FOUR - The Executive Collection					
Business Meeting Venues Guide & CD-ROM M+R	£40.00	£30.00	£10.00		
OFFER FIVE - The Holiday Pack					
3 Johansens Guides D+E+F	£18.93	£9.99	£8.94		
OFFER SIX - The Digital Collection					
3 Johansens CD-ROMs N+O+P PLUS Southern Africa CD-ROM Q FREE	£69.85	£59.85	£10.00		
OFFER SEVEN - The Chairman's Collection					
Business Meeting Venues Guide & CD-ROMs M+R PLUS 5 Johansens Boxed Guides A+B+C+G+K, PLUS 3 CD-ROMs N+O+P PLUS Southern Africa Guide/CD ROM Q FREE, PLUS Mystery Gift FREE	£200.53	£149.00	£56.53		
Privilege Card PLUS The Millennium Guide		FREE			
1 Presentation box for offers 1, 2 and 3		£5.00	£20.00		
			TOTAL 1		

JOHANSENS PRINTED GUIDES 2000

CODE	TITLE	PRICE	QTY	TOTAL
A	Recommended Hotels – Great Britain & Ireland 2000	£19.95		
B	Recommended Country Houses & Small Hotels – Great Britain & Ireland 2000	£11.95		
C	Recommended Traditional Inns, Hotels & Restaurants – Great Britain 2000	£10.95		
NEW D	Recommended Holiday Cottages – Great Britain & Ireland 2000	£4.99		
E	Historic Houses, Castles & Gardens 2000	£4.99		
F	Museums & Galleries 2000	£8.95		
G	Recommended Hotels – Europe & The Mediterranean 2000	£15.95		
NEW H	Recommended Hotels – Europe & The Mediterranean 2000 (French Language)	£15.95		
NEW J	Recommended Hotels – Europe & The Mediterranean 2000 (German Language)	£15.95		
K	Recommended Hotels & Inns – North America, Bermuda & The Caribbean 2000	£12.95		
NEW L	Recommended Hotels & Game Lodges – Southern Africa, Mauritius & The Seychelles 2000	£9.95		
M	Recommended Business Meeting Venues 2000	£20.00		

JOHANSENS CD ROMs DIGITAL COLLECTION 2000

N	The Guide 2000 – Great Britain & Ireland	£29.95		
O	The Guide 2000 – Europe & The Mediterranean (English, French, German Language)	£22.95		
P	The Guide 2000 – North America, Bermuda & The Caribbean	£16.95		
NEW Q	The Guide 2000 – Southern Africa, Mauritius & The Seychelles	£16.95		
R	Business Meeting Venues 2000	£20.00		
S	Privilege Card 2000 (Free with your order. Additional Cards £20 each)	£20.00		

Postage & Packing (UK) £4.50 or £2.50 for single order and CD-ROMs

Outside UK add £5 or £3 for single orders and CD-ROMs

TOTAL 2

GRAND TOTAL 1+2+P&P

Name	(Mr/Mrs/Miss)
Address	
	Postcode
Card No.	Exp Date
Signature	

I have chosen my Johansens Guides/CD-ROMs and

☐ I enclose a cheque for £ _____ payable to Johansens

☐ I enclose my order on company letterheading, please invoice (UK only)

☐ Please debit my credit/charge card account (please tick).

☐ **MasterCard** ☐ **Diners** ☐ **Amex**

☐ **Visa** ☐ **Switch** (Issue Number)

A15

GUEST SURVEY REPORT

Your own Johansens 'inspection' gives reliability to our guides and assists in the selection of Award Nominations

Name of Hotel: _____

Location of Hotel: _____

Page No: _____

Date of visit: _____

Name of guest _____

Address of guest: _____

_____Postcode _____

Please tick one box in each category below:	Excellent	Good	Disappointing	Poor
Bedrooms				
Public Rooms				
Restaurant/Cuisine				
Service				
Welcome/Friendliness				
Value For Money				

Occasionally we may allow other reputable organisations to write with offers which may be of interest. If you prefer not to hear from them, tick this box ☐

To: Johansens, FREEPOST (CB264), 43 Millharbour, London E14 9BR

ORDER FORM

Call our 24hr credit card hotline FREEPHONE 0800 269 397.

Simply indicate which title(s) you require by putting the quantity in the boxes provided. Choose your preferred method of payment and mail to Johansens, FREEPOST (CB 264), 43 Millharbour, London E14 9BR, England (no stamp needed). Your FREE gifts will automatically be dispatched with your order. Fax orders welcome on 0171 537 3594

CHOOSE FROM 7 SPECIAL GUIDE COLLECTIONS – SAVE UP TO £56

TITLE	Normal Price	PRICE	SAVE	QTY	TOTAL
OFFER ONE					
3 Johansens Guides A+B+C	£42.85	£36.00	£6.85		
OFFER TWO					
4 Johansens Guides A+B+C+G	£58.80	£46.00	£12.80		
OFFER THREE					
5 Johansens Guides A+B+C+G+K **PLUS** Southern Africa Guide **FREE**	£71.75	£56.00	£15.75		
OFFER FOUR - The Executive Collection					
Business Meeting Venues Guide & CD-ROM M+R	£40.00	£30.00	£10.00		
OFFER FIVE - The Holiday Pack					
3 Johansens Guides D+E+F	£18.93	£9.99	£8.94		
OFFER SIX - The Digital Collection					
3 Johansens CD-ROMs N+O+P **PLUS** Southern Africa CD-ROM Q **FREE**	£69.85	£59.85	£10.00		
OFFER SEVEN - The Chairman's Collection					
Business Meeting Venues Guide & CD-ROMs M+R **PLUS** 5 Johansens Boxed Guides A+B+C+G+K, **PLUS** 3 CD-ROMs N+O+P **PLUS** Southern Africa Guide/CD ROM Q **FREE**, **PLUS** Mystery Gift **FREE**	£200.53	£149.00	£56.53		
Privilege Card PLUS The Millennium Guide		**FREE**			
1 Presentation box for offers 1, 2 and 3		£5.00	£20.00		
			TOTAL 1		

JOHANSENS PRINTED GUIDES 2000

CODE	TITLE	PRICE	QTY	TOTAL
A	Recommended Hotels – Great Britain & Ireland 2000	£19.95		
B	Recommended Country Houses & Small Hotels – Great Britain & Ireland 2000	£11.95		
C	Recommended Traditional Inns, Hotels & Restaurants – Great Britain 2000	£10.95		
NEW D	Recommended Holiday Cottages – Great Britain & Ireland 2000	£4.99		
E	Historic Houses, Castles & Gardens 2000	£4.99		
F	Museums & Galleries 2000	£8.95		
G	Recommended Hotels – Europe & The Mediterranean 2000	£15.95		
NEW H	Recommended Hotels – Europe & The Mediterranean 2000 (French Language)	£15.95		
NEW J	Recommended Hotels – Europe & The Mediterranean 2000 (German Language)	£15.95		
K	Recommended Hotels & Inns – North America, Bermuda & The Caribbean 2000	£12.95		
NEW L	Recommended Hotels & Game Lodges – Southern Africa, Mauritius & The Seychelles 2000	£9.95		
M	Recommended Business Meeting Venues 2000	£20.00		

JOHANSENS CD ROMs DIGITAL COLLECTION 2000

CODE	TITLE	PRICE	QTY	TOTAL
N	The Guide 2000 – Great Britain & Ireland	£29.95		
O	The Guide 2000 – Europe & The Mediterranean (English, French, German Language)	£22.95		
P	The Guide 2000 – North America, Bermuda & The Caribbean	£16.95		
NEW Q	The Guide 2000 – Southern Africa, Mauritius & The Seychelles	£16.95		
R	Business Meeting Venues 2000	£20.00		
S	Privilege Card 2000 (Free with your order. Additional Cards £20 each)	£20.00		

Postage & Packing (UK) £4.50 or £2.50 for single order and CD-ROMs

Outside UK add £5 or £3 for single orders and CD-ROMs

TOTAL 2

GRAND TOTAL 1+2+P&P

Name (Mr/Mrs/Miss)

Address

Postcode

Card No.

Exp Date

Signature

I have chosen my Johansens Guides/CD-ROMs and

☐ I enclose a cheque for £ _____ payable to Johansens

☐ I enclose my order on company letterheading, please invoice (UK only)

☐ Please debit my credit/charge card account (please tick).

☐ MasterCard ☐ Diners ☐ Amex

☐ Visa ☐ Switch (Issue Number)

A15

GUEST SURVEY REPORT

Your own Johansens 'inspection' gives reliability to our guides and assists in the selection of Award Nominations

Name of Hotel: _____

Location of Hotel: _____

Page No: _____

Date of visit: _____

Name of guest _____

Address of guest: _____

_____Postcode _____

Please tick one box in each category below:	Excellent	Good	Disappointing	Poor
Bedrooms				
Public Rooms				
Restaurant/Cuisine				
Service				
Welcome/Friendliness				
Value For Money				

To: Johansens, FREEPOST (CB264), 43 Millharbour, London E14 9BR

ORDER FORM

Call our 24hr credit card hotline FREEPHONE 0800 269 397.

Simply indicate which title(s) you require by putting the quantity in the boxes provided. Choose your preferred method of payment and mail to Johansens, FREEPOST (CB 264), 43 Millharbour, London E14 9BR, England (no stamp needed). Your FREE gifts will automatically be dispatched with your order. Fax orders welcome on 0171 537 3594

CHOOSE FROM 7 SPECIAL GUIDE COLLECTIONS – SAVE UP TO £56

TITLE	Normal Price	PRICE	SAVE	QTY	TOTAL
OFFER ONE – The Basic Collection					
3 Johansens Guides A+B+C	£42.85	£36.00	£6.85		
OFFER TWO – The Extended Collection					
4 Johansens Guides A+B+C+G	£58.80	£46.00	£12.80		
OFFER THREE – The Full Selection					
5 Johansens Guides A+B+C+G+K PLUS Southern Africa Guide **FREE**	£71.75	£56.00	£15.75		
OFFER FOUR - The Executive Collection					
Business Meeting Venues Guide & CD-ROM M+R	£40.00	£30.00	£10.00		
OFFER FIVE - The Holiday Pack					
3 Johansens Guides D+E+F	£18.93	£9.99	£8.94		
OFFER SIX - The Digital Collection					
3 Johansens CD-ROMs N+O+P PLUS Southern Africa CD-ROM Q **FREE**	£69.85	£59.85	£10.00		
OFFER SEVEN - The Chairman's Collection					
Business Meeting Venues Guide & CD-ROMs M+R PLUS 5 Johansens Boxed Guides A+B+C+G+K, PLUS D+E+F, PLUS 3 CD-ROMs N+O+P PLUS Southern Africa Guide/CD ROM Q **FREE**, PLUS Mystery Gift **FREE**	£205.53	£149.00	£56.53		
Privilege Card PLUS The Millennium Guide		**FREE**			
1 Presentation box for offers 1, 2 and 3		£5.00	£20.00		
				TOTAL 1	

JOHANSENS PRINTED GUIDES 2000

CODE	TITLE	PRICE	QTY	TOTAL
A	Recommended Hotels – Great Britain & Ireland 2000	£19.95		
B	Recommended Country Houses & Small Hotels – Great Britain & Ireland 2000	£11.95		
C	Recommended Traditional Inns, Hotels & Restaurants – Great Britain 2000	£10.95		
NEW D	Recommended Holiday Cottages – Great Britain & Ireland 2000	£4.99		
E	Historic Houses, Castles & Gardens 2000	£4.99		
F	Museums & Galleries 2000	£8.95		
G	Recommended Hotels – Europe & The Mediterranean 2000	£15.95		
NEW H	Recommended Hotels – Europe & The Mediterranean 2000 (French Language)	£15.95		
NEW J	Recommended Hotels – Europe & The Mediterranean 2000 (German Language)	£15.95		
K	Recommended Hotels & Inns – North America, Bermuda & The Caribbean 2000	£12.95		
NEW L	Recommended Hotels & Game Lodges – Southern Africa, Mauritius & The Seychelles 2000	£9.95		
M	Recommended Business Meeting Venues 2000	£20.00		

JOHANSENS CD ROMs DIGITAL COLLECTION 2000

CODE	TITLE	PRICE	QTY	TOTAL
N	The Guide 2000 – Great Britain & Ireland	£29.95		
O	The Guide 2000 – Europe & The Mediterranean (English, French, German Language)	£22.95		
P	The Guide 2000 – North America, Bermuda & The Caribbean	£16.95		
NEW Q	The Guide 2000 – Southern Africa, Mauritius & The Seychelles	£16.95		
R	Business Meeting Venues 2000	£20.00		
S	Privilege Card 2000 (Free with your order. Additional Cards £20 each)	£20.00		

Postage & Packing (UK) £4.50 or £2.50 for single order and CD-ROMs

Outside UK add £5 or £3 for single orders and CD-ROMs

TOTAL 2

GRAND TOTAL 1+2+P&P

Name (Mr/Mrs/Miss)

Address

Postcode

Card No.

Exp Date

Signature

I have chosen my Johansens Guides/CD-ROMs and

☐ I enclose a cheque for £ _____ payable to Johansens

☐ I enclose my order on company letterhead, please invoice (UK only)

☐ Please debit my credit/charge card account (please tick).

☐ MasterCard ☐ Diners ☐ Amex

☐ Visa ☐ Switch (Issue Number) _____

A15

Johansens
FREEPOST (CB264)
43 Millharbour
London
E14 9BR